THE VALUE OF OTHERS

THE VALUE OF OTHERS

UNDERSTANDING THE ECONOMIC MODEL OF RELATIONSHIPS TO GET (AND KEEP) MORE OF WHAT YOU WANT IN THE SEXUAL MARKETPLACE

ORION TARABAN

Troilus: What is aught, but as 'tis valued?

Hector: But value dwells not in particular will;
It holds his estimate and dignity
As well wherein 'tis precious of itself
As in the prizer

Troilus and Cressida, II.ii.

CONTENTS

PREFACE

This is a book about relationships, principally about sexual relationships between men and women. Since this is a particularly sensitive topic fraught with potential difficulty, I considered it appropriate at the outset to provide some context for the book and my motivations for writing it.

Like anyone else, I'm not sure how much time I have left — and books are notoriously time-consuming. So my primary intention in undertaking this project was to write a book that I would not later consider a waste of time to have written. And this (I felt) would be the surest guarantee I could offer you that the book would not be a waste of time to read.

And to the extent that I accomplished this, I believe I did so by respecting your attention and intelligence. There is very little fluff in this book. Many sentences could be expanded into chapters; every chapter could be its own book. I readily concede that I have glossed over many topics and omitted others completely. Perhaps I will be able to address these deficiencies in future works. For the time being, however, I hope that the reader of the present volume will remember that this book is intended as a kind of survey text, incapable of providing greater detail without compromising its overarching goal.

As a survey, the book also needed to accommodate certain variables in my intended audience, two of which are of particular note, namely: differences in familiarity with the topic under consideration, and differences in gendered communication styles. With respect to the former, I've attempted to compile this overview of intersexual dynamics for the widest possible audience without sacrificing the integrity of the message. If I succeeded, then those already well-versed in the subject won't be bored, and those who possess no preexisting knowledge won't be lost. I've also striven to be as objective and value-neutral as possible. My goal is to present the sexual marketplace as it is — not as it "should" be or as we might like it to be. In this way, I've presumed on my readers' maturity and their ability to entertain ideas that may be different from their own without reactive judgment.

With respect to the latter, it's worth noting that this book was not written for men — at least, not exclusively. Rather, my intended audience is all those who participate in the game of mating and dating — especially those who are (or who have ever been) confused, frustrated, or dissatisfied by their experiences. For better or worse, these states usually arise due to flaws in participants' underlying models of reality. The objective of this book is to dispel the confusion, frustration, and dissatisfaction by providing an alternative framework for understanding relationships, ideally leading to clarity, success, and fulfillment. Like any other theory, it is true to the extent that it works — which, in this case, would mean more people getting more of what they want in the sexual marketplace.

Writing a book that is palatable to both men and women is a challenge in its own right, and I'm sure that I have included content that has (at least occasionally) failed in this regard. However, there is no way around it: any legitimate theory of the sexual marketplace must be able to explain the experiences of both men and women using the same set of principles. Otherwise, it is incomplete at best, and biased at worst. What's more, any set of strategies that achieves one gender's goals by sacrificing the other's is unlikely to produce sustainable and satisfying outcomes. To that end, my intention is to present the truth about relationships without enraging men or alienating women, as the world does not need more of either. If I am unsuccessful, I can only remind the aggrieved reader that offense is taken, not given.

And we often take offense because we maintain a number of unacknowledged taboos regarding the analysis of certain constructs — especially love, attraction, and sexual desire. Though intimate relationships generate an incalculable amount of unnecessary suffering every day, many would still prefer that we not look too closely at their fundamental operation. Despite all our modern pretensions to liberality and open-mindedness, we still largely treat sexual (versus "romantic") relationships like medieval corpses: they're imbued with a sacredness that makes their dissection feel transgressive.

Unfortunately, while laying bare the physical apparatus of the human body may have been uncomfortable for some, this squeamishness functionally prevented millions from receiving appropriate medical care for centuries. Until we could see the human organism clearly, physical maladies were treated with a combination of ritual, charisma, and superstition. If people improved, it was generally in spite of their treatment — not because of it. And even though the consequences of remaining ignorant were as obvious as they were deadly, those who sought to shed light on how the human body actually worked were often shunned, denounced, and excommunicated by the same people whose lives would have been improved by such discoveries.

By the same token, while laying bare the realities of the sexual marketplace may be uncomfortable for some, this squeamishness has functionally prevented millions from enjoying satisfying relationships for centuries. Without an understanding of the perception of value, relationship difficulties will continue to be addressed with a combination of moral exhortations, trite platitudes, and wishful thinking. If people succeed, it will generally be in spite of this advice — not because of it. And even though the consequences of mystifying these realities are as obvious as they are painful, those who seek to shed light on how relationships actually work are often shunned, denounced, and ostracized by the same people whose lives would be improved by such discoveries.

To the extent that my analysis is an infringement on moral sensibilities, I hope that my intentions will justify my actions. It is not a morbid curiosity that motivates me — nor an iconoclastic delight in destruction — but a desire to release others from pain. I've spoken with thousands of people who suffer at every stage of relationships. Some suffer when they're not in them. Others suffer when they are in them. Yet others suffer when they're out of them. And ignorance so often creates, maintains, and exacerbates this suffering.

And how could this not be the case? Our popular conceptualization of relationships is based on a model equivalent to the humoral theory of medicine: it is a metaphysical mishmash of demonstrated ineffectiveness. Under the circumstances, I consider refusing to take action to be more of an ethical lapse than breaking with cherished ideologies. The time has come to address the obvious failings in our understanding by creating a new model that exists in greater alignment with reality. And we'll know we have succeeded in this enterprise when we suffer less than we currently do.

This book is a first, fledgling attempt at sharing such a model. I have tried my best to pursue my inquiry — if not to its ultimate conclusion — then at least as far as I could manage. And I feel satisfied by my efforts in no small part because I was often surprised by what they produced. The ideas presented here are not casual opinions: they represent my best thinking on a subject to which I have devoted a good deal of study and careful observation over the years. That said, any truth contained herein can be attributed to what grace has been afforded me; any errors are my own.

You may appreciate at the outset that this book is essentially theoretical in nature. Those who expect every claim to be substantiated with empirical evidence will be disappointed. This is not necessarily because I couldn't substantiate my observations if I so wished — the fields of evolutionary psychology and behavioral economics provide a robust evidence base for this book — but because I find academic writing tedious to write (and even more tedious to read). In any case, most of the claims presented in this book are verifiable and so are subject to the principle of falsifiability. I will readily recant any assertion shown to be demonstrably incorrect.

I generally include citations to provide sources for any explicit statistics but not to offer corroboration for any claims. After all, if an idea presented here is wrong, then it wouldn't matter who else believed it was right. And if my ideas are right, then it shouldn't matter if they have no other support. This is not to say that all the ideas contained in this book are utterly unique (though I believe I do present a few original thoughts). Like most works, its originality is largely derived from the novel arrangement of preexisting components.

Nevertheless, I have made an effort not to repeat what I have already said elsewhere. This is out of respect for those who are already familiar with my content online. I'm proud to say that my episode scripts constitute a very small percentage of this text, which means that even the most avid followers of my work will be able to satisfy their appetites for new material. This book is not a recapitulation of previously expressed notions but a self-contained endeavor designed to stand (or fall) on its own merit.

That said, much of my content online naturally complements the ideas put forth in this volume. So rather than repeat myself in print, I've included a QR code at the end of each chapter that links to a playlist on my YouTube channel. Each playlist is comprised of episodes that dovetail with the specific topic under discussion. If you are interested in further exploring a subject, I encourage you to take advantage of these resources. I will add new episodes to the playlists as appropriate.

If nothing else, the present work has afforded me the opportunity to clarify my thinking on a subject that has shaped the man I have become in more ways than I could possibly articulate. I don't mind confessing that I'm particularly fond of the title, which can be read either sincerely ("The *worthiness* of others") or cynically ("The *price* of others"). In reality, both are true. And for us to approach a more mature understanding of relationships, we may need — like the title — to increase our capacity to accommodate both understandings simultaneously. It's a paradox — but what truth isn't?

April 2024
Napa, California

PROLOGUE

THE JUDGMENT OF PARIS

There is a story behind the painting[1] on the cover of this book, and it goes like this:

A wedding was held in ancient Greece. All the gods and goddesses were invited, except one: Eris, the goddess of discord, who inevitably showed up anyway. When she was denied entry to the festivities, she threw her wedding gift — a golden apple inscribed with the words "TO THE FAIREST" — into the crowd before departing in a huff. Predictably, three goddesses each assumed the apple was addressed to her, and Zeus was summoned to mediate the dispute. Wisely perceiving that there was no way this couldn't end poorly for him, Zeus asked Paris, the mortal prince of Troy, to cast the

1 Lorrain, C. (1645/1646). *The judgment of Paris*. [oil on canvas]. National Gallery of Art. Washington, D.C.

deciding vote. The painting depicts this momentous event: The Judgment of Paris.

To tempt the prince into choosing her, each goddess attempted to bribe Paris with a fantastic gift. Athena — the goddess of war — promised martial prowess and victory in battle. Hera — the queen of the gods — pledged great riches and worldly power. Neither was successful. Instead, Paris awarded the golden apple to Aphrodite — the goddess of love — who promised him the affections of the most beautiful woman in the world: Helen of Sparta. Unfortunately for all involved, Helen happened to be married to another man — a man no less than the king of Sparta — but a promise is a promise. Whether Helen was kidnapped or she followed Paris of her own accord is a detail that changes depending on who is telling the story. Either way, the prince received his due.

And thus began the Trojan War.

CHAPTER 1

RELATIONSHIPS ARE THE MEDIA IN WHICH VALUE IS TRANSACTED

People want things from other people. This is why other people represent both a potential solution and a potential problem. They are a potential solution when they have the things we want and are willing to give them to us. On the other hand, they are a potential problem when they don't have the things we want — or when they *do* have them but won't give them to us. And it's far from straightforward to determine which people are which — which is why other people are typically a problem until they prove otherwise.

Across cultures and throughout history, people have devised three general approaches to the problem of others.[2]

2 Psychoanalyst Karen Horney was the first to formulate this framework. Source: Horney, K. (1950). *Neurosis and human growth: The struggle toward self-realization*. W. W. Norton & Company.

Some choose to *move against* others. This involves taking what they want from other people using force, skill, or guile in conquest or competition. Others choose to *move away from* others. This involves eliminating the inner desire for things or the interpersonal dependence that makes it necessary to deal with people. Both of these approaches are essentially antisocial — albeit for different reasons.

However, the most common approach that people have adopted to address the problem of others is to *move toward* them. From the hunting parties of our ancient ancestors to the multinational alliances of the present day, people have found ways of getting what they want by joining into larger units. And they have discovered that the most effective way to entice others to join them is to give — or promise to give in the future — something these other people want in return. This is, by definition, a prosocial solution, as it creates the basis of society.

Now, these terms can trip people up. Because of the language involved, many believe that anything prosocial must be good, and anything antisocial must be bad. For instance, the word *prosocial* can conjure images of people working together in harmony toward a common goal. And while this can happen, the reality is rarely that simple — and it's easy to understand why. People typically don't join together because they want the same things. If you want what I want, how could I possibly give it to you? If I had it to give, I wouldn't want it from you. Keep in mind that *to want* has a double meaning: it can mean both *to desire* and *to lack*. This is why people who want the same things are generally useless to each other: each lacks what the other desires.

In most cases, people come together because they want different things. This is true even if they are aligned in terms of their superordinate goal, since a judicious complementarity of skills and resources significantly increases the likelihood that they will achieve their goal. If I have what you want, and you have what I want, then we have grounds for moving toward each other. And if we exchange the things we respectively want, then we enter into a *relationship*. And this explains — all by itself — why certain people are rich in relationship opportunities and others are not. It is neither the good nor the loving nor the virtuous who are desired for relationships, but *the people whom others want things from*. The person who has more of what other people want most will have more and better relationship opportunities than the person who has less. This is just the way it is.

A relationship is the medium in which value is transacted. Where value is transacted, a relationship exists. Conversely, where no value is transacted, no relationship exists. This is because people don't move toward others whom *they want nothing to do with*. Rather, they approach those from whom they hope to derive some benefit. When they do not hope to benefit, people will sometimes avoid others from whom they fear harm, but most of the time, they will simply do nothing. Most individuals do not walk around with either desire and admiration *or* fear and animosity toward other human beings: instead, they feel indifferent. And it's this neutrality that functionally stops them from rushing toward, or running away from, every person they happen to see. In general, people feel relatively disinterested until they perceive that someone has something they want: either to acquire or to avoid.

Anything that can be bought or earned can be transacted, and these transacted goods are what motivate people to form relationships. On the other hand, anything that can neither be bought nor earned — gifts that are given solely at the pleasure of the giver (and for which no reciprocity is expected) — *cannot* be transacted, and therefore do not form the basis of relationships. This is because relationships require exchange, and unilateral transactions don't meet the criteria. For instance, we wouldn't say that a fan is in a relationship with her idol any more than we would say a victim is in a relationship with his mugger. Relationships must go both ways.

In order for a relationship to exist, value must be transacted: it must be exchanged between the parties involved. However, this is no simple task, as value is neither static nor objective. As we'll see, it exists solely in the mind of the valuer, and it is subject to constant fluctuation as new information emerges and circumstances evolve. What's more, this valuation typically occurs beneath the threshold of awareness. This means that neither party can ever know the other's true valuation of a specific good (which exists in the inaccessible privacy of the other's mind), and also that each party typically doesn't entirely know his or her own valuation of the good in question. And to make matters even more complicated, people generally attempt to exchange unequal (i.e., different) goods in relationships, which further increases the likelihood that the goods will have unequal (i.e., different) valuations.

That said, these valuations must be comparable. People do not willingly exchange something they value highly for something they do not. This means that if the subjective valuations of the goods in question are too far off, then no exchange occurs (and no relationship is formed). In order to effect a transaction, that which is given must be valued similarly to that which is received. As a result, we can refine our definition of relationships even further to be *the media in which unequal goods of comparable value are exchanged.*

Since these values are both unequal and subjective, relationships must be negotiated — not just at their inception but through their entire duration, as well. The overtness of this process depends on the nature of the relationship. For instance, in a professional relationship, the terms of the transaction are expected to be rigidly and explicitly defined. On the other hand, adopting this approach in relations with friends and lovers would feel inappropriate and off-putting. Different types of relationships must be negotiated differently.

That said, this does not mean that these types of relationships are not predicated on the transaction of value. People do not hang out with (or sleep with) those they want nothing to do with. Without exception, people want something — they hope to benefit — from the people they choose to spend their time with, even if that something is merely the pleasure of the others' company (or an escape from the guilt associated with *not* discharging a duty). What this means is that the transaction of value in such relationships is typically negotiated covertly: it must be approached with subtlety, tact, and indirectness. When people take issue with my model of relationships, it is often because discussing their nature so explicitly violates a tacit social convention that friendships and romantic relationships more or less "just happen" and are maintained through altruistic "good will" (and also because the explicitness potentially reveals people's own self-interest where they would least like to encounter it).

There are rules and laws to relationships. *Rules* are more culturally informed and can be broken (though often not without *interpersonal* consequence). For instance, as a general rule, people expect their friends not to talk badly about them behind their backs. Obviously, some people violate this rule (so it *can* be broken); however, awareness of this violation can lead to conflict or the end of the friendship (so it can't always be broken without interpersonal consequence). Relationship rules can vary significantly from place to place and throughout time.

On the other hand, *laws* are more biologically determined and are much more difficult to break (and generally not without *intrapersonal* consequence). For example, it is a law that relationships are formed when people transact unequal goods of comparable value. If the goods are the same, then exchange is either unnecessary or impossible (so no relationship is formed). And if their values are too disparate, then the relationship becomes likely in inverse proportion to the size of the perceived mismatch in value: the greater the mismatch, the less likely the relationship. If the law is violated and a relationship is formed under a significantly mismatched valuation, this is generally due to the fact that the perception of value has shifted since the point of transaction. In any case, awareness of this violation can lead to a great deal of pain and distress for the under-compensated party (so it can't always be broken without intrapersonal consequence). Relationship laws are fairly constant and universal.

These relationship rules and laws, in conjunction with people's infinitely varied interpersonal objectives, collectively give rise to the *game of relationships*. Some people object to the word *game* used in this context; however, this is generally on the basis of the word's connotation. A game is not necessarily a casual thing: some games are played very seriously. And a game is not necessarily a trivial thing: some games are played for very high stakes. A game is *anything with rules and a goal*. And under this definition, human relationships are games. In relationships, people try to get what they want from others: this is the *goal*. And they have to go about doing this without violating — or, more realistically, selectively violating — various inter- and intrapersonal guidelines: these are the *rules*. If people get too little of what they want (or too much of what they don't want), they stop playing — which, incidentally, is another relationship law.

Every type of relationship constitutes a different game — as does every specific relationship of the same type. For instance, the game of friendship is different from the game of business, both in their rules and goals. What is considered an effective strategy in one game might constitute a rule violation in another. Furthermore, the game of friendship with a specific individual is different from the game of friendship with any other individual. After all, people don't want the exact same set of things from all their friends, and idiosyncratic patterns of interaction will emerge within the context of each friendship. So both the rules and the goals will vary from friendship to friendship. And since each specific friendship is nested in the larger game of general friendship, we find that the overarching category contains enormous variation at the individual level.

This is all to say that it's fairly difficult to talk about relationships. Any principle that seems to apply to the general category of relationship will likely be contradicted by a specific example on the individual level. However, we all recognize that different relationship categories exist: a friend is different from a lover is different from a colleague. And this means that there must be principles that vary from category to category but are consistent within each category itself. That said, the truer these principles are, the more abstract and unsatisfying they are likely to be. For instance, the statement "all people want to be happy" might be true in general, but it is useless in particular. Why? Because what makes one person happy will infuriate (or bore or terrify) another.

So we need to pick our poison. On the one hand, greater specificity at the category level will make any claim less valid and reliable because it will increase the likelihood that it is contradicted at the individual level. On the other hand, less specificity at the category level will make any claim less practical and actionable because it will decrease the likelihood that it can be effectively applied at the individual level. This is why the highest wisdom can often sound so vague and idiotic, while detailed advice can be so contentious and inapplicable. There are no perfect solutions here. My goal is to split the difference as best I can by providing insights that are as true as possible without compromising their usefulness.

This book is largely a discussion of the principles that govern a specific category of human relationships, namely: sexual relationships between men and women.[3] A sexual relationship exists whenever at least one of the goods transacted is sex. This means that when people have sex with each other,

3 To be fair, much of this discussion will apply to homosexual relationships, as well. However, this book would need to be significantly longer if it sought to cover every aspect of human sexuality in all its varied expressions — and I'm afraid I'm already taxing the reader's indulgence with the size of the current volume.

those individuals are in a sexual relationship (irrespective of whether they believe they are "in a relationship"). The duration of the relationship is unimportant: some sexual relationships last for an evening, others for a lifetime. It is also irrelevant whether sex is understood to be the ultimate objective of the relationship (i.e., the goal) or an instrument to achieve some other end (i.e., the means). What matters is the presence of sex: it is the necessary and sufficient element of a sexual relationship.

People enter into (and remain in) sexual relationships by playing the *game of mating and dating*. Like those pertaining to all other relationships, this game is subject to rules and laws that are culturally informed and biologically determined. Ignorance of the principles governing play is associated with a diminished likelihood of success. After all, if you don't know the rules of a game, you can probably only win through sheer dumb luck. On the other hand, awareness of these principles will significantly improve the probability of securing one's desired outcome. This is especially true considering that most people either don't understand or are (at best) only dimly aware of the game they are playing.

For instance, the most fundamental law of the game of mating and dating — the law that explains the lion's share of the variance behind who gets (and stays) with whom — is that people enter into (and remain in) sexual relationships with their perceived best options. The idea that — all other things being equal — individuals will forgo a better opportunity for a worse one is absurd. If humans were governed by this law, our species might have gone extinct ages ago. And if people enter into (and remain in) sexual relationships with their perceived best options, then the *perception of value* must be the mechanism that lies at the heart of sexual relationships.

Once we appreciate this, we can understand that the game of mating and dating is fundamentally governed by a synthesis of psychological and economic principles. This synthesis is partly psychological because it is informed by perception (which is a complex cognitive phenomenon), and it is partly economic because it is enacted according to principles regulating value exchange (which constitute economic action).[4] We can refer to this interdisciplinary framework as behavioral economics, which is why I call my theory the **economic model of relationships**. As we'll see, when applied to sexual relationships, the economic model can explain a great deal of people's mating and dating decisions using only a few underlying assumptions.

In all likelihood, this model will significantly deviate from your own subjective experience with respect to how you go about pursuing relationships. This is because most people enter into relationships for emotional reasons. Taken at face value, this is a contradiction in terms (i.e., emotion isn't *rational*). However, at a much deeper level, there is some truth in this phraseology. In fact, the economic model clarifies the reasons behind the emotions that motivate people to form relationships. And since the model can explain emotions

---

4 People often balk at this definition because they believe that economics is only concerned with *money*. As a result, they think that applying economic principles to sexual relationships is somehow crass and materialistic. However, this isn't necessarily the case. A better definition of economics was provided by Lionel Robbins, who wrote that economics "studies human behaviour as a relationship between ends and scarce means which have alternative uses." Under this definition, we can see that the game of mating and dating is heavily influenced by economic realities. Source: Robbins, L. (1932). *An essay on the nature and significance of economic science*. Ludwig von Mises Institute.

(but emotions cannot explain the model), this means that the model is more fundamentally true and should take precedence.

To understand why this is the case, we need to take a closer look at the concept of value: what it is and how it operates.

THE COVERT CALCULATOR[5]

Value is easy to define but difficult to pin down. Our everyday use of the word suggests a serviceable enough definition: *value* is something that people are willing to pay for. And *payment,* in turn, is the expenditure of resources. This does not necessarily mean money (though it certainly can). Time, effort, attention, and opportunity (among others) are all forms of resources. These resources must be expended both to acquire and to retain valuable goods, and resources — once expended — cannot be refunded.[6]

Any given individual possesses these resources in limited quantities. No one has infinite money, unlimited time, or inexhaustible energy. This means that people have to make decisions about how they allocate their limited resources most effectively. They can't have everything, and pursuing some paths will close off others. At the most basic level, the scarcity produced by our limited resources is what creates value to the individuals involved. This is essentially why the

5 This is probably the most abstract and difficult-to-understand section of the entire book. It's a shame it has to show up in the first chapter, but there's no way around it. If you can get through it, congrats! You'll have a deeper appreciation for what follows. And if you're getting lost or having a tough time, don't worry about it. Just skip ahead to the next section. Everything will be easier from here on out.

6 Even expended monetary resources can't be refunded. This is because the same quantity of money will have a different value to a specific individual at different points in time.

gods in Greek mythology envied man: mortality (i.e., scarce time) made his life valuable.

However, this definition doesn't explain *why* people value certain goods (and not others), nor does it clarify *how* people determine the value of these goods. The answers to these questions are fairly complex, but let's take a stab at them anyway. As previously stated, it's important to appreciate that value is never static. Just like a stock in an exchange, it is subject to perpetual fluctuation. What's more, value is never objective. As we'll see, it only exists in the minds of the valuers. Even the "objective" market price of a certain stock is really just an aggregate of countless subjective valuations. And this, of course, is what allows some individuals to determine that this aggregate valuation is wrong: they might think the aggregate is too high (and sell short) or too low (and buy more). Objective reality, on the other hand, can't be wrong (or right, for that matter): it simply is what it is. In any case, the determination as to whether something is "worth it" is always personal and subjective: the same price will be a steal to one person and highway robbery to another (or to the same person at different points in time).

There are two primary drivers of value fluctuation at the individual level: goal-relevance and information. People want lots of different goods, and — to the extent that the acquisition of these goods is governed by rules — that means that people are playing lots of different games simultaneously. In fact, the human experience means being embedded in a complex and interrelated set of nested games. The game of, say, making a presentation is embedded in the game of a job, which is embedded in the game of money, which is embedded in the game of society, which is embedded in the game of survival. Which game is most personally relevant at any one time depends on the never-ending stream of information that enters into our consciousness through our changing perception of the present moment.

For instance, perceiving a look of disapproval on your manager's face might motivate you to temporarily prioritize the game of your job over and above the game of your presentation. After all, you're likely not making a presentation because you find presenting intrinsically rewarding but because you understand that it is one of your professional responsibilities. So there would be little point in securing a lesser goal if it meant compromising a greater one (perfectionists: take note). By the same token, if you perceived that the building was on fire, you would likely try to escape using every available method — the disapproval of your manager notwithstanding.

The upshot is that nesting games will always take precedence over nested games whenever we become aware of new information that affects the acquisition (or maintenance) of the superordinate game. And it's this fluctuation in goal-relevance caused by new information that functionally explains why people value certain goods (and not others). This is because the more we perceive a specific good to be instrumental to achieving a personally relevant goal, and the higher we understand that goal to be in our nested hierarchy of games, the more we invest that specific good with value. People might scoff at paying ten dollars for a bottle of water — but a man dying of thirst would be willing to pay a great deal more. But he will likely *not* be willing to pay as much for a second bottle, as the new information provided by his body will tell him that his need is now not quite so great and urgent. The water is valued differently by different people (and by the same person at different times) because it is not perceived to be equally instrumental in achieving a personally relevant goal associated with an equally important game.

Okay — so how do people determine the value of any specific good at any given time? We've already touched on a few factors that influence this determination: the scarcity of the specific good, the perception of its instrumentality in achieving a personally relevant goal, and the importance of that goal in the nested hierarchy of games (among others). However, the valuation process is far more complicated in reality. This is because value is essentially the output of an extremely complex calculation comprised of a countless number of evaluations mediated by perception, memory, and imagination. This output is also calculated anew hundreds of times every second for an uncountable number of goods simultaneously. I'll try my best to explain what this means.

Once we become aware of new information that indicates a specific good might be instrumental in achieving a personally relevant goal, we begin to evaluate a great number of factors, including: the extent to which current conditions match previous conditions associated with an opportunity to acquire the good, the various ways we could go about obtaining that good, the anticipated costs (in terms of expended resources) associated with each method, the subjective value of these resources given their respective scarcity, the perceived likelihood of each method's success, the previous success rate of each individual method, and the degree to which (and for how long) successfully obtaining the good would achieve the personally relevant goal. We execute these evaluations using many different cognitive processes that utilize information from the present and the subjective past (e.g., perception, memory) to predict an outcome in the subjective future (e.g., imagination). Finally, all these evaluations are conducted for all the most relevant goods that we could acquire using a comparable amount of resources. So far, so good?

Now, all these evaluations influence valuation in constant and predictable ways. For instance, people will value a method of obtaining a specific good with a higher likelihood of success more than they would value a method with a lower likelihood of success. This tendency is universal: there is no culture in which it doesn't exist. This is because the principles of valuation are like the principles of logic: they do not change from place to place or moment to moment. What's more, neither can be empirically proven: we just somehow perceive them to be self-evidently true. And this is almost certainly because — like the ability to think logically — the ability to calculate value is hardwired into our brains. This, of course, doesn't mean that everyone always uses these abilities correctly. People can (and do) make mistakes in employing propositional logic. It just means that the same fundamental principles inherently exist within all of us — irrespective of our individual skill in applying them.

So why is this so complicated? Why don't people, say, simply choose the method of obtaining a specific good associated with the highest likelihood of success in all cases? For the "simple" reason that — in the real world — all other things are *not* equal. Like a physics textbook that instructs its readers to ignore friction and air resistance, considering all other factors to be equal is a thought exercise designed to help people understand how a single component operates within a complex, interdependent system. It doesn't generalize to reality. That said, if we could somehow understand how every component operated — both individually and interdependently — in a given system, then we might be able to create a model capable of increasingly approximating reality.[7] And while we might not be able to explicate every one of these components consciously, the covert calculator that exists within all of us *doesn't require our understanding to operate.* It goes about its calculations intuitively and unconsciously — whether we want it to or not.

It does this by assigning a *provisional value* to each individual component of the calculation, ascribing a *provisional weight* to the value of each individual component depending on the relevance of the component to the goal in question (and the relative position of that goal in the nested hierarchy of games), and aggregating them into a *provisional total value.*[8] We can call this output the value coefficient of a particular good. It represents how valuable an individual perceives a specific good to be at a distinct moment in time. The higher the value of a coefficient associated with a specific good, the more valuable a particular individual will perceive that good to be. This value coefficient is then compared with the value coefficients of all the most relevant goods that could be acquired using a comparable amount of resources. All other things being equal, people will choose to invest these

7 However, no model will ever completely align with reality due to its reliance on known unknowns and its vulnerability to unknown unknowns.

8 This could be represented mathematically as something like: $\Sigma = a_1(x_1) + a_2(x_2) + a_3(x_3)...$, in which the x terms represent the valuations of the various individual components, the corresponding a terms represent their respective weights, and the Σ represents the total value. Of course, this is an extremely simplified representation. The reality is far, far more complicated.

resources in the particular good associated with the *highest relative value coefficient*. And the difference between any two value coefficients will not only indicate a given individual's preference but the relative size of that preference, as well.

This is how people determine the value of something. The issue is that almost no one experiences the determination of value in this way. When presented like this, the valuation process feels alien or robotic or sociopathic. This is because the vast majority of this process occurs well below the threshold of awareness: individuals are generally cognizant of only a few aspects of the calculation, at best. And this can be off-putting, as it suggests not only that people are not aware of why they value the things they do but that their valuations might be influenced without their knowledge, as well. Both are true. However, if you pop the hood and look inside, you'll see that the brain is one enormously complicated organic computer. And among its most important functions — just behind keeping the body alive and rendering an accurate representation of reality — is the tireless calculation of value by means of the covert calculus I just described. This is how people actually determine the value of something — it's just not how they *experience* doing so within their own subjectivity.

So why is there a mismatch between the actual process of valuation and the experience of that process? Simple: under normal conditions, conscious awareness has a very limited bandwidth. Awareness of the actual process of valuation — and the billions and billions of calculations per second that this process entails — would be absolutely overwhelming. It would paralyze the individual in question, which would be a significant liability for an organism that has to move through reality. Even bringing a greater proportion of the process into conscious awareness would likely lead to behavioral hesitation, which would have consequences for time-sensitive decisions (including those that impact survival). So the mind effectively hides this process so deep in the unconscious that, much like the routines governing an individual's heartbeat, it can only be partially accessed with an inordinate amount of conscious effort.

That said, while awareness of the process itself is unnecessary (or even detrimental) to the individual, awareness of the output of the process is extremely important. So the question becomes: How can people be meaningfully made aware of the output of a process of which they must remain functionally ignorant? The mind has evolved an ingenious solution to this problem, namely: *the calculated value coefficient is transformed into an emotion*. This emotion contains the personally relevant significance of the value coefficient, and it transmits this significance in a manner that (typically) prevents individuals from being overwhelmed with unnecessary information and can motivate them into immediate action.

This is why no one thinks, "I've determined that a particular good would be greatly instrumental in helping me achieve an important self-relevant goal: not only because I anticipate that the benefits associated with acquiring it will significantly exceed the costs, but because I can also conceive of no better way of achieving the same goal to the same extent with a different good that could be acquired with comparable resources at an equivalent cost-benefit ratio." Instead, they feel: "I *need* this," or "*This* is the one," or "Wow! I *love* that!" The feelings behind these statements accomplish the same goal more elegantly than awareness of the valuation process ever could: they communicate to the individual (and potentially to others) that a particular good is subjectively *valuable*. And this communication is extremely useful because it is constituted by behavioral impulses that motivate action in alignment with this valuation: to approach, to acquire, to protect, to maintain.

So people *do* make decisions for emotional reasons. That is, the covert calculus of the valuation process provides the rationale for the emotion that motivates decisive action. Neat! And to the extent that it's true, this explanation can also help us understand a number of other potentially puzzling phenomena. For instance, it clarifies why feelings often seem to *come out of nowhere*. They don't really: they are the transmuted outcomes of the valuation process. It's simply because the process is normally so deeply unconscious that we experience the emotions as sort of arising within us. In the absence of a better understanding, we've even created a mysterious organ to help explain the origin of these feelings: *the heart*. When people talk about the heart in this context, they generally don't mean the electromechanical pump that circulates blood throughout the body, but a hypothesized seat of emotion capable of sensitively responding to environmental cues. And, of course, people *do* have hearts in this sense: they're just not where they think they are.

I could say much more about this topic; however, I'm probably already pushing my luck here. So let's abandon this disquisition in favor of less rarefied realms. I promise the remainder of the book will be easier to read.

THE GAME OF GAMES

Applying the concept of value to human beings — and the relationships they form — can be unsettling and contentious.

It's unsettling because we would prefer not to think that some people are more valuable than others, and it's contentious because we tend to disagree about what might contribute to those differences in value. However, we can largely avoid both issues by remembering that value is always assessed in relation to a personally relevant goal.

For instance, a plumber is neither inherently more nor less valuable than a cardiologist. However, if your toilet backs up, you'll be calling one and not the other. This decision is not unsettling — it's common sense. So to understand why individuals enter into relationships with certain people (and not others), it is extremely useful to identify the goal they are attempting to achieve. This is equivalent to asking the question: *What problem of living are they attempting to solve?* Fortunately, the bi-directional relationship between problem and solution helps us answer this question. That is, because your toilet is clogged, I can predict that you'll call a plumber (and not a cardiologist) — and because you called a plumber, I can deduce that you had an issue with your plumbing (and not your heart).

This personally relevant goal organically renders certain traits, skills, and attributes more valuable than others. For example, while we all might not agree on what makes for an ideal plumber, we can reasonably predict that we will tend to value signals of responsiveness, effectiveness, and affordability in a potential candidate more heavily than, say, signals of kindness, temperance, and humor, if and when we need to hire one. This decision is not unsettling — it's common sense. It's also important to appreciate that in most cases the traits, skills, and attributes we value more highly in those with whom we enter into relationships to solve a particular problem of living are much more influenced by the nature of the goal in question than by personal preference. This is because the value of a good is directly related to its perceived instrumentality in achieving a specific goal. If anything, it's probably more correct to think of our preference as the consequence of that perception (as opposed to the other way around).

Whether we're aware of it or not, we also seem to possess *exemplars* — or idealized constructs — associated with specific types of relationship partners. And since thoroughly examining each individual candidate for a relationship can be both time-consuming and prohibitively expensive, one of our most common decision-making heuristics is to (often unconsciously) determine the *perceived goodness of fit* between any specific candidate and its relevant exemplar. The greater the perceived fit, the more likely we will select a given option, all other things being equal.

What's more, this process is influenced by contextual factors in predictable ways. For example, the less important the goal a given relationship will attempt to achieve in an individual's nested hierarchy of games, the lower this individual's selection threshold will be with respect to the perceived goodness of fit. That is, for a less important decision, we're more likely to consider a decent match to be "good enough." However, for a more important decision, we would likely hold off until we found a "better" option (provided we weren't under an urgent time constraint).

To understand why individuals enter into relationships with certain people (and not others), it is extremely useful to identify the exemplars against which they are comparing candidates. Fortunately, the bi-directional relationship between exemplars and selection helps us in this process. That is, because I know your exemplar, I can predict that you'll choose to enter into a relationship with a specific person (and not another) to achieve a specific goal. And because you've chosen to enter into a relationship with a certain individual to achieve a specific goal, I can deduce the features of your exemplar (with sufficient data).

When we apply all these considerations to sexual relationships, it's easy to see why the game of mating and dating can be so confusing. In the first place, it's important to understand that — for the vast majority of people — this game is very high in the nested hierarchy of games. As the saying goes, "All's fair in love and war." To the extent that this is true, it is true because both of those games are fundamentally concerned about *survival*. And we generally expect the game of survival to take precedence over all other games for the simple reason that losing that game typically makes it impossible to win the others.

While the "game of war" is associated with the survival of the individual organism, the "game of love" is associated with the survival of the individual's genes. From an evolutionary standpoint, an organism that lives to a ripe, old age without reproducing not only dies — it goes extinct. At some level, it lost the game of survival because it did not find a way to perpetuate itself through time. Indeed, it seems that genetic survival is a more important goal than individual survival for perhaps all living beings (including humans). A mother who dies so her children might live exemplifies this phenomenon. Just as humans have evolved biological and psychological mechanisms to facilitate their own individual survival, they have evolved other mechanisms to assist with the survival of their genes.

As a consequence, the game of mating and dating ranks very highly in most people's nested hierarchy of games — in many cases, above their own individual survival. In many respects, it is the *game of games*: the game that makes all other games possible. This explains a number of things. For example, if the game of mating and dating is associated with the most superordinate goal of all (i.e., genetic survival), then we should not only expect a constant, passive surveillance for new information pertaining to that goal but also a willingness to prioritize this goal over all others when sufficiently attractive opportunities present themselves. This is why the sexual marketplace is functionally *everywhere,* and why people are subject to doing all kinds of hurtful, shameful, and desperate things in the service of this goal. A starving person is likely not proud of choosing to steal food — and we probably wouldn't uphold the behavior as an exemplar for ethical conduct — but we would almost certainly understand this person's decision.

Since the value of a good is related to its perceived instrumentality in achieving a particular goal and to how highly that goal is ranked in an individual's nested hierarchy of games, we can now appreciate why those with whom we enter into sexual relationships can be among the most valuable people in our lives — and why that value can fluctuate so dramatically over the course of a relationship. After all, a plumber is much more valuable to us before he fixes our clog than he is after he does so. People might balk at this, but no one continues to pay the plumber after the job is finished.

Though potentially challenging (and frustrating), the changing priority of our goals — and, therefore, the fluctuating value of any given person for a particular relationship over time — might be navigable were it not for two additional variables that significantly complicate the matter further, namely: goal conflation and lack of awareness. Let's look at each in turn.

It can be hard enough to get what you want from a specific person. However, this process becomes exponentially more difficult if you want many different things from that specific person. We can call this *goal conflation,* which occurs when a single means (i.e., a specific relationship) is used to pursue multiple goals (e.g., sex, security, friendship) simultaneously. Goal conflation makes every aspect of a relationship more challenging because completely satisfying options will be both rare and expensive.

As a result, most people will not be able to get everything they want from a single person. And this means — when it comes to relationships — there aren't any solutions, *only trade-offs*. And this system of trade-offs becomes increasingly more complicated in direct proportion to the number of things we want from any given person. Not only will the things we want fluctuate in importance over time, but they will fluctuate differentially, as well. This will alter the relative priority of what we want from any particular person, and this, in turn, will affect how much we value that person by influencing our perception of the trade-offs involved.

Let's say a given woman might not be the most beautiful, but she may be very good with children. This trade-off will not only cause different men to value the same woman differently, but it will cause the same man to value the same woman differently at different points in time. A husband who was willing to forgo an attractive sexual opportunity for the sake of a woman's maternal instincts will likely be less willing to do so once his children are grown up. This is because — if nothing else changes — the same woman will have become less valuable to him. This is not only because the woman can no longer help him achieve one of his personally relevant goals (i.e., raising children) but also because this goal is no longer highly ranked (for having been achieved). The cruel reality is that she will have become less valuable to him *for having given him what he wanted*. Remember: no one continues to pay the plumber. In light of this, we can understand why staying together over a lifetime can be such a difficult task — and why relationship longevity is so closely related to responding effectively to the way certain trade-offs evolve over time as a result of goal conflation.

That said, the man in the previous paragraph likely would not have consciously formulated his situation in those terms. And this brings us to the second significant complicator: *lack of awareness*. As you'll recall, most of the valuation process is buried in the unconscious most of the time. What's more, the individual is generally only made aware of the outcome of this process when the value coefficient is transmuted into an emotion. And with respect to sexual relationships, the emotion into which this value coefficient is transmuted is *desire*. The more a particular person is perceived to be valuable — that is, the more this person is perceived to be capable of achieving more of an individual's most highly ranked personally relevant goals as prioritized in that specific moment — the more this particular person will be desired by the individual in question.

This is the true (though, perhaps, unsatisfying) definition of a *high-value* man (or woman): it is a person we perceive as being able to give us more of what is most important to us, given the current prioritization of our goals. What's more, this person's ability to give us more of what is most important to us should not be compromised by any significant liabilities that would negate the benefits we hope to accrue in a relationship with him (or her). That is, a high-value person also gives us less of what we *don't* want.

When both of these are true, then the individual is perceived to be a *net positive* in the context of our hyperconflated goal set. The bigger the net positive, the higher the person's perceived value and the more desire we experience. Of course, whether we act on the impulses that constitute that desire (e.g., to approach, to acquire, to protect) depends on a host of other factors (e.g., perceived availability, intrasexual competition, available resources). However, we can't help but feel desire as a consequence of that perception. From this perspective, we can understand that saying people desire a high-value individual is a tautology, as desire is the natural emotional response to the perception of high value. It's equivalent to saying that people desire a desirable individual. And this is because *value and desire are the same thing experienced in different ways*.

As a result, our hypothetical husband probably wouldn't think of his wife as less valuable to him because she now provides less of what he wants (and, potentially, more of what he doesn't want) in the context of his evolving, hyperconflated goal set for the relationship, which thereby renders his marriage increasingly expensive (especially in the context of an optionality that may include more "affordable" alternatives) over time. And if he *does* think this way, he will likely feel guilty for doing so, as this type of thinking violates a tacit social convention with respect to sexual relationships.

It's much more likely that our hypothetical husband will respond to his circumstances *by feeling less attracted to his wife*. The diminishment of his desire is the result of his (potentially unconscious) perception that his wife has become less valuable to him, given his personally relevant goals. He may feel confused or frustrated or embarrassed in response to this diminishment, but — to the extent that desire represents the transmuted perception of value in sexual relationships — he won't be able to prevent it. That said, he may attempt to avoid experiencing this change in his desire in a variety of ways (e.g., drinking more, avoiding his wife, devoting more time to his work) with varying degrees of success.

In the context of sexual relationships, our emotional response to the perception of a high-value individual is desire. And this feeling motivates us to initiate (or maintain) a relationship with the individual in question. On the other hand, our emotional response to the perception of a low-value individual (i.e., someone we perceive to be a net negative in the context of our hyperconflated goal set) is *disgust*. And *this* feeling motivates us to avoid (or escape) a relationship with the individual in question. Finally, our emotional response to the perception of a mid-value individual (i.e., someone we perceive to be net neutral in the context of our hyperconflated goal set) depends on the number and intensity of the benefits and liabilities involved. If we perceive that a person might be capable of giving us a few things we kinda want (and a few things we kinda don't), we typically feel *indifferent*. We could take or leave the opportunity this person represents.

However, if we perceive that a person might be able to give us a lot of what we really want (and a lot of what we really don't), then we typically feel *conflicted*. And this is because both our desire *and* our disgust are active at the same time.[9] That is, we feel powerfully drawn to and repulsed by the same individual simultaneously. This is called an *approach-avoidance conflict*, and it can trap people in agonizing indecision for years.

Incidentally, the foregoing also helps explain why people ignore red flags — at least, in otherwise attractive individuals. Red flags are traits or behaviors that signify that a liability that is not (or only marginally) present now might be present (or much more present) in the future. The issue is that — just as the same benefit is always more valuable in the present than in the future — the same liability is always less detrimental in the future than in the present. This is because a chance always exists that neither the future benefit nor the future liability will actually come to pass, which influences the weighting of the value of each in proportion to the likelihood of its obtaining. This causes people to (rationally) undervalue potential future liabilities, which then contributes to tipping their perception of any given individual in the direction of a net positive.

When people perceive someone to have many of the goods they most want (right now), and few of the goods they don't want (right now) — that is, when they're dealing with an apparently high-value individual — then they will feel a

9 This suggests that more than one value coefficient is calculated for any particular good. Most likely, there is a coefficient associated with (at least) each of the inherent behavioral routines that constitute the primary emotions. Just like all visible hues can be created through various combinations of the three primary colors, all our feelings can be created through various combinations of the six primary emotions.

great deal of desire for this person (right now). And this positive emotion will reciprocally influence their valuation process in predictable ways, namely: by weighting values associated with current benefits more heavily, and weighting values associated with future liabilities more lightly. This is in the service of motivating action in alignment with their valuations. Given this feedback loop, it can take a fair amount of wisdom and forbearance to resist being emotionally swept away in the face of an extremely attractive option — virtues that are generally only cultivated as a consequence of the pain associated with *not* resisting such an impulse in the past.

On the other hand, people are typically better able to keep their wits about them when dealing with less obviously attractive individuals. Since they perceive these people to have fewer of the goods they most want, their valuation isn't quite so positive, even in the apparent absence of liabilities. This causes them to experience less desire, which mitigates the process described earlier. Ultimately, it is this reciprocal relationship between the perception of value and desire that explains why attractive people tend to receive all kinds of allowances that less attractive people don't — including the tendency to discount or minimize the implications of their bad behavior.

WHEN MODELS FAIL

While there are many ways in which a lack of awareness significantly complicates the pursuit and maintenance of sexual relationships, I'd like to discuss one final consideration that will be particularly relevant to our subsequent discussions. It is this: if the process of determining value is comprised of a countless number of individual evaluations, each associated with a specific weight that attempts to predict the importance of that evaluation to the achievement of a particular goal, and if the valuation process is almost entirely unconscious, then (to a large extent) *people will be unaware of precisely what they value and the extent to which they value those things.*

For instance, a woman who consciously thinks she wants a nice man to settle down with but who constantly finds herself getting involved in short-term relationships with exploitative bad boys is completely in the dark with respect to her actual goals and values, which are revealed by examining her choices. Such a woman might even vigorously deny that she has "a type," so profound the lack of awareness of her own preferences might be. This is hardly unusual.

Furthermore, irrespective of how progressive and open-minded we collectively consider ourselves to be, certain goals and values will always remain socially unacceptable. This means that even if we were aware of our valuation process, we would likely try to hide aspects of that process from others (and even ourselves). As a result, it is generally useless to directly ask people what they want in a sexual partner. Even if they could tell you the whole story (and they can't), they wouldn't. This is due to the fact that sharing some parts of that story would result in social censure and other parts might compromise the attainment of their goals. Just like a job interviewer can't be completely transparent about the actual criteria for selection — as doing so would significantly increase the likelihood that candidates would simply tell the interviewer what she wants to hear — people are generally forced into some measure of dissimulation when trying to get what they want from the opposite sex.

The most significant consequence of the unconscious nature of the valuation process is that — while there is always a rational basis for people's attraction (i.e., it is the transmutation of a value coefficient into an emotion) — what people are attracted to *is not always rationally aligned with their best interests* (or even their consciously explicated goals). This is due to the fact that — while the valuation process is inherent — the weights and evaluations used in that process are not.

People can't help but constantly (and unconsciously) value the objects of their perception according to their personally relevant goals. This tendency is baked into our neurobiology and might only be surmountable through enlightenment-level self-awareness and self-control. On the other hand, *what* people value — and *how much* they value those things — is not entirely biologically determined. It is both mediated by perception (which is not always reliable) and informed by culture (which creates significant variability across time and place).

As humans, we are born with the capacity to value, just like we are born with the capacity for language. However, precisely what we value often depends as much on the culture into which we are born as does our native language. People realize the potential inherent in both of these capacities primarily through observation of the world around them. In many respects, the brain is like a machine learning algorithm. It is hardwired with certain computational pathways, but it must be trained on data to function properly. And how accurately and efficiently such an algorithm performs its intended purpose is directly related to the data on which it is trained. These data not only constitute the inputs of the algorithm, they are also capable of altering the structure and process of the algorithm itself. These alterations can then influence the inputs of the algorithm in a reciprocal fashion. We can call the evolving outcome of this interdependent system the *valuation algorithm* when it is concerned with determining the instrumentality of perceived objects to our self-relevant goals.

With respect to influencing the development of the valuation algorithm for sexual relationships, the most significant culture into which people are born is their home environment. Whether they want to or not, children principally train their valuation algorithm on the data collected by observing the relationships of their primary caregivers. And while I can think of no better alternative, this is subject to creating difficulties for people further down the road for two reasons. Both are inevitable and inescapable in that they impact everyone to some extent.

The first reason is related to the *quantity* of our training data. If each of our valuation algorithms for sexual relationships is principally trained on data collected from just one relationship, then our algorithms will be unduly biased by the idiosyncratic features of that relationship. This is comparable to using one specific sparrow not only as the exemplar for all other sparrows but also *for all other birds*. Penguins, ostriches, and condors are fully just as avian as sparrows, but an algorithm trained exclusively on sparrows (let alone one specific sparrow) probably wouldn't even recognize them as birds.

We could call this the law of small numbers as applied to relationships, and it skews our valuations irrespective of the nature of the relationships on which they were trained. Consider that a child raised by a bitter and resentful single mother will likely develop a very different valuation algorithm than one developed by a child raised by two loving and engaged parents. Each will value different things differently; however, both will experience bias in their valuation algorithms in the same way. That is, unless their biases are subsequently corrected with additional data, both children will likely grow up thinking that the relationship on which each of their algorithms was trained *is the way all relationships should look*.

The issue is that no one relationship, no matter the relationship, can serve as the exemplar for *all* relationships. This is *not* to say there are no differences between healthy, functional relationships and unhealthy, dysfunctional relationships: there are. It *is* to say that there are many different ways for relationships to be healthy and functional (though, perhaps, not quite as many as there are ways for relationships to be unhealthy and dysfunctional). When people's valuation algorithms are skewed by the law of small numbers, their capacities to perceive the multiplicity of ways they can effectively structure their relationships — and the multiplicity of people with whom they can have those relationships — are compromised, even if they were raised under "ideal" conditions. Unfortunately, the unconscious nature of this bias can prevent people from even recognizing plausible relationship candidates, making the selection process even more difficult and restrictive. It may even be in people's best interests to deviate from the outputs of their algorithms, especially if those outputs constrain them to more costly methods of attaining their goals.

The second reason the home environment creates difficulties is related to the *quality* of our training data. If each of our valuation algorithms for sexual relationships is principally trained on data collected from just one relationship, and this one relationship (inevitably) achieves the goals of its constituents in a suboptimal (or even dysfunctional) manner, then all of our sexual relationship algorithms contain weights and values that *have no business being there*. To some extent and without exception, all people utilize algorithms that contain valuations that are either irrelevant or antagonistic to their goals. That is, they value things that don't matter too highly (because these things are not actually instrumental to getting what they want), and they (often) value things that *do* matter incorrectly (because they have been trained to approach what instrumentally they should avoid, and vice versa).

Irrelevant valuations are liabilities because they reduce the pool of satisfactory options for any given type of relationship, which has significant economic consequences. Including criteria that do not actually help you achieve your personally relevant goals will typically require you to spend more time and energy in the selection process and transact more resources to secure (and maintain) any satisfactory opportunity, if and when it finally presents itself. Focusing on irrelevant criteria can also distract you from more important considerations.

However, antagonistic valuations are even more problematic because they effectively sabotage goal-directed efforts. These valuations make it less likely that people will get what they want (and more likely that people will get what they don't want). The kicker is that they do this irrespective of the given individual's awareness. For instance, the hypothetical woman who doesn't understand why she keeps ending up in short-term relationships with exploitative men may not be aware of how her early experiences trained her relationship algorithm to highly value certain traits in a partner that are actually counterproductive to a healthy, long-term relationship (e.g., emotional volatility, spontaneity, fantasy) and to lowly value other traits that *are* related to that goal (e.g., emotional regulation, dependability, maturity). She is aware of her goal, but she is not aware of how her process (i.e., her valuation algorithm) is leading her astray.

But here's the thing: even if she *was* made aware of this process, *it wouldn't necessarily change her choices*. This is because awareness is technically insufficient to effect change, although it is potentially helpful in doing so. Even if this woman were to, say, go to therapy and come to understand how her childhood experiences influenced her unconscious valuation of prospective sexual partners in dysfunctional ways, she might *still* find herself in short-term relationships with exploitative men. This is because, if nothing else changes, this woman *will still continue to desire exploitative men* — even if she completely understands why she does so and why this desire is at cross-purposes with her best interests. Her awareness might prevent her from acting on this desire, but it won't prevent her from *feeling* the desire for the "wrong" men (or enable her to start feeling the desire for the "right" ones).

When people become aware of the extent to which their valuation algorithms have been trained on bad data, they become increasingly cognizant of a serious double-bind. Basically, within their subjective experience, they feel as though they are forced to choose between entering into a dysfunctional relationship with someone they authentically desire and entering into a functional relationship with someone they feel nothing for. Obviously, both options are problematic, but this double-bind will remain in effect until their valuation algorithms are appropriately corrected.

And the most effective way to correct them is to *flood these algorithms with better data.* It's not possible to erase the experiences on which these algorithms were trained. That would functionally require meddling with people's memories, which is problematic for a whole host of reasons. Rather, the idea is to expose people to so much good data that the bad data on which they were trained are rendered increasingly irrelevant. This could alter their valuation algorithms to be more aligned with their best interests, by means of the reciprocal process previously described. Doing so will literally change how individuals perceive actual and potential relationship partners. And as their perception changes, so too will their desire, as mediated by an altered valuation algorithm brought about through corrective experience.

My point here is that it is not necessary to judge the hypothetical woman for her relationship choices or the hypothetical man for his diminished attraction for his wife (any more than it would be necessary for these individuals, if they existed, to judge themselves). Rather, we can understand the desires of both constructs to be the rational and expected outcomes of an extremely complex (and almost entirely unconscious) valuation process and their decisions to be the reasonable and predictable consequences of their attempts to achieve as many of their (constantly fluctuating and) personally relevant goals as possible with the most economical expenditure of their available resources. All this neither eliminates personal accountability nor dispenses with free will. While our desires may not entirely be our fault, they remain our responsibilities. However, it's my hope that this understanding may open up new opportunities to relate to each other more humanely. And this is critical, as we can truly only love to the depth of our understanding.

In this chapter, I introduced some of the fundamental principles of the economic model of relationships. Because people want things from others, they enter into relationships. And because this process is subject to certain rules and laws, people must play the game of relationships to get these things. Individuals enter into relationships with their perceived best options, which means that the perception of value resides at the heart of all relationships. Value is calculated by an extremely complex and almost entirely unconscious process, the outcome of which is transformed into an emotion that impels people to act in line with that outcome. In the context of sexual relationships, this emotion is desire. However, desire remains mysterious — even to ourselves — due to goal conflation and a lack of awareness of our own functioning.

If people must transact their sexual relationships in the game of mating and dating, then there must be a field of play. In the next chapter, we'll discuss the nature of this field: the sexual marketplace.

If you'd like to further explore the topics presented in this chapter, please scan the QR code to access a curated playlist on the PsycHacks channel on YouTube.

CHAPTER 2

SEXUAL RELATIONSHIPS ARE TRANSACTED IN THE SEXUAL MARKETPLACE

That seems straightforward enough. However, despite the ubiquity of the sexual marketplace, how it tends to operate is not entirely obvious. So let's take a closer look, shall we? In the first place, it's important to understand that the sexual marketplace is not relegated to online dating sites or local meat markets. Quite the contrary: the sexual marketplace is *everywhere*. Though we may not like to admit it, the sexual marketplace is functionally coincident with the social world. This is because any two adults can initiate a sexual relationship at any time, irrespective of the differences in their age, wealth, attractiveness, or relationship status. Every day, new sexual relationships are initiated despite the ethical, moral, and — in some cases — legal prohibitions against doing so. That certain sexual relationships remain present even in contexts in which they are punishable by death is a testament to the irrepressible omnipresence of the sexual marketplace.

This makes people uncomfortable because the possibility represented by the marketplace is a potential chaos that is always threatening to disrupt the stability of their everyday lives. Sex — because of its connection to the propagation of life — remains an untamed (and untamable) force of nature. It is the Wild West that lurks at the heart of even the most repressive civilizations. It is a lawless free-for-all that will never be completely subjugated to order, and this is how it has always been. That contemporary sexual behavior is judged by some as increasingly shameless or permissive is less the result of a shift in sexual predilection than it is a change in the social reinforcement contingencies surrounding the acceptability of sexuality in the public sphere.

In any case, the sexual marketplace is everywhere, and the interaction between any two adults could potentially lead to a sexual encounter. The fact that most interactions do *not* lead to a sexual encounter does not necessarily mean that they couldn't in the future or that the interaction occurred outside of the marketplace. It simply means that at least one of the parties involved did not consider the projected benefits of such an encounter to sufficiently exceed the possible costs, risks, and liabilities. This contributes to a net neutral (or net negative) valuation, which is transmuted into indifference (or disgust).

If the sexual marketplace is coincident with the social world, then — on some level — we can't avoid locating ourselves within that marketplace. We don't have to opt in, and we can't really opt out. This can be distressing to a lot of people because it is generally uncomfortable to be sexualized against one's will. The best we can do is communicate on as many levels as possible that we are "closed for business." Just keep in mind that most shops are willing to transact after hours for the right price.

So if we can't avoid situating ourselves within the sexual marketplace, then it stands to reason that our best possible move is to learn how to navigate the marketplace as successfully and effectively as possible. To that end, I've developed an elaborate metaphor to help people understand what it is and how it operates. I'd like you to consider that the sexual marketplace is like a dock or a pier: a place where ships are moored. On the dock are two types of people: captains and passengers. Historically, captains have almost always been men, and passengers have almost always been women. However, in contemporary society, this is not the case, and we'll look into some of the consequences of this change later in the chapter. For now, it's enough to understand that these designations — captains and passengers — are technically gender-neutral (though, in practice, they typically aren't).

So how does the whole thing work? Simple. Captains stand in front of their ships and try to attract passengers onboard, while passengers walk the pier and attempt to secure a means to their chosen destination. Both parties need each other — two captains are only slightly less useless to each other than two passengers — and both parties will attempt to negotiate the best possible deal for themselves.

Negotiation is inevitable because — although they need each other — captains and passengers have *fundamentally different priorities*. From the perspective of passengers, a good captain is one who will safely take them exactly where they want to go as cheaply as possible. And from the perspective of captains, a good passenger is one who will pay well for the privilege of going where he or she is taken (or, at least, won't cause difficulties along the way). The party that needs the other more will be *less* powerful in the negotiation and more likely to deviate from his or her ideal position.

All people are passengers by default. This is because we all start off as children who can't go anywhere under our own power. If we do nothing to change this fact as we age, we will remain passengers throughout our lives. And since an option that requires action is typically less frequently chosen than an option that does not, this means that — in the sexual marketplace — there are more passengers than captains. This gives captains an advantage in their negotiations, as they effectively operate in a seller's market.

The sexual marketplace exists because enough people decide that the life of a passenger isn't for them, and they choose to devote their efforts to becoming captains. This is not an easy endeavor. In my experience, it takes about *ten years* to complete the transformation from passenger to captain. Most do not start, and many who start do not finish. And this is particularly dangerous for men because the marketplace isn't particularly kind to male passengers. If men fail to transform themselves into captains, they remain functionally invisible to others: unattractive to most women and useless to most men. There is no moral judgment here: it is what it is.

So how does one become a captain? To become a captain, you need to complete three challenges. You need to *build a boat*. You need to *learn to sail*. And you need to *chart a course*. The bad news is that any one of these is a lot of work and can take years to accomplish. However, the good news is that — since anything you spend that much time mastering is yours by rights — these achievements, once accomplished, cannot easily be taken from you.

And why are these the three challenges of the captain? Because they complement the three prerogatives of the passenger. And what are these? Passengers get to *inspect the ship*. They get to *test the captain*. And they get to *examine the itinerary*. The challenges of the captain are an adaptive response to the prerogatives of the passenger, and the prerogatives of the passenger are made possible by the challenges of the captain.

So how do captains and passengers find each other? What initially sparks an interaction is some kind of attraction, and this attraction is generally based on easily recognizable (and, therefore, superficial) characteristics. A passenger might like the external appearance of a given captain's ship and dawdle in front of it, while a captain might like the look of a given passenger and call out for his or her attention. If both parties are sufficiently interested, a negotiation ensues in which the two decide whether (and in what manner) they can do business with each other. This is effectively what dating is, and I will discuss this process at length later in the book.

For the time being, however, let's examine the respective roles of the captain and passenger in greater detail, as doing so will provide insight into how best to perform each. Let's start with the captain.

THE CAPTAIN'S CHALLENGES

As I stated before, captains have three fundamental challenges. They need to build a boat, learn to sail, and plot a course. Why is this the case?

Well, a captain without a ship is a captain in name only. Without one, a captain is play-acting at best and grifting at worst. Possession of a vessel is a necessary criterion to being a captain. However, it is not a sufficient criterion because possession merely makes one the owner of a ship.

Captains must know how to make the ship respond to their will — which is learning how to sail. However, even *this* is insufficient, as knowing how to sail a ship in one's possession merely makes one a mariner. A captain must be able to command the obedience of everyone else on board, which — at its most fundamental level — means having the authority to decide where to go and how to get there (i.e., plotting a course). A mariner with legitimate authority over his ship is a captain. Only by successfully completing all three of these challenges do people arrive at their captaincies.

The first challenge that captains must successfully resolve is to build a boat. Just as a ship is the vessel by which people navigate the seas, a lifestyle is the vessel by which people navigate their lives. It is the container that shelters captains through the vicissitudes of time and provides the means for them to continue the journey onward. Captains spend most of their lives on a ship. By the same token, people will spend most of their lives in their lifestyles. Given its importance, it may be surprising to learn that devoting too much time, energy, and attention to this aspect of their lives is a trap into which few people fall.

Building a boat requires two essential components: resources and knowledge. What does this mean? You can't build a boat out of *nothing*. You need resources to acquire the timber and cloth, more resources to transform them into planks and sails, and even more resources to assemble them into a ship. However, this alone is insufficient. To complete the task, you need accurate knowledge of the principles of ship-making: buoyancy, propulsion, and the like. Otherwise, you will only succeed in constructing a ship-looking sinker (as opposed to a seafaring vessel).

This analogy to building a lifestyle is sometimes obvious, sometimes not. The resources part is straightforward: *you need money*. Without money, it is difficult to navigate life. You can do it, but it's the advanced course, as you will need to compensate for your relative poverty by becoming rich in a host of different social virtues. And as difficult as it can be to acquire money, it is generally easier to do so than to acquire a host of different social virtues. Furthermore, money is the universal currency: you can be fairly sure it will be accepted wherever you go. And this facilitates an ease of movement that is otherwise difficult to achieve.

On the other hand, the meaning of knowledge in this context is not immediately apparent. By knowledge, I don't mean what is generally taught in schools or conferred with degrees. Rather, I mean knowledge in the sense of *an accurate understanding of reality* — or (at least) an accurate understanding of whatever subsection of reality you happen to be dealing with. For instance, money is good, but an accurate understanding of what money is (and how it works) is better. This is because money without that understanding is soon lost, and money with that understanding is preserved (and increased).

However, such an understanding is rare, as it demands that people be able to separate what money is from what they want money to be and what they think money should be. This is not easy. And if this understanding is uncommon enough when it comes to the reality of money, how exceptional must it be when it comes to reality, itself?

Many people suffer from the belief that such an understanding cannot be taught. This is not true — it absolutely can. The reason it is not taught even if it can be is that few people possess the understanding — and you must first have something before you can give it away. That said, real masters exist, and it's easier to find them today than it has ever been in human history.

If you want to find a master, you must take two steps. First, look for people who demonstrate through their actions that they have what you want. And second, implement their advice exactly as directed and observe whether it moves you in the direction of your goal. This allows you to responsibly enter into a kind of apprenticeship with the master, irrespective of whether you have an actual relationship (though this is preferable). This is precisely how most captains start their careers: as apprentices on *other* captains' ships. Ignorance is not a choice but remaining ignorant is.

In any case, with respect to the sexual marketplace, the challenge of building a boat is analogous to creating an emotionally compelling lifestyle and obtaining an accurate understanding of how the marketplace functions. Success in this endeavor will not only benefit the captains themselves — remember, captains spend most of their lives on their boats

— but will make it easier to attract qualified passengers on more favorably negotiated terms.

Now, having built their boats, captains must then *learn to sail*. And this doesn't simply mean the ability to make the boat move. A boat is in constant motion even if no one is at the helm. It also doesn't mean the ability to make the boat move where one wants. Even a child with little knowledge of navigation can make a boat move where it wants provided the seas are calm. Learning to sail is the ability to make the boat move where one wants when the water is rough. Everyone is a good sailor when the seas are calm. We only get a chance to observe who has learned their lessons when a storm sets in. Bad weather is the condition under which vast differences in skill become apparent, differences that are typically obscured by the insipidness of everyday life. Without this seafaring ability, a ship is little more than a floating casket.

In the context of personal development, learning to sail is a metaphor for *developing self-mastery*. It is the process of cultivating a suite of skills that will be useful out on the open seas of life — especially when the waters are rough. This suite includes abilities like logical problem-solving, emotional stability, and effective communication, and it includes virtues like wisdom, prudence, and courage. While good sailors don't seek out squalls, they see storms as opportunities to demonstrate their competence and further their mastery.

However, learning to sail has a special significance in the sexual marketplace because even wise, prudent, and courageous sailors will find it difficult to attract and retain passengers without first mastering two particular skills: *seduction* and *frame management*. Let's briefly discuss each in turn.

Seduction is the process of *inciting and directing sexual interest*. If sex only occurred under conditions of spontaneous attraction — the "spark" that many romantics chase through the years — then the human race would have died out long ago. Most attraction is not spontaneous. It is *responsive*, which means that it arises in the presence of certain stimuli. The ability to apply this stimulation intentionally is seduction. Both men and women can be seducers, although different tactics are more effective when performed by one sex than by the other.

Sailors who do not learn to seduce may be highly successful in other contexts but tend to get passed over in the sexual marketplace. These are nice guys who "any woman would be lucky to have," or women who are "like a sister" to men. Such people generally end up in satisfying relationships only through sheer dumb luck. More commonly, they set sail with one of the first passengers willing to come aboard, and at a steep discount. They often carry some form of baggage with respect to their own sexuality, and they can balk that they are not attractive enough to succeed.

Seduction has *little to do with attractiveness*. Indeed, the two are inversely proportional to each other in practice. The bitter truth is that the less attractive people are, the more they must become competent seducers to achieve comparable results. And this is good news because people can't learn to be attractive, but they can absolutely learn to be seductive. Many master seducers throughout history have, by all accounts, been nothing special to look at. Seduction is the means we can all employ to equalize the uneven distribution of attractiveness throughout the population. It is very difficult to achieve success — let alone the optionality from which success usually emerges — in the sexual marketplace without competence in seduction.

However, some ability in this domain is necessary but insufficient to the attainment of more abiding relationships. That is, master seducers may be able to cultivate many short-term sexual opportunities for themselves, but the ability to incite and direct sexual interest is typically not enough to keep people around for the long term. Depending on your goals, this may not be an issue. However, if you aspire to a satisfying long-term relationship, you will need to develop the second skill associated with learning to sail in the sexual marketplace: *frame management*.

Just like the frame of a ship is the structure of its hull, the frame of a relationship is the *structure of its negotiated arrangement*. As I will discuss later in the book, dating is a protracted negotiation in which — explicitly or not — both parties suss out what they hope to secure for the cost of what they're willing to give up. This typically occurs *before* the passenger boards the captain's ship in earnest and the two set sail for the open seas.

The issue is that time, circumstance, and personal agendas constantly challenge the original arrangement negotiated back on the dock. Consider your professional relationship. Assuming you're an employee, the arrangement you negotiated when the company first hired you will likely feel restrictive and inadequate even a few years later. However, as an employee, you're not in a position to dictate the terms of your employment. The most you can do is arrive at the willingness to leave if management remains unresponsive to your concerns.

This is why frame management is a required skill for captains. If they remain too rigid in their adherence to the original arrangement, then they run the risk of their passengers abandoning ship. But if they are not sufficiently steadfast in maintaining that arrangement, then they compromise the structural integrity of the ship, which will *also* motivate their passengers to seek transport elsewhere. And since this is a twofold disaster, it is generally better for captains to err on the side of being too rigid than being too flexible. The model for ideal integration is provided by the wood from which the ship is constructed: firm with a little give.

So now we understand that learning to sail in the context of the sexual marketplace means developing self-mastery, in general, and cultivating the skills of seduction and frame management, in particular. And having learned to sail a ship that we have built, are we now in a position to take on passengers?

Almost. The final challenge that aspirants must resolve in the path to their captaincies is *plotting a course*. After all, the whole point of building a boat and learning to sail was to create the means by which to go *somewhere else*. Without a destination, the pain and expense of cultivating those assets will go unredeemed. Competent mariners with fine vessels that sit at anchor in the harbor are of little use to anyone. They are certainly useless to passengers, who — by definition — seek passage. But even more importantly, they are useless to themselves. This is because a destination is the pretext for a voyage that will produce the opportunity to actualize, in themselves, what would otherwise remain potential.

In the context of personal development, plotting a course is analogous to *identifying your mission in life*. Where are you trying to go? By which star are you sailing? Cultivating an overarching purpose is vitally important for two fundamental reasons. In the first place, life is very difficult, and it is bounded on all sides by pain. And pain that is purposeless cannot be long supported. By extrapolating a personally compelling reason for living, you will be able to withstand the pain of existence with greater resilience. And in the second place, identifying an ultimate destination will allow you to resume your progress more easily after you are inevitably blown off course. No journey is a straight line, so it is wise to expect unexpected diversions (just ask Odysseus).

Much like learning to sail, plotting a course assumes a special significance in the sexual marketplace for a number of reasons. First, it's important to understand that taking on passengers is not a precondition of being a captain. That is, people who build a boat, learn to sail, and plot a course are captains — *whether or not they decide to take on passengers.* With their assets and skills, captains can sail around the ocean blue to their hearts' content all on their own — and this will be an ideal situation for a subset of captains.

So if captains technically don't need passengers in order to be captains, then if they *do* choose to take on passengers, it is important that they have a compelling reason for doing so. Why would it be necessary to have a passenger on board? This is the *manifesto* that justifies the *manifest*. Some destinations are difficult to reach on one's own; others are unobtainable with the excess weight. Ensuring that your destination is of the former type will not only provide a compelling enticement with which to attract passengers but will also supply the basis of frame management further out to sea.

I can't overstate the practical significance of this first point. Without a mutually agreed-upon destination, captains and passengers can't do business with each other. Think about it: would you get on an airplane if you didn't know where it was going? Most likely not. So why would a captain neglect the challenge of plotting a course?

Mariners who fail to plot a course often do so out of a scarcity mentality. This is because — as soon as mariners advertise their destination — *most passengers will have no interest in doing business with them.* A ship bound for Hong Kong is useless to everyone except those who want to go to Hong Kong. By not advertising their destination — or worse, by not having one — mariners are trying to secure the greatest potential customer base from which to derive their passengers. However, in their attempts to remain attractive to everyone, they generally succeed in attracting no one. On the other hand, captains who promote a destination that is attractive to even just 1% of passengers will have more potential business than they'll know what to do with.

Ultimately, plotting a course is a necessary precondition for captaincy; otherwise, the *passenger* will decide the course of the journey. The right to determine where to go and how to get there is the privilege of authority. And it is neither necessary nor helpful for passengers to be invested with this privilege. Passengers who are allowed to dictate the ways and means of the journey will likely never arrive, as they typically lack the knowledge and ability to support their decisions. For the safety and well-being of everyone on board, the highest authority on a ship must be the captain. And the best way to prevent passengers from commandeering the voyage is for captains to plot their courses well in advance of entering into negotiations on the dock.

So there you have it: the three challenges of the captain explained in the context of the sexual marketplace. Now let's turn our attention to the role of the passenger.

THE PASSENGER'S PREROGATIVES

Before we begin, it's important to appreciate the difference between a *challenge* and a *prerogative*. To become a captain, resolving the three challenges previously described is both necessary and sufficient. There is no way around them: you cannot become a captain without resolving the challenges, but resolving the challenges is enough to make you a captain. On the other hand, passengers technically do not have to complete any of the following actions. They *get* to; they don't *have* to. And it's this discretionary optionality that makes prerogatives out of the three tasks of the passenger.

And why is it useful to examine these prerogatives? For two reasons. First, just as captains display varying degrees of competence and ability, passengers do the same. It's wrong to think of passengers as passive. Like a captain, a passenger is a role that can be actively performed across a spectrum of talent and skill. There are good and bad passengers, much like there are good and bad captains. Understanding the differences between capable and incompetent passengers will help those who aspire to be the passengers of first-rate captains, and it will help captains who hope to take on top-notch passengers.

Second, taking time to examine these prerogatives will significantly improve a captain's ability to attract qualified passengers and negotiate favorable terms down on the dock. Think of it like doing market research. If captains can better understand *how* passengers make decisions about which ships to board, then they should be able to emphasize the aspects of their captaincies most salient to passengers' decision-making processes. And this will make it much easier for captains to do business.

So what are the three prerogatives of the passenger? As stated previously, they get to inspect the ship, test the captain, and examine the itinerary. Each prerogative provides the basis for one of the captain's challenges. You could think of the resolution of each of the captain's challenges as the ability to successfully prepare against each of the passenger's prerogatives. Let's look at each in turn.

Down at the dock, passengers walk up and down, looking for suitable captains. Even though there are more passengers than captains, passengers today enjoy a historically unprecedented degree of optionality. A ship is moored at every slip, and captains must effectively stand out if they hope to successfully compete. And the easiest way for captains to do this is through their ships.

Since different vessels can reasonably be expected to perform different functions, passengers first begin to inspect the ships on offer *at a distance*. Yachts are good for pleasure cruises. Ocean liners are ideal for transatlantic voyages. Submarines are perfect for clandestine rendezvous. For better or worse, passengers will rely heavily on the size and shape of a captain's ship in their decision to either keep walking or approach for a closer inspection.

This is because passengers are always constrained by two factors: time and money. *Money* is the value with which passengers hope to transact their passage, and it will become more important when we discuss the negotiation process in greater detail. *Time* is the medium in which decisions are made. If they already have a destination in mind, passengers typically don't have the luxury of idly strolling the pier or the means of thoroughly examining every ship they pass. As a result, they tend to rely on time-saving selection heuristics in inverse proportion to their available time. The more in a hurry they are, the more cursory their inspections will be and the more they will rely on easily recognizable *proxies of seaworthiness*.

One of the proxies passengers most commonly utilize is the *size of the crowd* in front of any given ship. Captains who — for whatever reason — have already succeeded in attracting attention are more desirable than captains who haven't. This is true for two fundamental reasons. In the first place, *people want what other people want*. Securing something in limited supply amid high demand is a status flex, as it communicates the securer's relative superiority with respect to some kind of transactable resource. And people like to feel superior to others — though they certainly don't like to admit it.

And in the second place, *it delegates due diligence to others*. If passengers neither have the time nor the inclination to thoroughly examine the captains on offer, then they can reasonably assume that at least some in the crowd of passengers in front of any given captain *did*, and that this subgroup found a particular captain especially attractive, given the relative competition. This approach isn't foolproof — as it is subject to all kinds of faddishness and caprice — but it mostly works (which is why it has survived as a heuristic).

If passengers are sufficiently interested in a captain's vessel and intrigued by the crowd standing on the dock, they will approach close enough to examine the captain, proper.

And on the basis of their own eyes and ears, they will begin to form judgments with respect to who this captain is. First, they will consider the captain's *physical appearance*. This means both the captain's dress and physique. Next, they will listen to the captain's *speech*. This means both the captain's words and tone. And, finally, they will consider the captain's *manner.* This means both the captain's emotional state and behavior. On the basis of a captain's appearance, speech, and manner, passengers will begin to cultivate fantasies (or expectations) of what it would be like to be on board the vessel.

That said, savvy passengers know that looks can be deceiving, popularity is fickle, and expectations are not always justified. These folks won't be content to only examine the ship from the outside. They will want to inspect the inside, as well. Among other things, the interior of a ship will give potential passengers a fairly good idea of the level of safety and comfort they will enjoy on board. Will they find lifeboats or water seeping through the planks? Will they sleep in a sumptuous stateroom or a hammock in the hold? And most importantly: has a place been created for them? If so, where is it? A poolside deck chair underneath an umbrella, or a seat at the helm at the captain's right hand? This interior examination will afford potential passengers a reasonable basis from which to extrapolate a vision of the voyage.

Now, before we continue, let's pause here and consider the significance of what has already been said for the sexual marketplace. Allow me to make a few aspects of the analogy explicit, if they weren't already obvious. The most important thing to understand about the selection process of passengers is that a good deal of it happens *before the captain is even aware of the passengers' presence*. If passengers don't like the look of a captain's ship, they will keep walking. If passengers observe that no one else seems to be interested in a captain's ship, they will keep walking. And if passengers don't like what they see and hear of a captain's appearance, speech, and manner, they will keep walking. All these filters are typically applied before a captain even has the opportunity to interact with a potential passenger.

And this awareness brings with it two important corollaries. First, if captains are not enjoying good optionality despite their advantageous position in the marketplace (remember: the demand for captains almost always outstrips the supply), then the problem lies somewhere in the inspection funnel: at the level of the ship, at the level of the marketing, or at the level of the personal presentation.

Each of these problems has a solution. If the problem lies at the level of the *ship*, then captains must invest resources to make their lifestyles appear more emotionally compelling. If the problem lies at the level of the *marketing*, then captains must make an effort to become more visibly competent. And if the problem lies at the level of the *personal presentation*, then captains must attend to their fitness, their fashion, and their communication. An issue at any one of these levels will significantly reduce the number of passengers any given captain can hope to engage.

And second, if several filters are applied by passengers prior to a first interaction, it means that passengers who enter into discussion with any given captain are *much more interested than they likely appear to be*. This is important for captains to remember throughout the negotiation phase, as passengers use all kinds of tactics to secure discounts for themselves by seeming to be uninterested in what's on offer.

The prerogative of passengers to inspect a captain's ship speaks to the paramount importance of lifestyle in the sexual marketplace. Captains must have something to invite passengers *into*, and that something is their lifestyle. If that lifestyle isn't supported with knowledge and resources, it probably won't last long. After all, no one wants to get on a boat that will fall apart in the middle of the ocean. So these components are essential to attracting *long-term passengers*. On the other hand, a lifestyle that appears fun and exciting is more useful for attracting *short-term passengers*. When people are looking to feel something, they might hire a speedboat for an afternoon, but they typically don't want to live on one. So the lifestyle components that captains should emphasize are fundamentally related to their relationship goals.

This suggests that an important component of the courtship process should be inviting passengers on board and giving passengers the opportunity to serve in the function expected of them at sea. Unless such activities constitute regular occurrences for them, rather than, say, mini golfing or dining at Michelin-star restaurants, captains should date by inviting passengers into the preexisting structure of their lives rather than creating an extraordinary fantasy for their dates. If anything, captains looking for long-term relationships should err on the side of being too boring. On the other hand, those looking for short-term relationships should err on the side of being too bold, as this helps to cultivate the fantasy upon which initial attraction is based. Finally, captains should waste no time in asking their passengers to serve in their intended capacities at sea. This means, for example, that captains shouldn't wait on their passengers hand and foot in the courtship process if they *actually* want their passengers to cook and clean later in the relationship. Just like in business, applicants should be evaluated according to their ability to discharge the responsibilities they will be expected to perform.

Now let's say that a given captain's ship passes a given passenger's inspection. Does that mean the passenger is ready to set sail? Not at all. It simply means that the passenger may then exercise the second prerogative: the right to test the captain. What does this mean?

Well, if everyone is a good sailor when the seas are calm, how much more difficult must it be to determine who is a good sailor *on land*? However, this is precisely the task set before passengers. And anyone who's been around the dock knows it doesn't take much to pretend to be a captain. Some folks dress the part but don't know how to play it. Others own the ship but don't know how to sail it. Things are not always what they seem to be.

This is why passengers have the right to test the captain before coming on board. And since they cannot directly assess a captain's sailing ability on land, passengers generally have to content themselves with evaluating a captain's character. And the surest way to do that is to *arbitrarily cultivate stress in their interactions*. How a captain responds to arbitrary stressors on land is a decent — though imperfect — proxy for how that same captain might respond to necessary stressors at sea.

With respect to the sexual marketplace, this second prerogative helps explain why certain passengers can be so difficult in the courtship process. Appreciate that the marketplace includes many deceptive signals. Some people wear designer clothes in the club but have no money in the bank. Others present highly curated images of their lives on social media but give little thought to their actual lifestyles. Still others appear confident and composed but lose their equilibrium at the smallest frustration. Testing is how passengers attempt to differentiate the real captains from the pretenders and the charlatans.

How do you treat a car on a test drive? If you're like most folks: *not well*. As soon as you're out of earshot of the dealership, you're probably stepping on the gas, slamming on the brakes, and whipping around corners. You'll look under the hood and kick the tires and honk the horn. In fact, if you have any sense whatsoever, you'll do everything you can to reveal any latent flaws or defects — anything that shows signs of falling apart or needing repairs — *before* you sign the contract. And of course, if you choose to sign, your behavior will change accordingly. No one drives a car with more care than a new owner.

Passengers do the same thing before coming aboard, except the vehicle they are stressing is the *captain's character*. They are creating an artificial storm on land in order to predict how a captain would weather an actual squall out at sea. Passengers can stress a captain's character in a near-infinite number of ways, including: being flaky, disrespectful, impulsive, uninterested, dishonest, or incompetent (just to name a few). This is because — no matter the person in question — all passengers eventually *will* be flaky, disrespectful, impulsive, uninterested, dishonest, or incompetent at some point on a long enough time line. This is analogous to the fact that — no matter the person in question — all drivers eventually will have to step on the gas, slam on the brakes, and whip around a corner at some point on a long enough time line. Just as drivers want to know a car's responsiveness before they need to know it, passengers want to know a captain's reactivity before they need to.

The prudence that underlies this passenger prerogative is important for captains to keep in mind because this testing can be both expensive and infuriating. If they're not careful, otherwise good captains — who may have already invested considerable resources into building their boats — will find themselves with few actual passengers amid a lot of apparent optionality. Consequently, it's useful for captains to remember that testing indicates a *high degree of interest*. Just like few people will test drive a car they are not seriously considering buying, few passengers will take the time and trouble to test a captain they are not seriously considering engaging. And this is also why testing the captain is the *second* prerogative: the condition of the ship always takes priority. So the presence of testing indicates that a captain has already successfully resolved the first challenge.

Now let's imagine that a given passenger has already exercised the first two prerogatives to satisfaction, that is: the ship is shipshape and the captain is capital. Is the passenger *finally* ready to head out to sea? Not quite. There's just one thing left to do, namely: examine the itinerary.

You would be forgiven for believing that this prerogative would be the most straightforward of the three. In most modern ports, a vessel's destination is clearly and unambiguously displayed. Cruises publish daily itineraries so that passengers know every port of call well in advance of disembarking. Exercising this prerogative is generally a simple confirmation: "Is this the boat bound for Barbados?"

This, however, is *not* the kind of dock on which we find ourselves. Rather than a safe and efficient transit center, the sexual marketplace is like a shady port in the 18th-century Caribbean. Pirates and buccaneers rub shoulders with soldiers and legitimate businessmen. Order and infrastructure contend with chaos and intrigue. Things are not always what they seem to be.

As we'll see, this is not due, as most people believe, to the dishonesty of certain bad actors. It's an *essential feature of the marketplace itself*. The dock will never *not* be a shady port. In any case, it falls to passengers to figure out, as best they can, where captains are going — and where captains are *really* going. What does this mean for the sexual marketplace?

Among other things, it means that neither captains nor passengers can rely on direct questioning to determine the nature and destination of the prospective voyage. And this is not because people are liars (although they are). It's because the more direct people are, the more transactional their relationships feel. And although all consensual relationships are transactional, most people want their intimate relationships *to feel as if they weren't*. This is true for both men and women and across the spectrum of relationships. A man who directly propositions a woman for sex generally enjoys as much success as a woman who directly propositions a man for a "serious relationship." These two offers are gendered equivalents of each other. Even if what's on offer might be what someone else is looking for, that someone might balk if it is emphasized too strongly or offered too forthrightly. The rules — though variable to time and place — must be observed.

In practice, what this often looks like is men pretending to be interested in commitment and provision in order to get sex, and women pretending to be interested in sex in order to get commitment and resources. This is because pretending *works*. Leaving aside the moral or ethical implications of such a strategy, pretending to be interested in giving the other party what he or she wants is a far more effective approach to securing a relationship than simply declaring one's own interest in the transaction. A salesman who says he wants to do business for the sake of his commission will not be rewarded for his honesty.

Note that pretending might not be a successful strategy for maintaining a relationship. However, a relationship must first be secured in order to be maintained. These are different problems requiring different solutions. As we'll see, the tacit agreement regarding how much sex is transacted for how much commitment and provision is an ongoing negotiation that transpires over the duration of the relationship, with the more powerful party securing a more favorable arrangement. For the time being, however, it's enough to understand that stated intentions (i.e., what people *say* they are going to do) and revealed intentions (i.e., what people *actually* do) are not always the same.

This is why examining the itinerary cannot be reduced to a structured interview or a written questionnaire — and why we probably wouldn't like it even if it could. Even assuming perfect honesty and transparency (both of which are anathema to seduction), this method could only hope to reveal where captains *think* they are going. If people are dishonest (and they are), then they are — first and foremost — dishonest with themselves. Even worse, asking people where they're going presumes they've given it some thought. In reality, most individuals do not have an extrapolated vision for their lives — though they will often use words to cover up this deficiency, if pressed.

When done correctly, examining the itinerary is a process of deducing where people are actually going through careful observation of their actions. This is why it is essential that captains formulate an overarching purpose for their lives: it is extremely difficult to remain in alignment with a mission that has not been clearly articulated. By extrapolating that vision, captains create a standard against which their behavior can be measured. And this, in turn, makes it more likely that prospective passengers will discern this vision in captains' actions.

It's also important to appreciate that — unless they're dealing with a ferry (and more on that later) — passengers generally cannot expect to go exactly where they want. After all, they just show up with a little money and a desire to go somewhere. Captains, on the other hand, have invested years in the construction of their boats and the mastery of their craft. Captains and passengers are not equally invested in the endeavor, so it stands to reason that they are not equally franchised to direct its course.

Ultimately, it is the duty of captains to create the itinerary, and the right of passengers to either accept or reject the itinerary, as they see fit. And just like there are *false captains* who advertise destinations at which they will never arrive, there are *false passengers* who feign acceptance only to attempt mutinies once they've lost sight of land (more on this later). Both parties must be careful.

That said, while passengers cannot reasonably expect to go exactly where they want, they are unlikely to get on a boat unless it seems to be headed in the general direction of where they want to go. And while captains can technically go where they please, they won't enjoy much demand for their services if they voyage where few passengers are interested in visiting. Just like in the commercial marketplace, in which products and services emerge out of an ongoing dialectic between producer and consumer, the itineraries of relationships, in practice, are created from the mutual interdependence of captain and passenger. And like consumer products, relationships are subject to larger market forces more often than we would generally care to admit.

In any case, those are the three prerogatives of the passenger with respect to the sexual marketplace. If passengers like the boat, approve of the captain, and accept the itinerary, are they — at long last — ready to set sail? If only life were that simple. Rather, if these conditions are met, it's a signal that negotiations for the price of the passage are ready to begin in earnest. We'll examine what that process looks like in more detail in chapters 4, 5, and 6.

THE TWO-BODY PROBLEM

At the risk of making this chapter overlong, we have one more important consideration to address before moving on. As I previously stated, the terms *captain* and *passenger* are technically gender-neutral, and I've been careful to avoid gendering the terms in the forgoing discussion. However, in practice, this is hardly the case. So let's briefly discuss the intersection of gender and role in the sexual marketplace.

Historically, throughout nearly every age and in nearly every culture, men have always had/gotten to be captains, and women have always had/gotten to be passengers. I'm using this awkward construction, *had/gotten*, intentionally to keep the reality that both roles are associated with benefits and liabilities in the forefront of our awareness. For instance, there is no power without responsibility, and there is no safety without restriction. Most men were not kings of the Earth, and most women were not chattel in bondage. This is a retconning of history.

However, the last few decades have seen a tidal change in the sexual marketplace. The advance of modernity, the proliferation of certain technologies, and the influence of particular social movements have done much to liberate gender from role — at least, for women. Throughout the Western world, women are supported, encouraged, and incentivized to "ascend" to their captaincies: to build boats, learn to sail, and plot a course. And I don't think this is inherently a bad thing. I'm generally in favor of greater freedom and optionality for the individual. And I can appreciate that — in certain corners of the world — there may be a dearth of good male captains for women to engage. Personally, I would rather try my own luck than bind my fortunes to an incompetent captain in a leaky dinghy.

However, the converse has not been true for men. It has never been acceptable for young men to aspire to one day settle down with a good woman who will provide for him while he raises her children — nor will it likely ever be. This has less to do with "toxic masculinity" or some unyielding machismo that prevents men from accessing their capacities for tenderness and child-rearing, as some theories purport, and much more to do with the fact that women — on the whole — generally find the prospect of providing for a grown man *distasteful*. Most would rather remain single than take on such a liability. Since women do not generally prioritize the suite of traits and skills that make for good "house husbands" in their selection processes, and since men tend to conform to women's preferences to secure sexual opportunity, the passenger role will never truly be open to men — especially since many of these preferences, though shaped by culture, are grounded in biology. This is not a complaint, just a reflection on reality.

In most cases, if a man does not succeed in becoming a captain, he does not get to sail as a passenger (though, as we'll see, many captains end up as passengers on their own ships). He just sort of gets left on the dock. On the other hand, it is perfectly acceptable nowadays for women to become captains, sail as passengers, or — increasingly — deploy a mixed strategy: build a boat and (eventually) secure passage on an *even bigger* ship. They are rarely left on the dock. That said, this mixed strategy often does not produce the desired outcome. However, in practice, women now have twice as many options as men do in the sexual marketplace.

As might be expected, while these new circumstances have created historically unprecedented opportunities, they have also given rise to difficulties that have never before been encountered. The foremost of these difficulties with respect to the sexual marketplace is the *two-body problem*.

If you're not familiar with the term, the two-body problem originated in academia. Let's say you're foolish enough to pursue a doctorate. Not only is this experience extremely stressful, joyless, and isolating, it will also devour a significant portion of your life. Nearly half of all liberal arts candidates, for example, do not complete their doctorates in less than ten years.[10] And because they undergo this difficult (albeit arbitrary) crucible with only a few other individuals who are uniquely situated to understand something of their suffering, these people tend to enter into relationships with their classmates: the shared trial brings them together. It happens all the time.

Now here's the thing. Eventually, these two budding scholars will graduate and enter into an insanely competitive job market. The number of new doctorates awarded every year dwarfs the number of new tenure track positions created by an order of magnitude.[11] Most will not be offered a job, and most of those who do will not enjoy much optionality. Given the gargantuan imbalance between supply and demand, new doctorates simply cannot afford to be picky if they hope to pursue a career in academia.

Given these realities, what do you think are the odds that both members of the couple will be offered tenure track appointments at *the same university*? Functionally zero. Assuming both receive offers — and that's far from a guarantee — their placements might not be within a thousand miles of each other. And if that occurs, given the struggle and sacrifice demanded of the doctoral process, what do you think are the odds that either person will give up his or her ambitions just to accommodate a relationship — especially considering that each person worked just as hard for just as long as the other? Again: functionally zero. This is the two-body problem: it

10 Just one of many good reasons to think very carefully about pursuing an advanced degree. Source: https://100rsns.blogspot.com/2010/09/4-it-takes-long-time-to-finish.html

11 Degrees also often have a shelf life. If new doctorates aren't offered a tenure track position within a year or two of graduating, it's unlikely they ever will. Source: https://100rsns.blogspot.com/2010/09/8-there-are-very-few-jobs.html

essentially asks people to choose between their careers and their relationships.

It should be easy enough to understand what this has to do with the current state of the sexual marketplace. Like earning a doctorate, it can take ten years (or more) to become a captain. The amount of time, energy, and money required to build a boat, learn to sail, and plot a course is considerable, to the say the least. It's one of the largest investments people can make in their lifetimes. And given the struggle and sacrifice demanded of the captaincy process, what do you think are the odds that someone will give up his or her position just to accommodate a relationship? Functionally zero.

Few people who become captains will ever truly be comfortable as passengers on someone else's boat. And that's how it should be. People don't pour their hearts and souls into their life missions just to walk away from them for someone else's preference or convenience. That's not the Way of the Captain. If it ever *does* happen, the offer would need to represent a substantially better opportunity than anything the captains could create for themselves, or it would need to arrive at a time when the captains were thinking of retiring from their positions. And this is precisely what we see when we observe the behavior of female captains: many of them only consider leaving their ships as they approach the end of their fertility windows, and only for a significantly better opportunity. This is the mixed strategy mentioned earlier. So why doesn't this generally work? Well, if a woman decides to follow the Way of the Captain, and if she resolves the challenges set out for her, she earns the right to moor her ship down at the dock and compete for the attention of passengers — *like all the male captains*. The men whose attention she would likely be much more interested in attracting — the male captains — will probably not be among the crowd in front of her boat for a number of reasons.

First, there's the two-body problem. These captains have invested considerable resources into their own ships, so they're unlikely to abandon their posts for passage on another. And this is especially true given the fact that women enjoy more optionality in the sexual marketplace. If it is socially acceptable for women to be captains *or* passengers, and *only* socially acceptable for men to be captains, and if *someone* has to leave the captain's quarters to accommodate the other, on what rational basis would it be the man?

And second, flouting these realities often leads to the dissolution of the relationship as a consequence of the woman's diminishing attraction. Most women are attracted to the suite of skills and traits embodied by captains: confidence, competence, courage, and capital. And a captain cannot remain a captain *if he's a passenger*. If she succeeds in luring a male captain off his boat, female captains can inadvertently destroy the bases of their own attraction by turning a daring leader into a devoted follower. They lose by getting what they want.

So if male captains are probably not going to leave their ships to become passengers on female captains' boats, what about the other way around? As previously stated, this is a more likely outcome given women's greater marketplace optionality. However, this maneuver can also prove difficult. This is because what makes for a good captain *is not what makes for a good passenger*. The two roles generally constitute completely complementary skill sets. A woman who has spent ten years (or more) mastering her captaincy is unlikely to have invested much time and effort into developing ideal passenger traits. And while every captain's individual preferences differ, most good captains are looking for good passengers. The suite of skills and traits a second captain would bring to the voyage is redundant at best, and competitive at worst.

This means that, at the end of the day, most female captains end up competing for the attention of male passengers — who might be more accurately described as the *men who are left on the dock*. These are generally not the kind of men with whom these women dreamed of becoming involved when they first started on the path to their captaincies. If good men are hard to find, they're even harder to find loafing about the dock. This is because the good ones spend most of their time *out on the open seas*. And since most women would prefer to remain single than provide for a grown man, an increasing number of modern women are capably sailing their boats right through their reproductive windows. According to a recent meta-analysis, 80% of childless women never intended to be.[12] The mixed strategy pursued by most women these days provides more freedom and optionality but comes with additional risk and responsibility. And, on some level, this is fair: people shouldn't be allowed to win more if they're not willing to stake more. There are two common objections to this assessment. The first believes that the previously described difficulties could be mitigated by making it more socially acceptable for men to be passengers. However, while this might make it easier for some women to retain their captaincies in the

12 Educational attainment and a stable career were associated with childlessness in women but not in men. Source: Keizer, R. (2010). *Remaining childless: Causes and consequences from a life course perspective* [Doctoral dissertation, Utrecht University]. Research Gate.

two-body problem, *it completely disregards how female attraction operates*. On some level, this social engineering scheme would only work if it also succeeded in fundamentally altering what women wanted and somehow motivated them to begin offering provision and protection to men. The second believes that these difficulties can be skirted with communication and compromise. These objections often take the form of questions like: "Why can't the captains take turns leading the ship?" or "Why don't they sail their own ships separately to the same destination?" My rebuttal to these objections is that, if these were good ideas, we would see them implemented in paid enterprise. The fact is that these solutions — while not impossible — are impractical: they are inefficient, ineffective, and undermine the role of the captain. They are also expensive, as they demand that a greater share of resources be devoted to the relationship — instead of to whatever the relationship was trying to accomplish. The point is that these solutions come at a cost, and that this cost must often be paid with resources that would be better allocated elsewhere.

In this chapter, I described the sexual marketplace as a dock where captains and passengers compete for the right to do business with each other. This led to a discussion of the complementary relationship between the three challenges of the captain and the three prerogatives of the passenger. I also briefly touched on the relationship between marketplace role and gender, and some of the implications of this intersectionality.

That said, mastering a role is not enough to secure a relationship. All relationships — from casual hook-ups to lifelong partnerships — are comprised of three stages: attraction, negotiation, and maintenance. In some cases, these stages transpire over a matter of minutes; in others, decades. However, if you look carefully, these three stages are always present.

In the next several chapters, we'll discuss how each of these stages operates. I'll begin by tackling that thorny and often misunderstood component of attraction: sexual marketplace value.

If you'd like to further explore the topics presented in this chapter, please scan the QR code to access a curated playlist on the PsycHacks channel on YouTube.

CHAPTER 3

EVERYONE HAS A VALUE IN THE SEXUAL MARKETPLACE

If relationships are the media in which value is transacted, and the sexual marketplace is the context within which sexual relationships are transacted, then this means that — whether they like it or not — everyone who exists within the sexual marketplace has a specific value at which they are trading in the hopes of entering into a sexual relationship and its attendant privileges. We can call this value *sexual marketplace value,* or SMV. As we'll see, SMV has a great deal to do with the game of mating and dating.

Many people are uncomfortable with the idea of SMV — at least, when the concept is applied to *themselves*. However, I've never met someone who doesn't make use of the idea in his or her own selection process. Such individuals may not be cavalier about their valuations, but they seem to have fewer qualms about applying the concept of SMV to potential suitors. When well-meaning friends tell you that "you could do better," they are referring to sexual marketplace value — if not as a number, then at least as a quantity.

This is because, though people generally seek to exchange unequal goods, comparable valuations are a prerequisite for a non-coercive transaction. Remember: in practice, relationships are transacted when individuals exchange unequal goods of comparable value. And this mutual interdependence is fundamentally based on self-interest: each party, in providing value to the other, tries to secure the best possible outcome for itself. As we'll see, in the sexual marketplace, this takes the form of an endlessly evolving suite of strategies that attempt to either increase one's own perceived value or (more nefariously) decrease the other's self-value.

As I mentioned in my discussion of the captains' challenges and the passengers' prerogatives, much of the filtering that passengers do with respect to potential captains occurs well before captains even realize they are being considered for selection. By the same token, captains can also see passengers at some remove, and they can (and do) make decisions about who they are interested in inviting closer for an interaction. That said, captains typically can't see passengers as far away as passengers can "see" captains: the ships and crowds advertise the presence of a captain long before the individual comes into view.

The important idea to understand here is that a great deal of the selection process occurs *before* the first interaction. And given (in many cases) the complete absence of more personally relevant information, SMV is the primary metric by which people make decisions at this stage. This makes sexual marketplace value — while not a determinant of sexual relationship opportunity — a powerful driver of marketplace optionality. So, it's essential that we understand this concept clearly, especially since SMV is much more complicated than most people appreciate. Let's take a closer look.

THE CULTURAL YARDSTICK

In its most rudimentary form, individuals are assigned a sexual marketplace value on a linear scale from 0 to 10. This conceptualization gives rise to statements like: "Ooh, he's a 9," or "Eh, she's a 5.2." As we'll see, this framework mystifies the reality of transacting sexual relationships in practice, mostly due to the fact that it suggests that SMV is both objective and inherent. It is neither. That said, SMV isn't entirely subjective and extrinsic either. So what is it?

This conceptualization of sexual marketplace value is essentially a quantification of the degree to which a specific individual *matches a given culture's archetype of an attractive man or an attractive woman*. And this archetype is determined by both culturally specific *and* biologically constrained factors. In order to differentiate it from other forms of SMV that I discuss later in this chapter, I will refer to this conceptualization as *normalized sexual marketplace value*, or nSMV.

Even the most cursory examination of beauty standards reveals these standards are not only involved in a process of continual evolution but also fluctuate significantly across time and place. The most attractive woman in a Bantu village probably wouldn't enjoy the privileges associated with that perception if she were dropped in the middle of Tokyo (and vice versa). This is because beauty is (at least partly) presentation, and *presentation is communicative*: it attempts to transmit a message. Like any other message, it will be understood to the extent that the receiver is fluent in the language of its transmission. As a result, it's difficult to pin down exactly what constitutes an ideal standard of beauty, as these ideals can't really exist outside of the culture that elaborated them.

That said, these standards are not entirely culturally relative, either. Certain attributes tend to be associated with beauty archetypes across time and place — such as lower waist-to-hip ratios in women,[13] higher shoulder-to-waist ratios in men,[14] and higher facial symmetry in both[15] — which strongly suggests that our perception of attractiveness is (at least partly) rooted in our biology and maintained through evolutionary pressures of sexual selection.

For instance, one primary function of a sexual relationship is to create children, which can only be borne by women and only within a certain reproductive window. This reality alone does much to explain why men — across time and place — tend to prefer younger women, as younger women tend to be more fertile and capable of bearing more children across a longer time frame. The fact that modern women, over the

13 Women with low waist-to-hip ratios are also more fertile and less prone to chronic disease. Source: Cashdan, E. Waist-to-Hip ratio across cultures: Trade-Offs between androgen- and estrogen-dependent traits. *Current Anthropology, 49*(6). doi:10.1086/593036

14 The ideal shoulder-to-waist ratio in men is 1.6. Source: Horvath, T. (1981). Physical attractiveness: The influence of selected torso parameters. *Archives of Sexual Behavior, 10*, 21-24. doi:10.1007/BF01542671

15 In this study, the face artificially manipulated to be even *more* symmetrical than the most symmetrical natural face was selected as the most attractive face the overwhelming majority of the time. Source: Harun, N., Adam, K., Abdullah, N., & Rusli, N. (2023). Is a symmetrical face really attractive? *International Journal of Oral Maxillofacial Surgery, 52*(6), 703-709. doi:10.1016/j.ijom.2022.09.031

past 50 years, are waiting longer to have fewer children does little to change a sexual preference in men that has been cultivated by millions of years of evolution. Unsurprisingly, sexual preference in mate choice is significantly influenced by reproductive role.

It's also important to appreciate that these standards are *sexually dependent*. While the roles of captain and passenger are technically gender-neutral, the archetypal standards of attractiveness are decidedly not. This means that the same standards are used to measure the attractiveness of, say, male *captains* as of male *passengers* — which create opportunities for synergy and dissonance between marketplace role and biological sex that will significantly impact outcomes. These role-independent standards of attractiveness are largely responsible for the fact that male passengers and female captains don't fare as well in the sexual marketplace as do male captains and female passengers.

To my knowledge, no society has used the same standard to measure a man's attractiveness and a woman's attractiveness. If attractiveness were entirely culturally determined, and if a culture were highly invested in the notion of equality (i.e., interchangeability) between the sexes, then these different standards would be redundant at best and inconsistent at worst. However, the gendered standards continue to exist even under these conditions because it's not possible to completely remove either factor — nature *or* nurture — from the calculus of desire. Campaigns to influence the culturally determined component of attractiveness — even if completely successful — would have only a fractional effect on the overall standards.

So what exactly are the modern standards of attractiveness: the ideal archetypes against which nSMV is measured? It's an oversimplification, but it kinda breaks down like this: men want *Barbie,* and women want *all the things the Ken doll comes with.* As the recent film (correctly) depicted, Barbie isn't all that interested in Ken himself. All other things being equal, the closer a given individual approximates the attractiveness ideal for his or her sex, the higher his or her normalized sexual marketplace value will be. Obviously, this is a caricature (remember: nSMV is a complex and evolving concept), but — like a caricature — it should exaggerate the most prominent features so they are easier to recognize.

Let's start with male mate selection. For better or worse, male mate selection is visually dominated. Men highly value the physical appearance — the shape and structure — of a woman's face and body: the doll. This is why many women are displeased with physical compliments from men and attempt to redirect attention to a cultivated aspect of their interior selves: they are uncomfortable with the *objectification that exists at the heart of male attraction.* Taken to its extreme, male attraction cares nothing for a woman's career, intelligence, interests, or personality. It is entirely concerned with the woman's body and what that body can do for him (i.e., sexual pleasure and reproduction). To many men, the woman herself is irrelevant at best and obstructive at worst.

We know this is true by considering the type of men that women find most distasteful in the sexual marketplace: *players.* I'm not here using this word in the general sense of "those who participate in a game." Within this understanding, both men and women are players in the game of mating and dating. Rather, in the context of this particular discussion,

I'm using "player" in the pejorative sense to mean a man who is only interested in a woman for sex. He doesn't provide protection or provision — let alone commitment or long-term partnership — and may be completely indifferent to the woman as a person. He may not even plan a date, preferring instead to simply "cut to the chase." And this is distasteful to women not only because, under such an arrangement, they are treated almost exclusively as sexual objects but also (and more to the point) because they receive little by way of compensatory value in the transaction. Women don't like players because the latter are fundamentally hustlers: they succeed in transacting *something for nothing*. This causes women to feel "cheated" by the exchange, even though they were — in most cases — enthusiastic and consenting participants.

On the other hand, female mate selection is much more complex. It's not that women are insensitive to physical appearances — after all, Ken is a handsome doll in his own right — but rather that they do not afford physical attributes the same primacy as men do. What seems to be most important to women — broadly defined — is *lifestyle*: all the things the Ken doll comes with. To a large extent, the male doll is a cipher: interchangeable and unremarkable. It assumes its value by virtue of its context: its accessories, possessions, and surroundings. This is why Ken comes in an infinite variety of "flavors," each associated with a specific fantasy: there's Malibu beach Ken (with dream house and surfboard), and veterinarian Ken (with stethoscope and puppy), and cowboy Ken (with Stetson and quarter horse), and bridegroom Ken (with tuxedo and wedding rings).

When a woman is engaged in selecting a man for a long-term partnership, she isn't looking so much at the man himself as at everything the man is surrounded by. She uses the man's circumstances as a proxy for the kind of life that might be in store for her should she succeed in securing that relationship. This is why — as attractive as wealth is to women — women are more directly attracted to emotionally compelling lifestyles (which typically, but not always, require wealth to elaborate). And this is how even physically unattractive men secure relationships with beautiful women: they provide access to a lifestyle that the women could never hope to create for themselves. That the converse (i.e., a beautiful man in relationship with a physically unattractive woman) is so rare speaks to the general validity of these respective valuations.

We also know this is true by considering the type of women that men find most distasteful in the sexual marketplace: *gold diggers*. "Gold digger" is a pejorative term for a woman who is only interested in a man for his lifestyle. She provides only as much sexual access as is required to keep the man from leaving, and she indicates with her behavior that the relationship is contingent on the provision of resources. And this is distasteful to men not only because, under such an arrangement, they are treated almost exclusively as financial objects but also (and more to the point) because they receive little by way of compensatory value in the transaction. Men don't like gold diggers because the latter are fundamentally hustlers: they succeed in transacting *something for nothing*. This causes men to feel "cheated" by the exchange, even though they were — in most cases — enthusiastic and consenting participants.

Players and gold diggers are gendered expressions of exploitation in the sexual marketplace. And these expressions, as caricatures, reveal gendered differences in normalized sexual marketplace value. Women complain that players want sex and *nothing else*; men complain that gold diggers what *everything else* and not sex (at least, not sex with *them*). Though it is theoretically just as possible, it's revealing that the converse is almost never encountered in the real world. For instance, I've never heard a woman complain that, even after paying all his bills and buying him a car and providing entirely for his comfort and lifestyle, a man *still* won't sleep with her. And I've never heard a man complain that a woman *only* seems to be interested in him for sex. So there must be some truth to this caricature, namely: in the sexual marketplace, women are primarily valued for what they can provide physically (i.e., sexual pleasure and reproductive fertility), and men are primarily valued for what they can provide materially (i.e., lifestyle and resources). It is what it is.

These differing standards of valuation are reflected in the gendered application of normalized sexual marketplace value. The more a given woman approximates the physical standards of, say, a beauty pageant contestant or a sexy lingerie model, the higher her nSMV, and the more a given man approximates the material standards of, say, a movie star or a wealthy noble, the higher his nSMV. As we'll see, this isn't necessarily what any given individual finds most attractive, but — if you listen to the murmurings of culture — this is what we have collectively determined to be the gendered paragons of attractiveness.

Why is this important? More than any other single factor, the normalized sexual marketplace values of the individuals involved *not only determine whether an interaction actually occurs down at the dock but the relative costs associated with the negotiated relationship, as well*. People who fail to surpass certain nSMV thresholds are functionally invisible in the sexual marketplace, though these thresholds can vary considerably from person to person (and in the same person across time). What's more, *favorable nSMV gaps* (i.e., when one's normalized sexual marketplace value is higher than the other party's) can both unlock relationships not available to others and secure relationships at less overall expense to the privileged party.

And this, of course, is why we see so many social campaigns to influence what constitutes these paragons of attractiveness. The stakes in the game of mating and dating are very high: those who do not succeed are afforded few reproductive opportunities, and that which they *can* secure must be purchased dearly. Those who, for whatever reason, despair of approximating their respective sex's attractiveness ideal will be priced out of the market unless the ideal can somehow be manipulated to reflect what they have to barter.

THE BASIS OF FAIR TRADE

If people trade unequal goods of comparable value, and if sexual marketplace value is grossly approximated using the metric of nSMV, then we can begin to make predictions about mating and dating behavior as it is actually practiced in the marketplace. In light of the differing standards by which men and women are measured, and the fact that men and women continually change across their lifespans, we can assume that there must be an age at which — all other things being equal

— men and women attain to their respective *peak normalized sexual marketplace values*.

We can also assume that these ages will be *very different*. In the sexual marketplace, women are primarily valued for their physical attributes (e.g., fertility, youth, and beauty), while men are primarily valued for what their material assets can secure (e.g., provision, security, and lifestyle). So we should expect women to reach their peak nSMV earlier in their lifespans — as fertility and beauty typically decrease as a function of time — and men to reach their peak nSMV later in their lives — as wealth and status typically increase as a function of time.

These expectations are confirmed in a myriad of ways. For example, the average age of *People*'s sexiest man alive is 39 years old,[16] while the average age of *Maxim*'s Hot 100 winner is 24 years old.[17] The average age of a Mr. Olympia winner is 33 years old,[18] while the average age of a Miss Universe winner is 21 years old.[19] And these discrepancies only widen

16 The youngest winner was 27 years old (John F. Kennedy, Jr.), and the oldest winner was 59 years old (Sean Connery). Source: https://newsfeed.time.com/2012/11/15/so-you-want-to-be-the-sexiest-man-alive-heres-the-secret-formula/

17 The youngest winners were 20 years old (Jessica Alba, Miley Cyrus, and Hailey Baldwin), and the oldest winner, crowned in 2023, was 35 years old (Ashley Graham). Source: https://en.wikipedia.org/wiki/Maxim_(magazine)

18 And this title is trending older. The average age is 36, if you don't include the first three winners. The youngest winner, in 1970, was 23 years old (Arnold Schwarzenegger), and the oldest winner, in 2018, was 43 years old (Shawn Rhoden). Source: https://barbend.com/mr-olympia-bodybuilding-competition-facts/

19 This title is *also* trending older. The youngest winners were 17 years old (Armi Kuusela, Christiane Martel, and Gladys Zender), but no one that young has won since 1957. The oldest winner, crowned in 2022, was 28 years old (R'Bonney Gabriel). Source: https://en.wikipedia.org/wiki/List_of_Miss_Universe_titleholders

when the individuals in question are being considered for a relationship. For instance, a recent study of revealed preference on a popular dating app found that, across millions of data points, women at age 23 were most attractive to men, while men at age 50 were most attractive to women.[20]

Collectively, this evidence makes sense. At 23 years old, a woman is at her peak fertility, has many good childbearing years left, is often the most physically attractive she will be in her life, and may have few to no previous relationships. From a sexual and reproductive standpoint, a woman at this age is in her prime. On the other hand, at 50 years old, a man might have an established position in society, a fully developed career, some degree of renown in his field (or beyond), a fair degree of wealth, and an emotionally compelling lifestyle. From a wealth and status perspective, a man at *this* age is in his prime. I understand that women generally want to be seen as baby factories about as much as men want to be seen as meal tickets; however, if taking offense changed how people mate and date, *it would have worked by now*.

If people trade unequal goods of comparable value, then approximating gendered nSMV as a function of time should predict that certain pairings between men and women would be significantly more common than others. First, it suggests a rational basis for the older man-younger woman pairing. In no culture in the world is the woman's average age at first marriage greater than the man's.[21] And while the size of this

---

20 As might be expected, this contrasts starkly with men and women's stated age preferences. Source: Bruch, E., & Newman M. (2018). Aspirational pursuit of mates in online dating markets. *Science Advances, 4*(8). doi:10.1126/sciadv.aap9815

21 The largest age gap is 8.5 years (Eritrea), and the smallest is 0.8 years (St. Kitts and Nevis). Source: https://en.wikipedia.org/wiki/List_of_countries_by_age_at_first_marriage

gap is at historical lows in the Western world, we see larger contemporary gaps in cultures that continue to practice arranged marriage or polygamy — as well as evidence of much larger gaps in the historical record cross-culturally.

And this makes sense if men exchange their resources for women's sexual opportunities. The more resources a man can offer, the more desirable the sexual opportunity he can typically attract (and vice versa). This not only aligns with an evolutionary perspective — in which more resources and higher fertility would predict the survival of more viable offspring — but also with an economic perspective — in which exchange occurs at comparable valuation in the context of competitive self-interest. And this tendency becomes increasingly exaggerated as we approach the highest levels of society. The average age gaps in celebrity pairings, for instance, are much higher than those in couplings at the population level.[22] Taken to the extreme, we would expect the highest-status men in any given society to maintain a harem of young and beautiful women — which is typically what occurs in cultures where the practice is allowed.[23]

Differences in gendered normalized sexual marketplace value also predict that younger man-older woman pairings are likely — provided that the man is under 30 and the woman is under 40 when they first initiate the relationship. Nothing is inherently wrong with men in their early 20s: it's just that women generally don't seem to want them. This is likely

22 A recent model predicted that a 40-year-old male celebrity would enter into a new relationship with a woman on average 9.8 years younger. Source: https://www.curiousgnu.com/age-differences-celebrity-couples

23 It's also (incidentally) what happens in cultures where the practice is *not* allowed. See, in particular, the section entitled "Men who achieve their desires" in the following. Source: Buss, D. (1994/2003). *The evolution of desire: Strategies of human mating*. Basic Books.

because they still lack the resources, status, and lifestyle that would make them more compelling options for long-term relationships. And nothing is inherently wrong with women in their late 30s: it's just that men generally don't seem to want *them*. And this is likely because declines in their fertility and attractiveness have rendered them less appealing options for long-term relationships.

However, their respective "discounts" mean that they trade at parity in the sexual marketplace. This is also why pairings of men in their 20s and women in their 30s are more common than, say, pairings of men in their 40s and women in their 50s. Even though the absolute age gap remains the same, the average man's nSMV will have increased (and the average woman's nSMV will have decreased) across that time period, rendering the underlying value proposition more imbalanced. All other things being equal, a relationship becomes increasingly unlikely as the perceived value of the goods proposed for transaction become incomparable.

As we've seen, normalized sexual marketplace value — the degree to which a given individual conforms with the culturally influenced and biologically determined attractiveness ideal for his or her sex — explains a good deal about who interacts with whom down at the docks. However, this is not the whole story. And that's because people enter into relationships with *specific individuals* — not with statistical abstractions.

Predictions of mating and dating behavior based on nSMV are kind of like predictions of particle flow based on the laws of aerodynamics. Given their statistical nature, such predictions can forecast very accurately that, say, half the particles will flow over (and half will flow under) an ideal airfoil. However, these same laws won't be helpful in predicting the movement of any specific particle over any specific airfoil. To do that, it would be necessary to look at the interactions involved on a different scale.

THE EYE OF THE BEHOLDER

People don't just make their decisions in the sexual marketplace based on nSMV — and this becomes increasingly true in the context of mating (or long-term relationships). For instance, men very well might choose to enter into a short-term sexual relationship with a woman based primarily — or even exclusively — on her physical appearance. However, fewer men would elect to start a family with a woman on these grounds alone. The more significant the relationship, the more other standards are brought to bear.

By the same token, many women have checklists with respect to what they are explicitly looking for in a long-term partner. For instance, they might want a handsome man with a good job, who is loyal and caring and family-oriented. That said, women don't actually enter into a relationship on the basis of a consciously extrapolated rationale, and they won't offer sexual opportunity *purely as a response to the satisfaction of their criteria*. If their attraction is high enough, they might dispense with their checklists entirely, and if their attraction is too low, they may create new criteria that suddenly need to be fulfilled. In most cases, the satisfaction of a certain proportion of a woman's criteria is a necessary but insufficient prerequisite to securing a relationship with her.

At the end of the day, it's attraction that runs the show (and the perception of value that calls the shots behind the scenes). And this is why I call the individual elements that constitute the ideals upon which normalized sexual marketplace value is based *attraction proxies*. Many men and women believe that if they only possessed these elements in greater quality or quantity, they would more effortlessly attract more desirable partners. And while possession of these proxies will likely improve their overall optionality in the sexual marketplace, possession doesn't — in and of itself — guarantee either a sexual opportunity or a committed relationship from any person in particular.

For instance, things like a bigger bank account or larger breasts are attraction proxies because while they will likely improve a given individual's nSMV in general, they are too often utilized as substitutes for attraction in particular. The fallacy is to believe that since — statistically speaking — women prefer wealthier men,[24] or men prefer women with larger breasts,[25] you will be more attractive to the specific individual you are dealing with simply as a consequence of having a higher net worth or a larger cup size. And this belief is especially insidious because it can lead people to think that they don't need to do anything else to cultivate attraction should they succeed in possessing the proxy. Neither of these beliefs is necessarily true. You can't have a relationship with an abstraction like "men" or "women." You can only have a relationship with a *particular* man or a *particular* woman. And these particular individuals can and do have interests and preferences that deviate significantly from the cultural ideal.

24 Turns out women prefer lots of things. Source: Buss, D., & Shackelford, T. (2008). Attractive women want it all: Good genes, economic investment, parenting proclivities, and emotional commitment. *Evolutionary Psychology, 6*(1), 134-146. doi:10.1177/147470490800600116

25 But apparently not too large. Source: Zelazniewicz, A., & Pawlowski, B. (2011). Female breast size attractiveness for men as a function of sociosexual orientation (restricted vs. unrestricted). *Archives of Sexual Behavior, 40*(60), 1129-1135. doi:10.1007/s10508-011-9850-1

This is why, in interactions down on the dock, normalized sexual marketplace value doesn't matter nearly as much as *perceived sexual marketplace value,* or pSMV. This is true for several reasons. First, it is very difficult to evaluate the character (or even the net worth) of another person, and it absolutely cannot be done on sight. That said, if appearances don't succeed in sufficiently stimulating attraction, few people will put in the time and energy required to do the assay. In this way, we can certainly imagine a man who, according to the standards of his culture, has an "objectively" high nSMV (e.g., high net worth, interesting lifestyle, powerful position) but who is consistently passed over for sexual relationships because he doesn't present himself in a way that makes his value observable to women. He will be treated in accord with the pSMV associated with him in the minds of the women who observe him — not according to some "objective" metric that (ironically) they cannot see. It is *pSMV* — consisting, as it does, of the *perception* of value — that will be instrumentally related to these women's attraction (or lack thereof).

The discrepancy between nSMV and pSMV affects women less intensely. This is because their normalized sexual marketplace values are principally derived from alignment with certain standards of physical attractiveness, which tend to be more immediately recognizable. That said, women get a taste of the gap with which men must constantly contend when they experience a change in perceived interest as a consequence of wearing makeup or dressing in certain ways. However, since these behaviors are generally designed to approximate certain beauty standards (by, say, manipulating the shape of the body or obscuring signs of age), women's gaps move in the opposite direction from men's. As a result, a given woman's pSMV is more likely to be higher than her nSMV, while a given man's pSMV is more likely to be lower than his nSMV.

The primacy of pSMV to the decision-making process in the sexual marketplace gives rise to a whole suite of strategies designed to *influence the perception of others*. This is because there is no such thing as "objective" sexual marketplace value. There is only the value that exists in the minds of others. Ever since our ancient ancestors figured out that — at least some of the time — they could achieve the same outcome more cheaply and easily by *seeming* as opposed to *being*, we have been dealing with a host of behaviors ranging from bald-faced lies and deception to, let's say, "playing to your strengths" and "putting your best foot forward." These are all degrees of lying, and everyone does it.

Women lie when they wear makeup to look younger than they are. Men lie when they say they're looking for marriage and commitment in order to get a date. Women lie when they get implants or fillers to create curves they don't have. Men lie when they splurge on designer clothes and extravagant gifts they can't afford. Women lie when they play hard to get with men they like. Men lie when they pretend to care about women they don't even know. Women lie when they say they would "never do that on a first date." Men lie when they say they're "not talking to anyone else."

Neither sex is above lying: each just does so in its own way. And both do so because they believe that certain forms of lying will *increase the chances of getting what they want by catering to what they think the other sex wants to see or hear*. Through lying, men and women are often able to secure more desirable sexual opportunities more cheaply by allocating resources toward increasing pSMV (rather than toward increasing nSMV). This is possible because — morality aside — lying *works*, at least for a while and at least for some of the time. These gendered forms of lying *do* tend to make men and women more attractive, and they work according to the proposed mechanism of action: by positively influencing pSMV. And this should come as no surprise: if these expressions of lying didn't work, they would have disappeared long ago. Down on the docks, things are not always what they seem to be.

Another reason perceived sexual marketplace value is important is because people have "types," or certain kinds of individuals to whom they are consistently attracted. Some people will swear up and down that they don't have a type, but their revealed preferences often tell a different story. More often than not, people's types are not completely in line with their given culture's paragons of attractiveness. As discussed in chapter 1, this is often due to the idiosyncratic development of any given valuation algorithm. Some women like funny gingers with big butts. Some men like ambitious Asians with small hips. Personally, I tend to have a thing for cute nerds. None of these types comes remotely close to approximating the gendered archetypes on which nSMV is based, but each could serve as the exemplar against which a given individual's standard for pSMV is measured. Sexuality is strange: one person's "ick" can be another person's "yum." And the sexual marketplace bears witness to a broad spectrum of taste: from likes and preferences on the one hand, to kinks and fetishes on the other.

And this is why — down on the dock — it's important to shoot your shot. Ultimately, it's not the normative standards of the culture (nSMV) but the personal valuation of the individual (pSMV) that determines whether an interaction occurs (and how it transpires). And while we all — more or less — collectively understand our culture's gendered archetypes of attractiveness, the standards of personal attraction are often locked up in the unconscious minds of the individuals in question. In any case, it's not only a mistake to conflate pSMV with nSMV but also to assume your pSMV in the minds of others. Ultimately, since attraction is based on perception, if you believe that someone is "out of your league," you're right.

So the decision to initiate an interaction in the sexual marketplace is most directly influenced by perceived sexual marketplace value. Does this mean that SMV is completely relative or entirely subjective? Not at all. While the price of a cup of coffee at a neighborhood café may seem arbitrary if you zoom out far enough (say, to the conceptualization of money as a fiat currency whose value is derived from the belief of those who use it), it is also rationally determined by reference to local market forces (most notably, to the price of coffee at rival cafés). Value is an illusion constrained by reality. And as we'll see, value operates in a similar fashion in the sexual marketplace as it does in the commercial marketplace.

THE POINT OF SALE

Have you ever been flabbergasted at a modern art museum to learn that a white canvas painted white sold for $50 million? Or rendered speechless when you found out that someone is being paid $300 million to throw a ball a few times a year? Or dumbfounded to discover that a misprinted postage stamp can fetch eight figures at auction? If you've ever shook your head at these (or similar) valuations and judged that they weren't worth their price tags: *you're wrong*. In every case, the commodity in question was worth exactly what was paid for it: no more, no less.

This is extremely important to understand. Value is *only created at the point of transaction*. Until a transaction is executed, value remains entirely hypothetical: it becomes actual when the goods change hands. And once it does so, value becomes anchored at that price point. So an athlete who signs a $300 million contract is worth $300 million. If the same person could have signed a $500 million contract, he would have been worth $500 million; if only a $10 million contract, then only $10 million. The fact that someone believes the athlete in question is worth less than he was awarded is just as irrelevant as the fact that someone else might believe he is worth more than what he accepted (including the athlete himself). He was worth *exactly what he was paid*, and until he was paid, no one (including the athlete himself) knew exactly what he was worth.

The same holds true in the sexual marketplace: value is created at the point of transaction (albeit in slightly different ways for men and women). To differentiate it from other forms we've already discussed, we can call this *transacted sexual marketplace value*, or tSMV. Transacted sexual marketplace value is the closest we can come to approximating an individual's "true" value in the sexual marketplace. Until the point of transaction, value is conjecture at best and self-delusion at worst. Transaction is the reality that constrains illusion.

So, how is tSMV calculated? In most sexual relationships, resources aren't explicitly exchanged for sexual opportunity, so the negotiated value at the point of transaction isn't as obvious here as it is in professional relationships. However, just as prices in the commercial marketplace are not determined by measuring the inherent value of the given commodity (whatever that is) but by examining the *average price of comparable transactions* in the market in question, we can develop a similar workaround for the sexual marketplace.

Here it is. A man's transacted sexual marketplace value is the median normalized sexual marketplace value *of the women from whom he has secured sex*. On the other hand, a woman's transacted sexual marketplace value is the median normalized sexual marketplace value *of the men from whom she has secured commitment*. Let's break this down.

Transacted sexual marketplace value is always based on actual relationships, where the individuals have secured — as opposed to where they believe they could secure — the goods in question. And since the comparable transactions are the previous relationships of the individual under consideration, fewer potential confounds exist than in other methods of calculation. Finally, the averaging helps to equalize outliers in either direction to prevent skewing.

The most significant feature of this definition, however, is the transaction standard against which men and women are differentially measured. Each sex is considered against the transaction that is more challenging for it to secure. It's harder for women to secure commitment from men than it is to secure sex, and it's harder for men to secure sex from women than it is to secure commitment. This is generally why we say that women are the *gatekeepers of sex*, and that men are the *gatekeepers of commitment*.

It also goes a long way toward explaining why men generally seek sex from women and women generally seek commitment from men: each is hoping to secure the scarcer (and therefore, relatively more valuable) good from the other. That these are not the goods that each sex inherently prefers is demonstrated by observing the behavior of men and women when they have the typically scarcer good in abundance. Male celebrities eventually tire of playing the field and seek a meaningful connection. Married women grow bored of security and seek out passionate affairs. However, since many people do not experience this abundance, economic forces are often mystified as biological differences.

Within this framework, we can also understand why many women suffer an inflated sense of their own sexual marketplace value. Many men would have sex with a woman to whom they would never seriously consider committing. As a result, it can happen that certain women are able to have sex with handsome, high-status men and believe — on the basis of these encounters — that they must enjoy a comparably high sexual marketplace value. However, since most of these men would be unlikely to offer commitment to the same woman, her value in this exchange isn't a reflection of the men's nSMV nearly as much as the men's value is a reflection of the woman's nSMV. In reality, the men who are likely to offer her commitment possess a lower nSMV than the men who can secure sex *without it*, as the former must compensate for being less attractive in other ways. This is why many women can encounter unexpected difficulties in securing marriage and long-term commitment after years of dating casually. They (incorrectly) believe the ease with which they have historically secured attractive sexual partners predicts an effortlessness in finding an attractive husband.

So that's my best attempt at approximating the *actual* value of men and women in the sexual marketplace: for men, it's the median nSMV of the women from whom they have secured sex, and for women, it's the median nSMV of the men from whom they have secured commitment. And since this definition obviously utilizes an asymmetrical metric, I might as well explain everyone's favorite double standard before closing the chapter.

OF LOCKS AND KEYS

I am, of course, referring to the *sexual double standard*. The sexual double standard is the belief that it is acceptable (or positive) for men to have had many previous sexual partners, but that it is unacceptable (or negative) for women to have had the same. On the surface, this appears hypocritical and unfair. However, in many respects, it is simply par for the course: in the sexual marketplace, *asymmetry is the rule, not the exception*. What is equal isn't always fair, and what is unfair isn't always unequal. Let's take a closer look.

A popular explanation for this double standard is that is an unfortunate cultural artifact: a vestige of a patriarchal past that simultaneously glorified men's sexual conquest of women while constraining women's sexual freedom. And while there may be some truth to that, allow me to offer another explanation of this phenomenon that doesn't require quite as many ideological assumptions.

It goes like this: the outcome that can be accomplished through no action will always be valued *less* than the outcome that can only be achieved through the application of effort and skill. This is inherently true. People don't become stronger, richer, wiser, or more desirable by doing nothing. They attain these valuable attributes through the application of effort and skill. And all other things being equal, the more applied effort and skill, the greater the value. This is why a cake will cost more than the sum of the cost of its ingredients: the effort and skill applied to the ingredients make the finished product a more valuable commodity. Reasonable enough, right?

Now let's apply this principle to the topic under consideration. If a man does nothing, *he does not have sex*. The average guy can sit alone at a bar — day after day, week after week, month after month — and he will be approached by no one. And while there are pros and cons to this reality, the fact is that a man cannot enter into a sexual relationship *by waiting until it is offered*. Vanishingly few contexts exist in which male virginity is prized. This is because a man can do nothing and remain a virgin, so it can't really be celebrated. For a man to acquire (and retain) a sexual partner — which is to say, for a man to be sexually selected by a woman — more effort and skill are required than we would generally like to admit.

Now compare this to the experience of a woman. How long would *she* be able to sit alone at a bar undisturbed? This woman may not be approached by the person she would prefer to be approached by. However, sooner or later, she will likely be approached by *someone* with some kind of proposal, ranging from "Can I buy you a drink?" to "Want to get out of here?" In fact, some women are propositioned — in both direct and indirect ways — many times a day, nearly every day of their lives. If we include digital propositions via dating apps or social media platforms, this number can grow exponentially. Women can even be propositioned *without being aware that they are being propositioned*. Stark asymmetries exist between the experiences of men and women.

And these asymmetries collectively produce an unavoidable consequence, namely: that there are *gendered differences in the application of effort and skill in the sexual marketplace*. For instance, surrendering to every man who would have her doesn't require nearly as much effort and skill from a woman as, say, appropriately vetting her options and discerning the men who might be the best investments for her (necessarily limited) time and opportunity. *Discernment* is a skill that requires some degree of knowledge, experience, and savviness. Because it requires effort and skill *not* to believe every Tom, Dick, and Harry who crosses her path with a proposition, value is created by a woman's reticence.

So, the situation is (unsurprisingly) complementary: for men, action is generally required to make something happen, and for women, inaction is generally needed to prevent the squandering of her resources. This is especially true for people in their 20s. In the case of both men and women, the outcome associated with effort and skill is valued more highly than the outcome that is not. However, since effort and skill are typically applied by men and women to achieve different outcomes, this gives rise to the apparent double standard under discussion.

But here's the kicker: *this isn't inherent to men and women*. Rather, it's an emergent phenomenon that arises wherever value is unequally distributed. For instance, you find an analogous situation when dealing with the unequal distribution of money. Those with no money have to hustle to get it, while those with money have to find a way to resist squandering it on every two-bit "investment opportunity" that comes their way. You even find this phenomenon naturally occurring in sports that deal with the unequal distribution of points. Those with fewer points shift to offense, and those with more points shift to defense (and these shifts generally become more pronounced in inverse proportion to the available time).

The upshot is that, in any game, the player at a disadvantage is incentivized in the direction of acquisition, while the player at an advantage is incentivized in the direction of maintenance. And given the relative distribution of normalized value in the sexual marketplace — especially among younger cohorts — *women are decidedly the more advantaged players*. As a consequence, men are incentivized into an offensive role and play to win (and are rewarded for doing so, since skill and effort are required for this outcome), whereas women are incentivized into a defensive role and play not to lose (and are rewarded for doing so, since skill and effort are required for *this* outcome).

So the sexual double standard is culturally determined but not in the way that most people think. That is, it's not simply a superficial attitude — like a belief — that can be altered with education and awareness. Rather, it's deeply embedded in culturally normative rules that govern who approaches whom and who is valued for what — and these rules probably aren't changing anytime soon. The sexual double standard will privilege men *as long as women are perceived to be more valuable in the sexual marketplace*. Until the day arrives when it is as easy for the average man to find a willing sexual partner as it is for the average woman to do the same, the sexual double standard will exist. A key that can open any lock will remain a good key, and a lock that any key can open will remain a bad lock.

In this chapter, I discussed several conceptualizations of sexual marketplace value. This detour was necessary because — like it or not — these valuations have a profound influence on all three stages of relationships. All other things being equal, a person with a higher sexual marketplace value will attract more desirable partners for mating and dating, negotiate more preferential relationship terms, and maintain relationships more successfully against intrasexual competition, relative to a person with lower SMV. Furthermore, an individual's perceived sexual marketplace value does more to determine whether an interaction occurs that could lead to a sexual opportunity than any other single factor. What is written here is far from the whole story, but it will have to serve for now.

At this point, let's assume there is sufficient initial mutual attraction to motivate an interaction in the sexual marketplace. While each party's pSMV will continue to fluctuate in the other's mind as the interaction unfolds, the two have functionally entered into the negotiation stage of the relationship. As we'll see, this stage is exceedingly nuanced and involved. It also begins long before an actual proposition is offered. Learning to play this phase of the game well will dramatically improve an individual's bargaining posture once the proposal becomes explicit.

If you'd like to further explore the topics presented in this chapter, please scan the QR code to access a curated playlist on the PsycHacks channel on YouTube.

CHAPTER 4

EVERYONE IS TRYING TO NEGOTIATE THEIR BEST POSSIBLE OFFER

Marketplaces are fascinating. One fundamental feature of a marketplace is that it incentivizes the production of value. And this value is generally produced by transmuting self-interest into prosocial behavior. In a marketplace, actors typically learn that the best way to get their needs and desires met is to fulfill the needs and desires of others. As a consequence, most people spend a significant amount of their lives serving others as an indirect (but reliable) means of serving themselves. Self-interest is the primary driver of mutuality.

Consider the commercial marketplace. If somehow, overnight, every person on the planet suddenly possessed enough money to purchase everything they wanted or needed, that currency would instantly inflate into worthlessness, and the world would start to fall apart in a matter of days (if not hours). Most people are only motivated to work because they believe they don't yet have enough money to stop working. That is: they believe they don't yet have the means to provide for their wants and needs *indefinitely*. By a continuous process of value adjustments, the marketplace intentionally prevents the vast majority of people from ever arriving at this point. And while this might disappoint and frustrate the individual, it is absolutely essential for the community, which has come to depend on the prosocial behavior of transmuted self-interest for its survival.

However, it would be wrong to argue that the marketplace sacrifices the individual for the sake of the community. Just as the community is improved as a result of the collective prosocial behavior, the constituent individuals are improved as a result of the transmutation of their self-interest. This is because marketplaces don't have illusions about human nature. They understand that people are inherently self-interested and tend to prioritize pleasure, comfort, and convenience over difficulty, discomfort, and growth.

Consider how people spend their free time. When they're not working, they *could* be volunteering at orphanages, checking in on their elderly neighbors, helping with their friends' childcare, feeding the hungry, or (really) serving others in any way whatsoever. But what do they do instead? They anesthetize themselves in a hundred different ways under the name of "relaxation" and attend to their own pleasure. If most people did this indefinitely, the result could not possibly be a healthy and thriving community because its constituent parts would be sickly and disordered.

People are not altruistic. Some have the capacity for altruism at times, but it would be foolish to believe that most people are altruistic most of the time. And because people are not altruistic, they need to be motivated to be prosocial. In the commercial marketplace, people are so motivated by a social fiction called money. Money has no intrinsic value: it is just a piece a paper or — increasingly — some ones and zeros. However, I pretend to believe it has value because you pretend to believe it has value because I pretend to believe it does. Over time, we generally forget that we're pretending. The upshot is that once this social fiction becomes established, you can just tell people they're working for something called money, and they will spend all day *helping other people*.

Of course, once a society establishes a currency, the individuals who live in it will want as much of it as they can lay their hands on. In this way, ambitious individuals can be guided to assume more dangerous or unpleasant or difficult or complex roles in the network of prosocial behavior with the promise of more of that value. This not only benefits the larger community but (more to the point) the individuals in question, as well. This is because these people must become increasingly courageous, competent, disciplined, and responsible to acquire that value. Despite (or rather, *because of*) the frustration of their tendencies toward pleasure, comfort, and convenience, these individuals are generally healthier, happier, and more fulfilled than they otherwise would be. In pursuing their own self-interest, they are forced to better themselves and serve their communities — and the world is made a more desirable place to live as a consequence of this effort. Contrary to popular belief, the necessity of work is not a tragedy. Rather, the tragedy would occur if work were no longer necessary.

That said, marketplaces are not utopias. Their actual practice will always deviate (sometimes significantly) from their ideal operation. Every marketplace contains fraud, deceit, theft, corruption, and exploitation — if not as actualities, then at least as continually threatened potentials. And every marketplace inevitably nurtures bias and error, since inherent value (if such a thing exists) cannot be objectively measured, and transacted values must be negotiated within unequal power dynamics. However, despite these flaws and liabilities, I still maintain that marketplaces are *net positives* — both for individuals and their communities.

And why did I make this long-winded detour into the commercial marketplace? Hopefully, because it provided some necessary context within which to better examine the sexual marketplace and the transactions that occur within it. That's because the essential features of a marketplace *don't change as a consequence of the kinds of value being transacted.* At the highest levels, the principles that govern the commercial marketplace remain just as true when applied to the sexual marketplace. And since people are far more cognizant of the commercial marketplace than the sexual marketplace, I often use the former to explain the latter. Let's take a closer look.

A VIRTUOUS NECESSITY

As we've discussed, people want things from other people, and relationships are the media in which value is transacted. A sexual relationship is one in which *one* of the goods being exchanged is sex, and these relationships are transacted in the sexual marketplace. In this space, actors typically learn that the best way to get their needs and desires met is to fulfill the needs and desires of others. They do this by exchanging unequal goods of comparable value in a negotiated transaction that begins the moment the actors begin to interact with each other.

In the beginning, most actors attempt to negotiate a transaction by offering what they, themselves, would want. This is typically due to a lack of understanding or a failure in perspective-taking. Unsurprisingly, this strategy is rarely successful — for what should be obvious reasons. Successful negotiators don't offer what they want but what the other party wants. What they want is what someone else has. And if someone else already has it, why would this someone else want it? Remember: *to want* means *to lack*. Instead, negotiators achieve success by offering something they have that the other party wants. In this way, actors learn to indirectly get their wants and needs met by satisfying the wants and needs of others. Self-interest is transmuted into prosocial behavior.

If somehow, overnight, every person on the planet were suddenly (and completely and indefinitely) satisfied with respect to their sexual needs and desires, the value of sexual opportunity would instantly inflate into worthlessness, and the world would begin to look like a very different place. Society wouldn't collapse as quickly as it would under the hyperinflation of money, but it would experience a gradual — and irreversible — decline. Men typically catch a glimpse of what that world might look like immediately following orgasm. In that instant of sexual satisfaction, in the first moments of the refractory period, the value of sexual opportunity functionally falls to zero. And it's in that time that men can experience a radical re-evaluation of both their sexual relationships and their behavioral priorities.

The psychological delta that occurs across this time period reveals the extent to which ostensibly non-sexual attitudes and behaviors are *actually cultivated for the purpose of satisfying sexual needs and desires*. Because we live in communities with laws and social norms, people can't give full rein to their sexual appetites. Acting in this way would result in the imprisonment, expulsion, or execution of the individual. However, these appetites don't disappear just because they are socially proscribed. Instead, they are channeled — or *sublimated* — into behavior that (on the surface) appears prosocial and non-sexual but is (in fact) inexorably linked to sexual ends. The complete and indefinite satisfaction of sexual desire would not simply lead to the end of sexual relationships: *it would lead to the end of all sublimated prosocial activity, as well.*

By a continuous process of value adjustments (which are rooted in biological mechanisms at least as much as in cultural forces), the sexual marketplace intentionally prevents the vast majority of people from ever arriving at this point. And while this might disappoint and frustrate the individual, it is absolutely essential for the community, which has come to depend on the sublimated prosocial behavior of transmuted sexual self-interest for its survival.

However, it would be wrong to argue that the sexual marketplace sacrifices the individual for the sake of the community. Just as the community is improved as a result of the sublimated prosocial behavior, the constituent individuals are improved from the transmutation of their sexual self-interest. This is because the sexual marketplace does not harbor illusions about human nature. It understands that sexual desire — linked, as it is, with life itself — constitutes a deep, existential drive. This drive cannot ever be fully satisfied with culture or reason, nor can it ever be fully constrained by vows or taboos: it is older — much older — than any of these. If nothing else, the sexual marketplace has consistently borne witness to the fact that people will apparently go to incredible lengths — and will undertake a considerable amount of pain, discomfort, and inconvenience — to cultivate the value with which to barter for more (and more desirable) sexual opportunity.

The necessity of negotiating sexual opportunity is the *fundamental driver of self-improvement*. Individuals who — for whatever reason — enjoy seemingly limitless and effortless sexual optionality often become tyrannical, narcissistic, and entitled. The fact that they often choose not to grow themselves in dimensions they believe to be unconnected to that optionality is another indication of the extent to which self-development is rooted in the necessity of negotiating sexual opportunity. For instance, actors who can successfully transact in the sexual marketplace without being, say, kind or educated are much less likely to develop these attributes than those who cannot. Abundant sexual optionality, especially if acquired precociously, is often a long-term liability for the individuals who enjoy it.

On the other hand, individuals who — for whatever reason — despair of *ever* negotiating a successful sexual transaction often become hopeless, frustrated, and depressed. Their physical and mental health deteriorate considerably. They can even stop investing in themselves altogether because they believe they do not have (nor could *ever* have) anything of value with which to barter for a sexual relationship. Obviously, neither of these options is desirable.

And that's fortunate because — for better or worse — the vast majority of humanity is somewhere between these two extremes. Whether we like it or not, most of us are forced to negotiate for sexual opportunity, but we typically do so hopefully. And this *hopeful necessity* is what incentivizes the production of all kinds of value. Despite (or rather, *because of*) the frustration of their immediate sexual wants and needs, these individuals are motivated to engage in sublimated prosocial behavior and are generally more attractive, accomplished, and resourceful than they would otherwise be. After all, it's the sexual marketplace that affords individuals the inestimable opportunity to become captains, who — in turn — generally improve the overall quality of life of passengers. Contrary to popular belief, the necessity of negotiating sexual opportunity is not a tragedy. Rather, the tragedy would occur if the negotiation were no longer necessary.

That said, sexual marketplaces are not utopias. Every such marketplace contains fraud, deceit, theft, corruption, and exploitation — if not as actualities, then at least as continually threatened potentials. And every such marketplace inevitably nurtures bias and error, since inherent sexual marketplace value (if such a thing exists) cannot be objectively measured, and transacted sexual marketplace values must be negotiated within unequal power dynamics. However, despite these flaws and liabilities, I still maintain that sexual marketplaces are *net positives* — both for individuals and their relationships.

Since most of us are neither willing nor able to completely dispense with the necessity of negotiating sexual opportunity, let's spend some time examining the principles and processes that govern that negotiation. Since we can't *not* play, we might as well learn the rules so we can make our best showing. Over the next few chapters, we'll start by taking a bird's-eye view of the entire dock and gradually work our way down to examining the moment-to-moment interactions between two actively negotiating individuals.

Readers might balk that they've never haggled for a sexual relationship in their lives. My rebuttal would be that they've never *consciously* haggled for a sexual relationship in their lives. The fact that they may not have been cognizant of the negotiation process is not enough to refute the existence of that process. An absence of evidence is not evidence of an absence. As usual, we must look at what people *do* — as opposed to what they say, think, and feel — in order to approach the truth. If awareness were a necessary precondition of action, then the world would look like a very different place, indeed.

A FUNDAMENTAL TENSION

Like in any other marketplace, at any given moment, everyone is trying to negotiate the best possible offer with their best available option down at the docks. No one is interested in paying more for any given option when it can be bought for less, regardless of its desirability. Everyone will choose the most desirable option among goods of comparable value, regardless of the cost. And if individuals can acquire a comparable good more cheaply, more easily, or more safely somewhere else, then they will pursue that alternative. All of these are rational. It's not possible to argue against them: they are axiomatically true. And they all profoundly influence what happens when people begin to interact with each other in the sexual marketplace.

These statements all derive their truth from two essential features of any true marketplace: *antagonism* and *competition*. No one could buy anything if no one were selling. And no one could choose the most desirable option if there weren't any options. We need both antagonism and competition for negotiation to occur at every scale and across all time points.

To appreciate how antagonism operates in the sexual marketplace, let's first consider how it does so in the commercial marketplace. There will always be an irreducible antagonism between, say, management and labor. All other things being equal, management will always try to get as much productive effort out of labor as cheaply as possible, and labor will always try to get as much money out of management for the least amount of productive effort. The two sides need each other, but they're definitely not friends. This is because their goals are fundamentally opposed to one another. However, it's precisely this *antagonism* that creates the necessity for them to do business with each other.

Now, in the sexual marketplace, there are two forms of antagonism: one based in *marketplace role*, and the other rooted in *biological sex*. Remember: marketplace roles are technically gender-neutral, whereas biological sex (by definition) is not. This creates an opportunity for *role-sex interactions* that, as we'll see, greatly affect the negotiation process.

In the first place, a fundamental antagonism exists between marketplace roles, that is: between captains and passengers. All other things being equal, captains want to sell as many passages on their ships as they can, for as much as they can, to passengers who won't cause any problems. Just consider how commercial airlines operate: they try to cram as many obedient travelers into their cabins as possible — typically overselling their flights to ensure capacity — for as much as they can get away with. On the other hand, passengers want to buy passages on ships, for as little as they can, from captains who will treat them with as much consideration as possible. Just think about how you *wish* commercial airlines operated: cheap, direct flights with gourmet meal service and plenty of legroom. Of course, each convenience provided by the airline is an expense incurred by the carrier, which compromises the airline's overarching goal. On the other hand, if the carrier dispensed with these conveniences entirely, it might find it difficult to attract any paying customers (which would *also* affect its bottom line). The two sides need each other, but they're definitely not friends. This is because their goals are fundamentally opposed to one another.

However, this is not the only tension that drives negotiation. In the sexual marketplace, a fundamental antagonism also exists between men and women. Like the attractiveness ideals that serve as the standards against which normalized sexual marketplace value is measured, this antagonism is both culturally informed and biologically determined. All other things being equal, men want as much sexual opportunity for as few resources as possible, and women want as many resources for as little sexual opportunity as possible. This is because *men fundamentally trade resources for sexual opportunity, and women fundamentally trade sexual opportunity for resources.*

There are many reasons for this. Women are the gatekeepers of sex: they decide whether sex is transacted and with whom. However, this is mostly a cultural (rather than a biological) role. Women are endowed with this privilege because societies generally frown on using force or coercion to secure sex, and not because women, themselves, can unilaterally prevent unwanted or non-consensual sexual experiences. The upshot is that women in society have been given a *monopoly on sexual opportunity* — a monopoly that is typically (and understandably) protected by societies' most severe moral and legal prohibitions.

Couple this with the reality that sex — with the potential consequences of pregnancy and childbirth — is inherently riskier for women than it is for men. Women's capacities to secure resources for themselves and their babies are (at the very least) compromised during late-stage pregnancy and early-stage postpartum, in particular. As a result, women (or females, more generally) tend to hedge their reproductive risk by mating with men (or males, more generally) who seem capable of offering provision and demonstrate a willingness to do so.

Because women have something in abundance that men do not — namely, sexual opportunity — it is the most obvious good with which they can barter for something (at least, historically) that men have in abundance that women do not, namely: resources. I'm using this term very broadly to mean any transactable good besides sex, such as: money, food, time, shelter, devotion, attention, affection, protection, childcare, excitement, emotional support, practical assistance, companionship, entertainment, opportunity, and commitment. A woman's sexual opportunity is the closest thing to money than actual currency: it can be used to acquire pretty much any good or service, albeit in a (generally) much more indirect fashion. The only real difference between sexual opportunity and money is the marketplace in which each is accepted.

This last resource demands special attention. Whereas most (or all) of the other resources listed can be provided in other relationships (or by the woman herself), *commitment* (at least, in its ultimate form: marriage) can only be provided by a man in a sexual relationship. This is because men are the gatekeepers of commitment: they decide whether a commitment is transacted and with whom. And this role is *also* mostly cultural. Sex occurs in nature; commitment typically does not. While sex can be non-consensual, commitment can never be: even if it is forced or coerced (which societies, also understandably, frown upon), it must be consented to.

And this is why — even though nothing in either culture or biology prohibits men from offering sexual opportunities to women or women from offering commitment opportunities to men — successful transactions in the sexual marketplace generally don't assume this form. As stated previously, naive negotiators begin by offering what they, *themselves,* want: men mistakenly offer women sexual opportunity (which women already have in abundance), and women mistakenly offer men commitment opportunity (which men already have in abundance). This is why you almost never see men trading sexual opportunity for commitment, or women trading commitment for sexual opportunity, despite the fact that nothing should technically prevent such transactions from occurring. The economics just don't support these events.

All things being equal, the more desirable her sexual opportunity, the more resources a woman can secure in the transaction. This is because people trade unequal goods of comparable value. However, value is an elusive and evolving thing, and the relative value of any good typically diminishes *as it is acquired*. For example, a poor man would likely work all week for another thousand dollars; however, a rich man probably wouldn't. The relative value of that thousand dollars is significantly less to the rich man because he already has a lot of money.

This is known as the *law of marginal utility*, and it's as valid in the sexual marketplace as in the commercial marketplace. It (at least partly) explains why a man is more likely than a woman to work overtime rather than catch an evening yoga class. Becoming slightly richer will be marginally more useful to the man — who will attempt to trade resources for sexual opportunity and must compete with other men who will do the same — than to the woman. And becoming slightly more physically attractive will be marginally more useful to the woman — who will attempt to trade sexual opportunity for resources and must compete with other women who will do the same — than to the man. Money is valuable to everyone — *but it is more valuable to men*. This is because, in addition to all the other goods money can represent (e.g., security, freedom, convenience), money has one additional signification for men that it doesn't hold for women, namely: *reproductive optionality*.

Neither men nor women may be aware of these incentives, but people do not need to be conscious of incentives to be influenced by them. In the Western world, the marginal utility of resources in the sexual marketplace does more to account for absolute earning inequality between men and women than sexual discrimination does. And as we'll see, this idea also goes a long way toward explaining many of the current trends in the sexual marketplace, including the decline in sex, committed relationships, and marriage. But one thing at a time.

One final word before we move on. As mentioned previously, marketplace roles interact with biological sex to create synergistic (or antagonistic) effects in the attraction phase of relationships. This is why male passengers and female captains tend not to fare as well in the sexual marketplace as female passengers and male captains do: there is a mismatch between the expectations of the role and the culturally informed, biologically determined attractiveness ideals. On some level, this makes the former pairings harder to see than the latter, which reduces the likelihood that male passengers and female captains will be selected for relationships.

However, our recent examination into the antagonisms that lie at the heart of the negotiation phase of a relationship suggests another (at least partial) explanation for this phenomenon. If female captains want to trade sexual opportunity for resources (because they're *women*), and they want to sell passage on their ships for as much as they can get away with (because they're *captains*), then the vast majority of male passengers *will be priced out of the transaction*. They just won't be able to do business. This is because female captains sell passage for *resources*, and the marginal utility of those additional resources to female captains is so low that an extraordinary amount of resources would be necessary to make it worth their while. And if male passengers had the capacity to trade on that level, well, they probably wouldn't be passengers. This is why we don't see a lot of transactions between female captains and male passengers: the former typically decide that the marginal utility of the relatively insignificant addition of resources offered by the latter isn't worth the risk and cost of the transaction.

On the other hand, it's much easier for male captains and female passengers to negotiate a transaction. Here's why. If male captains want to trade resources for sexual opportunity (because they're *men*), and they want to sell passage on their ships for as much as they can get away with (because they're *captains*), then female passengers — who have a monopoly on sexual opportunity (because they're *women*) — can trade at a comparable valuation. This is because male captains sell passage for *sexual opportunity,* and the marginal utility of additional sexual opportunity for most men is so high that only a negligible amount of opportunity would be required to make it worth their while.

In any case, there would be grounds for a negotiation. All other things being equal, the more desirable the ship, the more expensive the passage — but the more desirable the passenger, the less expensive the ticket. Specific male captains may not be able to negotiate successfully with specific female passengers, but the marketplace is full of transactions between these two classes of individuals. The economics make sense.

From their first interaction, men and women start trying to suss out how expensive it will be to board a given ship or to take on a given passenger. This occurs in a myriad of ways: consciously and intentionally *and* unconsciously and unintentionally. And if this weren't complicated enough, both parties are (on some level) aware that any given negotiation occurs in the context of the larger marketplace. So let's now turn our attention to that other feature of the sexual marketplace that gives rise to the necessity of negotiation: *competition.*

A DOUBLE-EDGED SWORD

If neither party had other options, then negotiation would be an empty ritual at best, and a total sham at worst. The existence of other options doesn't just create the necessity for a negotiation: it also creates the necessity for a negotiation *bounded by reality.* This is because people don't trade in inherent values. They trade in estimated values informed by comparable transactions.

If the going rate in your town for a coffee is $3, a café couldn't charge $20 for a cup of Joe and expect to do business. The fact that the café has competitors offering a similar product is good for consumers, who won't get hosed by price gauging. On the other hand, if the going rate in your town for a coffee is $3, a café could charge 10 cents for the same drink and steal customers away from other businesses. The fact that the café has competitors offering a similar product is bad for business owners, who constantly contend with the possibility of being undersold. And while most people won't lose any sleep about a café going under — because most people typically identify with being consumers — the reality is that people in any economy are always *both producers and consumers.*

In the sexual marketplace, every buyer is also a seller, and every seller is also a buyer. Consequently, competition is always a double-edged sword: it is both a threat and an opportunity. And this is why so many games in sexual relationships revolve around attempts to *control competition.* From a purely self-interested perspective, an ideal situation would be one in which I fully retain all my optionality (i.e., your competition) while I completely eliminate all my competition (i.e., your optionality). All other things being equal, this would provide me with the most advantageous position from which to negotiate terms for myself.

The commercial equivalent to this would be something like the marketplace in a company town — which, because it lacked competition, wasn't a true marketplace. In many communities built around a particular industry, workers weren't historically paid with cash (which was universally accepted and created optionality) but with *scrip* (which was only accepted at the company-owned stores and eliminated optionality). The workers could only buy from the company, but the company was free to sell to consumers besides the workers. And since the company enjoyed a monopoly on the workers' business, the workers predictably paid more for the same good at the company store than they would have needed to on the open market.

It goes without saying that this arrangement was only made possible by the significant power imbalance between the company and the workers. In general, the more powerful party can secure more advantageous terms for itself in any transaction. And this privilege is roughly proportional: the greater the power imbalance, the more advantageous the terms. Another takeaway is that *exclusivity is expensive*: the company's monopoly allowed it to charge more for the same good than it otherwise would have been able to.

In most sexual relationships, couples typically regulate competition by forming *symmetrical commitments*, for instance: I will be your exclusive sex dealer, and you will be my exclusive sex dealer. However, the economics of this arrangement only make sense if the values of the respective exclusivities are comparable. Remember: equal isn't always fair, and proceeding in this fashion can potentially compromise relationships in the long term.

As a counterexample, if one actor has many options (and may enjoy even more in the future), and if the other has few options (and may enjoy even fewer in the future), then a symmetrical commitment probably wouldn't be in the former's best interests. The second actor's lack of options already creates a *de facto* exclusivity, so the first actor would be giving up something (presumably) of great value in return for something that he or she already had. It doesn't make sense. On the other hand, the second actor would likely advocate hard for a symmetrical arrangement, as securing one would allow him or her to enjoy a desired good at functionally no additional cost. In any given sexual relationship, it is generally *the actor with less optionality who pushes for exclusivity*. Another conclusion from the same principle would be that the smaller the perceived optionality disparity between the two actors, the more likely they will enter into a symmetrical arrangement, and the greater the disparity, the more likely an asymmetrical arrangement will emerge.

On the docks, before passage has been secured, the general rule is that captains are interacting with multiple passengers, and passengers are examining multiple captains. This is as it should be. An informed consumer is a powerful consumer. Since people trade in estimated values informed by comparable transactions, it makes sense that both parties would conduct some measure of due diligence prior to entering into a transaction in earnest. After all, it's impossible to know whether you're paying more than you need to, or securing the most desirable option at a given price point, if you don't do a little research first.

This is one reason why aggressively targeting actors as soon as they first enter the sexual marketplace will indefinitely remain a negotiation tactic — for both men and women. Freshly minted captains and newly arrived passengers are much less likely to have the knowledge and experience necessary to understand whether a given offer is actually compelling in the context of the larger marketplace. As a result, more savvy and experienced actors can sometimes secure transactions with very desirable options at a fraction of the usual cost.

Conversely, it can also prove nearly impossible to transact with new captains and passengers, as their self-valuations have not yet been tempered by the constraining forces of the marketplace. Given that sellers almost always value the good they are selling more highly than buyers do, and the reality that new actors in the sexual marketplace do not yet have a tSMV from which to anchor a negotiation, some of these self-valuations can be absurdly high. So this tactic enjoys a variable degree of success.

Even though due diligence is a reasonable strategy for both marketplace roles, passengers will generally spend more time in the research and evaluation phase than captains. Indeed, "testing the captain" is one of the three prerogatives of the passenger. This occurs as a result of another inherent asymmetry between the two roles, namely: *a ship can have multiple passengers, but a passenger can only be aboard one ship at a time*. Let's consider some implications of this fact.

Since captains generally want to sell as many tickets as possible, while passengers typically only want to buy a single passage, captains and passengers evaluate each other differently. Consider what happens in commercial air travel. When you're looking to buy a ticket to a specific destination, you will likely research various carriers, across various dates, to determine with whom to book your passage. All other things being equal, you will choose the cheapest, most convenient, and most comfortable option.

Carriers don't do this. They don't research all the travelers looking to book a ticket and offer passage *only* to the most compliant, highest-paying ones. In fact, it might look as if carriers conduct no research whatsoever into their travelers and that they're functionally willing to fly anyone who pays. But that isn't strictly true. Carriers do conduct research — *they just do it at the airport*. It's called security screening. To get on the airplane, you must consent to your person being searched and your baggage being examined. Otherwise, best of luck boarding that flight. Unlike travelers, carriers don't conduct research to secure their best options — they do it to avoid their worst ones.

The same holds true in the sexual marketplace. Since passengers can only be aboard one ship at a time, they will generally conduct more due diligence using the available competition with the ultimate goal of *securing their best overall option*. After all, a given ship can have a profoundly influential effect on the experience of a single passenger, who must — in any case — forgo all other ships to secure his or her passage on this one.

In contrast, since a ship can have multiple passengers, captains will generally only conduct enough diligence to ensure that they are *not taking on a catastrophic option*. This is because a single passenger does *not* have a profoundly influential effect on any given ship — unless, of course, he or she is a terrorist or the only one aboard. In fact, the more passengers on board, the less the non-catastrophic influence of any one passenger matters, since this influence will be averaged across the entire manifest. The upshot of this is twofold. First, it means that passengers typically mate and date with the intention of *maximizing benefit in a minimized domain*, that is: with the goal of securing their single best option. And second, it means that captains typically mate and date with the intention of *minimizing loss in a maximized domain*, that is: with the goal of securing as many non-terrible options as possible.

We see these same economic incentives reflected in the reproductive behavior of men and women, which informs mating and dating to a considerable degree. With respect to initiating a sexual relationship, men notoriously have *much* lower standards than women do, and fewer barriers to entry. This is partly because, in any given month, men produce billions of sperm, capable of impregnating many, many women. From an evolutionary perspective, they are incentivized to secure as many non-terrible options as possible, as this will increase the likelihood that at least some of their offspring will survive to sexual maturity. From the perspective of most men, it is enough that a woman simply not be undesirable to entertain a sexual relationship.

On the other hand, women typically have *much* higher standards than men do, and higher barriers to entry. This is partly because, in any given month, women produce a single fertilizable egg, capable of being impregnated by a single man. If this occurs, it comes with the risks and liabilities of pregnancy and childbirth, as well as an opportunity cost that prevents them from reproducing with anyone else for the better part of a year. From an evolutionary perspective, they are incentivized to secure their single best option, as this will increase the likelihood that their offspring will survive to sexual maturity. From the perspective of most women, a man must be desirable (often, very desirable) to entertain a sexual relationship.

These realities create yet another synergistic effect between marketplace role and biological sex in the case of male captains and female passengers: *their role incentives align with their reproductive capabilities*. Female captains are hampered by the difficulty — if not the sheer impossibility — of taking on multiple passengers. Consequently, they are more or less forced to operate under a different business model than male captains in order to remain solvent. If male captains can operate as commercial airliners, which defray the risk and expense of their operations by negotiating affordable passage with a multitude of low-paying travelers, then female captains generally operate as private jets, which defray *their* risk and expense by negotiating a costly passage with a single, high-paying traveler. The issue is that most men who could afford such a ticket are captains themselves and won't lightly surrender their posts. Most male passengers would not be able to afford such a service.

There is much more I could write about the consequences of marketplace role asymmetry, but I will content myself with just one more observation, namely: it predicts differences in how men and women pursue sexual opportunities outside of their committed relationships. In other words, it predicts *how people cheat*.

Basically, since a ship can have multiple passengers, captains are much more likely to cheat *simultaneously*. This is cheating in the most commonly understood sense: someone is having an affair behind his or her partner's back. While an obvious ethical breach, this strategy aligns with captains' overarching incentive to pack their cabins with as many paying customers as possible. And the bitter truth is that a preexisting commitment may not be enough to satisfy this objective. And since male captains trade passage for sexual opportunity, we would expect this form of cheating to be most prevalent among this demographic.

On the other hand, since a passenger can only be aboard one ship at a time, passengers are much more likely to cheat *consecutively*. This is cheating in a less commonly understood sense: someone immediately leaves one relationship in order to enter into another. The ethical breach in this case is less obvious — as there may, technically, be no overlap between the two relationships — but it exists, nonetheless.

To understand *why* this is a breach, consider, for example, the ethics code for psychologists.[26] Unsurprisingly, the code establishes that it is unethical for psychologists to enter into sexual relationships with their patients (i.e., to enter into a simultaneous relationship). However, this statute would be functionally useless if psychologists could get around this restriction by simply *ending the therapeutic relationship* (i.e., to enter into a consecutive relationship). This is why they must (among other things) wait two years from the point of termination to initiate a sexual relationship with a former

26 Statutes 10.05 and 10.08 are the relevant guidelines here. Source: https://www.apa.org/ethics/code

patient. Consecutive relationships must also be unethical to close the obvious loophole on simultaneous relationships.

And while this is an ethical breach, "jumping ship" is a strategy that aligns with passengers' overarching incentive to travel to their chosen destination as comfortably as possible with their best available option. The bitter truth is that a preexisting commitment may not be enough to satisfy this objective. And since female passengers trade sexual opportunity for passage, we would expect this form of cheating to be most prevalent among *this* demographic. Of course, this doesn't mean that male captains can't (or don't) cheat consecutively, or that female passengers can't (or don't) cheat simultaneously. It just means that we should expect these forms of cheating to be less common in the indicated demographics than the ones previously described.

STRATEGIES FOR OPTIMIZATION

Given what we've discussed so far, we're well-positioned to extrapolate an overarching strategy on how to approach negotiation in the sexual marketplace at a high level. Consider the following. Men trade resources for sexual opportunity, and women trade sexual opportunity for resources. Captains try to secure as many non-terrible options as possible, and passengers try to secure their single best option. All transactions must be secured within a larger context of open competition, and no actor will pay more for a given option when it can be bought for less, regardless of its desirability. If all these statements are true, then what strategies would best position each actor in the negotiation process as a function of role-sex interaction?

Male captains would be strongly incentivized to prioritize resource acquisition. If invested into their ships, these resources would not only increase the likelihood that more passengers will consider these captains to be their single best option, but they would also facilitate access to more desirable passengers, as well. This would allow male captains to access more desirable sexual opportunities from more female passengers, optimizing both their role and their sex incentives. Male captains should also position themselves in sectors of the market where they can be reasonably assured of being considered the single best option for the greatest number of female passengers, even if that means being considered less desirable to more overall passengers. They should also consider marketing features of their ships in order to generate interest and cultivate intrasexual competition among the passengers — both of which drive up the price of fares. Finally, since resource acquisition tends to increase as a function of time, male captains are typically at their most disadvantaged position at any given time point. Their default strategy is *to wait*.

On the other hand, female passengers would be strongly incentivized to prioritize their physical attractiveness, as this is the primary metric by which men measure the desirability of any given sexual opportunity. Investing in their appearance would not only increase the likelihood that captains will commit more resources to access their sexual opportunity, but it would also attract attention from more desirable captains, as well. This would allow female passengers the best possible chance of securing more resources from their single best option, optimizing both their role and sex incentives. Female passengers should also position themselves in sectors of the market where they can be reasonably assured of being considered attractive relative to the greatest number of direct female competitors, even if that means being considered more desirable by fewer overall captains. They should also consider marketing features of their attractiveness in order to generate interest and cultivate intrasexual competition among the captains — both of which drive down the price of fares. Finally, since physical attractiveness tends to decrease as a function of time, female passengers are typically at their most advantaged position at any given time point. Their default strategy is *to act*.

Next, we come to female captains. If optimizing for both incentives, we would expect a female captain to trade sexual opportunity for resources from as many non-terrible options as possible. In the modern age, this needn't look like actual prostitution (though the oldest profession is alive and well today). For example, female captains can use technology to leverage their sexual opportunity for resource acquisition across a wide swath of men. Doing so would not technically require the initiation of a sexual relationship. Remember: resources are only directly exchanged for sex in prostitution. In most sexual relationships, resources are exchanged for sexual *opportunity* only.

Female captains need only suggest the possibility of sex to motivate the transaction of resources. And since the value of their sexual opportunity is primarily measured by their physical attractiveness, which tends to decrease as a function of time, female captains would be incentivized to secure as many resources as possible from as many men as possible as quickly as possible. Once the value of their opportunity decreases past a certain threshold, these women would likely attempt to *switch roles* and secure as many resources as possible from their single best option as a female passenger. In this way, they could maximize the transaction of resources for their sexual opportunity across their lifespans.

As for male passengers, if optimizing for both incentives, we would expect them to trade resources for sexual opportunity from their single best option. However, this poses some difficulty, as male passengers typically don't have as many resources with which to transact as male captains do. This means that male passengers not only consistently lose out to their intrasexual competition for both classes of women but that they also rarely have enough interest to make selecting their single best option a meaningful decision.

Male passengers overcome this difficulty by offering something that goes against the fundamental incentive of male captains: *exclusive commitment*. As we've discussed, the value of exclusivity can vary considerably from person to person as a function of their optionality. It's also something that men — as the gatekeepers of commitment — have to give. Since most male passengers are *de facto* exclusive (i.e., they have little to no optionality), they conjure value out of nothing by offering women an exclusive commitment, which enables them to beat out (at least some of) their intrasexual competition. This is facilitated by the fact that many women value exclusivity very highly, not only because it eliminates her own intrasexual competition for the same resources but also because it's the resource that male captains (who would find the arrangement too expensive) are least likely to offer. Consequently, the optimal strategy for male passengers is to *get married to the most desirable woman who will have them*. In this way, they offer the provision of resources in an exclusive commitment to their single best option.

In this chapter, I discussed some of the most salient features of marketplaces and argued that the necessity to transact with others is a net positive for both individuals and their communities. In particular, I focused on two essential properties of marketplaces — antagonism and competition — that give rise to the necessity for negotiation, and I described some of the ways these properties influence the sexual marketplace on a high level. Finally, I offered optimization strategies for each of the four role-sex combinations. All other things being equal, these strategies should help to position actors most advantageously in their respective negotiation processes.

All these considerations affect negotiation on a macro scale. In the next chapter, I will discuss the game of negotiation on a micro scale — that is, in the moment-to-moment exchange of an interaction — and the strategies that people predictably employ in their attempts to get what they want.

If you'd like to further explore the topics presented in this chapter, please scan the QR code to access a curated playlist on the PsycHacks channel on YouTube.

CHAPTER 5
NEGOTIATION IS THE FUNDAMENTAL GAME OF HUMAN RELATIONSHIPS

Psychology is not my first career. Many years ago, I got my start as a theatre actor. I received my conservatory training at the Experimental Theatre Wing (ETW) at New York University's Tisch School of the Arts, and I worked as a professional actor in New York City for many years afterward. Though it may sound strange, my experiences as an actor taught me more about psychology than all my graduate school coursework combined. Let me explain what I mean.

At ETW, I had a unique introduction to acting. We didn't read plays or analyze characters or rehearse scenes. In fact, the entire first semester of my training was devoted to a single game. And though this was not how it was presented to me, I've since come to understand that this game is actually *the fundamental game of human relationships*. As we've discussed, relationships are the media in which value is transacted. So people enter into relationships because they want things from other people — usually things that help them solve important problems of living. The issue is that these other people are problems in and of themselves.

If they have what we want, other people represent a potential satisfaction of our desire. However, they are unlikely to give us what we want simply because we want it. This is because *wanting is free*. It costs the wanter nothing to want, but it costs the giver something to give. And the most prevalent — and prosocial — method of navigating this asymmetry is to enter into a trade agreement: the exchange of unequal goods of comparable value. Since value cannot be objectively measured, and since valuation changes from moment to moment and from person to person, the process by which an exchange is executed is a complex, ever-evolving, infinitely varied operation. It is both an experimental laboratory in which new tactics and strategies are continually developed, and the principal stage on which people seek to secure their well-being and survival in society.

The fundamental game of human relationships is *how to get what you want from other people*. Those who excel at this game thrive, while those who fail (or refuse to play) do not. This is because all the games humans play with each other are simply context-dependent variants of this archetypal game. At ETW, we called this game **the Game of Please/No**. And since this game will deeply inform our understanding of the negotiation phase in the sexual marketplace, allow me to explain how it works.

The Game of Please/No is simple. There are always two players. One player — whom we'll call *the wanter* — can only say the word "please." This is the *only* word this player can use. The other player — whom we'll call *the giver* — can only say the words "yes" and "no." This player must begin the game from a "no" posture. The game ends when the wanter succeeds in changing the giver's "no" into a "yes" using only the word "please." That's it. It's a fascinating game.

In the Game, the giver's default posture is "no" because this reflects a fundamental truth about life. In the real world, *the universe lives closed.* The things we want are generally inaccessible to us and require effort to obtain. This is wise from the point of view of material reality, since most of the things people want — in their specifics — tend to be acquired through a zero-sum game. For example, if I want a certain job, you can't get it. If I want a certain house, you can't buy it. And if I want to marry a certain woman, you can't have her too. So there is scarcity with respect to specifics.

This is why the default response to wanting any specific thing is "no." If the default response were "yes," then the planet would have been stripped of all its resources by now. Preservation of the individual — no less than the Earth itself — requires that it *not* simply cater to all the desires of other human beings. So the default answer to any question in life is "no." "Can I have some money?" "No." "Can I take you out?" "No." "Will you help me with my problem?" "No." No, no, no, no, no. This rejection isn't personal: *it's a feature of reality.*

However, this feature doesn't stop people from wanting things. So the game of all human relationships is how to transform the default "no" to a request for any specific good into a "yes." This is why it makes sense that the wanter initiates the game. After all, their wanting serves as their motivation to act, and this action serves as the minimum necessary effort to overcome the default withholding of the giver. Sometimes asking is all it takes to receive — though it generally requires more. However, this is precisely why simply asking will never disappear as a strategy in the Game. Since wanting is free and giving is costly, and since (at least sometimes) wanting is accommodated by the mere request for something, wanters occasionally succeed in conjuring value out of nothing *simply by asking*. It's kind of like getting a free pull on a slot machine: it costs functionally nothing, and you could hit the jackpot.

That said, it should be noted that — if their asking isn't immediately accommodated — the wanters put themselves in a disadvantaged position vis-à-vis the givers as a consequence of their asking. This is because they have functionally confessed that they believe the givers have something they want and the givers can give that something to them. As a result, a good that may not even have been worthy of the givers' attention is suddenly invested with some measure of value as a consequence of the wanters' request — which, of course, serves to drive up the price of any subsequent transaction.

Deep appreciation of this economic reality leads to several important understandings. First, it reveals the (perhaps) counterintuitive truth that in the Game of Please/No, wanters don't maximize their success by maximizing their effort. Doing so generally results in their being priced out of the exchange. However, completely minimizing their effort is generally insufficient to overcome the default withholding required by the asymmetry between giving and wanting. That means we should expect the most accomplished wanters to strike a balance between these two extremes. I call this the *"take it or leave it" posture,* and it is indeed associated with a high degree of success in many real-world interactions.

Second, the unfavorable position of the wanter gives rise to the most abiding strategy in the Game of Please/No: *deception.* If wanters are disadvantaged to the extent that givers accurately recognize the degree of their interest — or even the object of their interest — then wanters are incentivized to *keep givers in the dark about their true desires for as long as possible.* And while no player can ever endorse deception as an interpersonal strategy — as deception is only effective to the extent it is unrecognized, and communicating a willingness to engage in deception would compromise the effectiveness of the player's own deceptions — almost every player uses deception to some degree or another. Indeed, when people express indignation at deception (which is not uncommon), their outrage is typically not directed at deception *per se* but at where to draw the line between "acceptable" and "unacceptable" forms.

Regardless, deception is an extremely common interpersonal strategy. For example, one of the most common forms of deception is *reversal*: feigning disinterest (or disappointment) in something of great value to the wanter or pretending interest (or enjoyment) in something of little value to the same. In the sexual marketplace, this can look like men pretending they "aren't like the other guys" (i.e., feigning disinterest in sex) in order to access sexual opportunity ("the nice guy"), or women feigning they "really like you" (i.e., pretending interest in the person) in order to acquire more resources ("the long con"). However, as we'll see, deception can also be very subtle and nuanced, as people succeed in deceiving themselves at least as often as they succeed in deceiving others.

Third, the economic asymmetry between wanting and giving provides the rationale for one of the Game's most effective interpersonal tactics, namely: *getting the other person to be the wanter*. In the game we played at ETW, the roles were explicitly determined in advance: both players knew who was who. But that's not the case in the real world. Anyone can be a wanter, and anyone can be a giver. What's more, the same person can be the wanter in one game and the giver in another — even across concurrent relationships. The upshot is that if players can succeed, despite their own desires, in provoking the *other* player into initiating the negotiation, they can typically secure a much more favorable bargaining posture for themselves. Successful application of this tactic requires, on the one hand, some measure of discipline and self-sufficiency (in order to abide in their own discomfort of wanting), and on the other hand, some degree of marketing acumen (in order to stimulate the discomfort of the other player's wanting). After all, no one can want something from you if they don't yet know you have it.

With the right presentation, you may even succeed in cultivating a desire for something other players *didn't even know they wanted*. This gives rise to the various strategies men and women devise to advertise the goods with which they hope to transact in the sexual marketplace. It also helps to explain why modern women — despite all their "enlightened" ideas about power, sex, and gender — have never campaigned to normalize, say, proposing marriage to men. Women are loath to dispense with this gendered tradition — and for good reason. On some level, women understand that it is more advantageous for them to continue to wait for a man's offer than it is to suffer the disadvantage inherent in the wanters' position by acting first.

This is also (at least part of) the reason why women tend to react so negatively to any attempts to regulate their dress or appearance. Over and above the indignant reactance most people experience in response to attempts to control them, this reaction belies some degree of awareness with respect to their advantaged position in the sexual marketplace as givers. We can assume that women would not be so opposed if the proposed regulation improved their positioning. Restricting women's ability to freely market their sexual opportunity would compromise their general strategy of awaiting the offer *by cultivating desire in men*. It is by means of this cultivated desire that men are motivated to approach and initiate a negotiation from the disadvantaged wanters' position. This is also why relationships are much more likely to be arranged by third-parties in societies where women's appearance is highly regulated, relative to more permissive cultures. Open marketplaces depend on the ability to market directly to consumers in order to operate; closed marketplaces depend on the inability to do the same.

So if both parties understand that whoever acts first is at a disadvantage, then how does any negotiation ever get transacted? Wouldn't the game end in a stalemate before it even began? No, it would not. Just look around you: people successfully transact negotiations all the time. The reason this happens is twofold, namely: ignorance and impatience. Most people have no idea they're playing the Game of Please/No — let alone the optimal strategies for getting what they want within that Game. That's *ignorance*. What's more, unsatisfied desires are painful, and people vary significantly in their ability to tolerate this pain. When the pain of unsatisfied desire is strong enough for long enough, then players are compelled by their own temperaments to act. That's *impatience*.

Having discussed the fundamental mechanics of the Game, let's now turn our attention to the process by which the negotiation unfolds.

LEARNING TO LISTEN

It doesn't take long for novice players of the Game of Please/No to come up against their own communicative limitations. Most people — and especially most men — overly rely on the semantic information contained in verbal language in order to get what they want from other people. However, if the only word they can say is "please," then wanters quickly learn that they will need to come up with other methods of communicating their intentions to givers if they stand any chance of winning the Game.

It turns out that people communicate with each other in a myriad of ways: body language, posture, gesture, proxemics, rhythm, duration, motion, and — most importantly — facial expression and tone of voice. You might be surprised at how many ways the word "please" can be said. This is possible because every word is simultaneously the representation of a concept and the container of an emotion. In their conceptual aspect, words are specific and defined. However, in their emotional aspect, words are general and undefined. They are containers of emotion, and (like all containers) they can hold anything they *can* hold. In any case, the Game teaches people not to depend on semantic language. And this is extremely relevant to negotiation in the sexual marketplace since the games of attraction and seduction are typically executed on non-verbal levels of communication.

Players also quickly realize that no two games of please/no are the same. Wanters can play the Game with one giver today, and it will be a completely different game with the same giver tomorrow. Much to their chagrin, wanters discover that the strategies that finally succeeded in unlocking the "yes" from a specific giver yesterday are no longer effective today — even with the exact same giver.

This is because the Game of Please/No unfolds in the present moment — which is always new and never repeated. Players can't rely on scripted strategies or previous victories. They must be continually present with their partners and carefully attend to every step of the interaction. The most successful wanters are highly attuned to the constantly fluctuating internal state of their partners. Since no two games are alike, wanters must attend as closely to the moment-to-moment exchange with their partners on their first playthrough as on their thousandth.

And the way they do this is by listening to their partner with a kind of "third ear." Since "no" is also a word, and all words are indifferent containers of emotion, then the word "no" can be said in just as many ways as the word "please." This is extremely fortunate. If the word "no" did not contain any emotional content, and no other semantic information were provided, then every game would either end after a single exchange or devolve into a series of random stabs in the dark. However, wanters are afforded one means by which to secure victory in a game that would otherwise be functionally impossible: *the way givers say "no" always contains a clue about how they would say "yes."* Wanters need only learn how to listen.

In this way, the Game of Please/No is similar to the childhood game of hot/cold, in which one player hides something in a room and another tries to find it. If seekers move away from the hidden item, hiders tell them they are getting "cold... colder... freezing," and if they start to move in the right direction, hiders tell them they are getting "warm... warmer... boiling!" Both games require that feedback be given to the seeking party. Otherwise, play could only progress stochastically (if at all). This feedback is both emotional and semantic in the game of hot/cold — which makes the game easier and more appropriate for children — but it is *only* emotional in the Game of Please/No — which makes the game far more subtle and complex. And since people can't *not* communicate — though they can get very good at muting that communication — wanters always receive feedback clues, whether or not givers intend to provide them.

The idea here is to become increasingly sensitive to the *emotional timbre* of the response. For instance, a sharp, loud, forceful "NO!" almost always means that the wanter is "freezing cold," whereas a soft, hesitant, quivering "...n..o" often means that the wanter is "boiling hot." The more negative the feedback, the more likely a diametrically opposed tack would be appropriate; the more positive the feedback, the more likely only a subtle shift (if not mere perseverance) is needed. By growing increasingly sensitive to smaller and smaller changes in "temperature," wanters can zero in on the "please" most capable of unlocking the "yes" through a kind of emotional triangulation.

These are the attributes that make for highly skilled wanters in the Game of Please/No: mindful attention, emotional sensitivity, behavioral flexibility, and mastery of non-verbal communication. And this goes a long way toward explaining women's relative success in the sexual marketplace: they are generally more adept than men in most (if not all) of these capacities. Since this game is the fundamental game of human relationships — which are never negotiated once and for all but are subject to a constant and evolving negotiation process (more on this later) — it should come as little surprise that *relationships more often come to accommodate women's needs and desires over time* than vice versa. To put it another way: women are better at getting what they want from men than men are at getting what they want from women.

However, the attributes in the prior list are not sufficient in and of themselves to secure a "yes": they must be actualized using specific behavioral strategies. Let's now turn our attention to what those strategies might look like.

THE WANTER'S PLAYBOOK

In bounded games, like chess, no two games are exactly alike. However, as the game iterates over hundreds (or billions) of playthroughs, recognizable patterns begin to emerge in player behavior. Top performers typically are not better at considering a greater number of hypothetical permutations but at perceiving more patterns more quickly with less information. Once the pattern is recognized, play (at least for a time) is coherently oriented in a specific direction, and a player needs to expend fewer cognitive resources to determine the next right move. Among other things, that's what patterns do: they save us time and energy by relying on the mind's ability to fill in the gaps of perception.

However, this is precisely where players are also most vulnerable. On some level, the mind can't *not* look for patterns. This instinct is so deeply unconscious that — for better or worse — it can't be overridden by our conscious intentions. And if players' capacities to recognize patterns have been trained on bad or limited data, then they are much more likely to be oriented in incorrect or unhelpful directions — without ever being consciously aware that they are going off track. This is why master players of any game *need to play thousands and thousands of times with as many different partners as possible*: they need to train their capacities to recognize patterns on robust data sets in order to minimize the potential for bias and error inherent in small sample sizes.

The same is true for the Game of Please/No. Remember: few rules exist regarding how to proceed with play. There also isn't a time limit. I've played games that were over in seconds, and I've played games that have lasted for years. Given this spaciousness and permissiveness, you might expect an endlessly varied proliferation of strategies. However, this isn't the case. Certain recognizable patterns reliably emerge across players over thousands of playthroughs. I call these patterns *core strategies*.

Core strategies are important because they facilitate the perception of intention. By acting in certain ways, wanters can more reliably communicate their inner states (or at least, what they want givers to *believe* are their inner states). On some level, if wanters' behavior doesn't fall within one of these patterns, givers won't be able to recognize it as *communication*: it will be received as all noise and no signal.

Suffice it to say, incomprehensible communication is unlikely to prove effective. Master wanters not only have to understand what behaviors constitute meaningful communication in a given context, but they also have to improve their ability to execute those behaviors and determine which are most likely to secure the desired outcome in real time. This is the elegance of the Game: it takes a minute to learn and a lifetime to master.

Much of this will make more sense with concrete examples. To that end, I will briefly describe a dozen core strategies in the Game of Please/No. The list is far from exhaustive and in no particular order. What's more, inclusion here doesn't necessarily constitute a moral endorsement of the strategy. Whether they're "right" or "wrong," these strategies predictably emerge in radically different players across thousands of playthroughs. They are also associated with some measure of success; otherwise, they wouldn't persist through time. I'm sure you'll recognize many of them from your own experience.

The first core strategy is **intimidation**. This strategy uses the *threat of harm* to secure a desired outcome. The threat in question can run the gamut from vague, emotional harm to specific, physical harm, which is why it's wrong to associate intimidation exclusively with lumbering bullies. It is most effective when executed across a significant power imbalance from high to low. This is because givers must believe wanters possess both the ability and the willingness to make good on their threats. Intimidation from a perceived equal typically provokes hostility, whereas intimidation from a less powerful wanter generally evokes mirth or indifference. Keep in mind that power (as we'll discuss further in the next chapter) is psychological: being physically bigger or stronger does not necessarily translate into being more dominant. Intimidation functions through the manipulation of *fear*.

The next core strategy is **seduction.** This strategy cultivates the *hope or expectation of a sexual encounter* to secure a desired outcome. Like all the core strategies, seduction is gender-neutral: it's something both men and women can do. However, it's a much more effective strategy for women. This is because most men are open to a sexual relationship with most women, but most women are not open to a sexual relationship with most men. Just be aware that the more seduction is utilized as a strategy to obtain a desired good other than a sexual encounter, the less likely a sexual encounter will actually take place. This is because givers are far more motivated to provide seducing wanters with the desired good before the encounter, when they believe giving to be the means of relieving their sexual tension, than after the encounter, when they are already sexually satisfied. And to the extent the good can be obtained by seducers merely by cultivating the hope or expectation of a sexual encounter, the encounter itself becomes redundant and unnecessary. Seduction functions through the manipulation of *desire*.

Next is **pity**. This strategy stimulates givers' *distress* into providing a desired outcome through corrective action. By acting sufficiently unworthy, desperate, or pathetic, wanters hope to obtain their desired good by means of a dual reinforcement mechanism existing in givers' minds. The idea here is that giving groveling wanters their desired good will not only relieve the felt discomfort experienced from observing another person's misery (negative reinforcement) but will also inspire positive experiences of self-regard (positive reinforcement). It is most effective when executed across a significant power imbalance from low to high. Pity functions through the manipulation of *disgust*.

Another approach is **victimization**. This strategy attempts to secure a desired outcome through the *remediation of damages incurred through acknowledged wrongdoing*. Unlike all the other strategies, victimization is always reactive: it can never be implemented as an opening move. This is because victims must first establish that they were undamaged at the onset of the interaction. To utilize this strategy, wanters must both communicate that they were hurt as a consequence of givers' actions (which requires a non-hurt baseline for comparison) and convince givers that they are responsible for this hurting (which serves as the rationale for remediation). Victimization functions through the manipulation of *guilt*.

Yet another strategy is **surprise**. This strategy tries to secure a desired outcome by *bypassing expected defensiveness*. Otherwise known as a "pattern interrupt," the idea here is that givers might surrender the good in question as a thoughtless reflex. This is generally accomplished by means of a radical shift in the tone or rhythm of an interaction, which is why it is most effective when preceded by the induction of a trance-like state. Surprise functions through the manipulation of *awareness*.

Next up is **friendliness**. This strategy leverages positive regard to *lower the perceived cost to the giver* of surrendering a desired good. People transact more valuable goods at lower costs with those they like and love. They are also much less likely to look closely at value discrepancies in an exchange between confederates, allowing friends to obtain goods more cheaply and easily than they otherwise would. The expression of familiarity, warmth, and equality can also lower defensiveness and stimulate a sense of reciprocal obligation — making it a mainstay of close relations and con men alike. Friendliness functions through the manipulation of *affection*.

Straightforwardness is also a core strategy. This strategy tries to secure a desired outcome through *unemotional direct request*. When people claim they "don't play games," they're functionally expressing a preference for this strategy when they play the Game of Please/No. Successful implementation of this strategy depends on the ability to express sufficient sincerity and transparency to instill wanters' requests with an aura of safety and credibility. In essence, wanters use this strategy in an attempt to convince givers that they have no strategy, which lowers defensiveness. Straightforwardness functions through the manipulation of *trust*.

Another common strategy is **humiliation**. This strategy attempts to secure a desired good as the means of *escaping a socially compromising situation* contrived by the wanter. It is essentially the blackmail of status, prestige, or position. As a strategy, it is most effective when executed across a significant power imbalance from low to high (after all, "humiliation" implies a "humbling"), and when the giver is emotionally identified with the attribute under threat. Humiliation functions through the manipulation of *shame*.

Our next strategy is **charm**. This is a strange one. This strategy attempts to secure a desired good as the means of *facilitating identification with an attractive other*. The idea here is essentially superstitious (i.e., a "lucky" charm): givers are allowed to partake in some of the positive attributes with which wanters are imbued by virtue of their sacrifices. Charm doesn't have the overt sensuality that seduction does. Instead, it relies on *charisma*, which mesmerizes givers into believing they can become more powerful, attractive, or prestigious through association with the wanter. In the Game of Please/No, the desired good is typically held out as the price of that association. Charm functions through the manipulation of *hope*.

Now we come to **authority**. This strategy tries to secure a desired outcome by communicating that it is *the giver's expected duty* to render it. By expressing assertiveness, confidence, and poise, authority implies an elevated station and presumes the honor and respect due to that station. This is why it is most effective when executed across a power imbalance from high to low. It commands with the expectation of obedience and succeeds because it assumes it cannot fail. Authority functions through the manipulation of *awe*.

Another strategy is **playfulness**. This strategy attempts to secure a desired outcome by *changing the meaning or context of the transaction*. It can be difficult to secure a "yes" in the Game of Please/No. However, by creating a game within the Game, players may be able to secure a "yes" in the nested game that remains valid in the nesting game with different stakes and under different pretexts. To the extent that it is successful, playfulness cultivates a shared illusion within which certain objects or behaviors assume context-dependent meanings that can radically deviate from their conventional significance. *Humor* is an archetypal form of play because it blurs the line between the truth and "only kidding." It's also an excellent way to reduce defensiveness and inspire engagement: "yes, and..." is the essence of play. Playfulness functions through the manipulation of *meaning*.

And, finally, **quitting** is a core strategy. In the Game of Please/No, the giver enjoys an inherently more powerful position. Among other reasons, this is because it's *not possible* for wanters to transform a "no" into a "yes" if they're playing with a giver who — for whatever reason — refuses to surrender the desired good. History is full of the stories of givers who have preferred to suffer even death than to comply with wanters' demands. They take their "nos" to the grave and can be transfigured into religious or political martyrs as a result. And this was why — when we played the Game at ETW — there was an informal rule that givers be good faith actors. This meant that if givers genuinely felt an impulse to say "yes," they would do so. Otherwise, the Game would be impossible for wanters to win.

This is important to keep in mind, as wanters will sometimes find themselves playing with givers who will never say "yes." These people are *not* good faith actors because they will choose not to surrender to an impulse that they (on some level) have no choice but to feel. And unless wanters are willing to escalate the game of power to its ultimate conclusion, these bad faith givers are just a waste of time.

However, quitting — or at least *threatening* to quit — is a useful strategy for testing the resolve of a recalcitrant giver. This is because givers only have a more powerful position *in the context of the Game*. By threatening to end the game, quitting wanters are attempting to remove the basis of the givers' power. The idea here is to communicate that the maintenance of the givers' privileged position is predicated on the wanters' obtaining their desired good. Otherwise, wanters will just take their ball and go home, leaving no one to play the Game that givers can't lose. What a waste! Quitting functions through the manipulation of *disappointment*.

So those are twelve core strategies in the Game of Please/No. And since all these strategies depend on the manipulation of a human emotion or a feature of human consciousness, they are functionally universal. These strategies appear in the moment-to-moment transaction of negotiations of all kinds, across time and place: from corporate boardrooms to trading bazaars to cocktail lounges. They are tried-and-true methods for turning "nos" into "yeses."

It's also important to appreciate that all these strategies are forms of bartering. We typically think of bartering as a *quid pro quo* — I'll give you this, if you give me that — so it might sound strange when applied to the preceding examples. However, the good being exchanged may not be as concrete as an object or a service. In fact, the good being exchanged in most of these strategies is not material at all: it's emotional. Let me explain.

The ability to stimulate an emotion in another person is *manipulation*. This word has a negative connotation, but it needn't have. Not all manipulation is predatory, and not all manipulation is unwanted. Manipulation does not require that manipulators even be conscious of their intentions to manipulate. However, all manipulation succeeds in evoking emotion in its target. It's almost as though someone were able to reach inside of us and "pull our heartstrings" (or, in a more pejorative sense, "play us like a fiddle"), which speaks to the root of the word in the sense of "to handle with skill."

In the Game of Please/No, nearly every effective strategy in the wanter's playbook depends on its capacity to stimulate a specific emotion in a particular giver. And it's this stimulated emotion that serves as the basis of the proposed barter: a "yes" is transacted for an emotion. That said, this transaction looks different depending on the *valence* (i.e., the positivity or negativity) of the emotion in question.

In strategies that rely on the stimulation of positive emotion (e.g., friendliness, charm, playfulness), the idea is to cultivate a desirable experience in the giver (e.g., belonging, pride, relief) *of comparable value to the good proposed for transaction*. Most people consider positive emotions to be intrinsically valuable, so the successful manipulation of these emotions will create a value discrepancy in which both parties recognize that one person has benefited from the efforts of the other. And since value discrepancies are often difficult to tolerate (especially in more egalitarian relationships), the giver is motivated to give the desired good not only as a reward for the intrinsically valuable emotion the wanter succeeded in invoking but also as a means of escaping an otherwise uncomfortable relational dynamic.

Of course, these intentions are rarely conscious. Friends aren't friendly in order to cultivate a value discrepancy advantageous to the transaction of goods. We wouldn't consider such a person a friend at all! However, we can appreciate that friendliness, like all the other core strategies involving positive emotions, has persisted through time and place because it *works*. Humans have evolved to have friends because this strategy has been reliably associated with getting what they want (i.e., turning "nos" into "yeses"). And friendliness — like all the other core strategies — works not because of magical vibes but because of the (largely unconscious) calculation of value that serves as the basis for decision-making.

And what of the strategies that rely on the manipulation of negative emotion? Such strategies (e.g., intimidation, pity, victimization) attempt to cultivate an undesirable experience in the giver (e.g., fear, disgust, guilt) *of comparable but inverted value to the good proposed for transaction*. Basically, these strategies work to the extent that they succeed in evoking an emotional experience so painful or aversive to givers that they consider the value of the proposed good to be comparable to the value of escaping the undesirable experience. In these situations, givers give to avoid further exposure to their own negative emotion. They barter the proposed good for the removal of an undesirable experience.

These strategies constitute what people generally consider to be manipulations, and they are what give the word its bad reputation. This is because, relative to strategies that attempt to manipulate positive emotions, they are much more likely to be conscious and predatory. In this class of strategies, there is no real prospect of securing good, just the chance of avoiding harm. Fortunately, givers aren't without their countermeasures. After all, these strategies only work to the extent that (a) givers validate the judgments that give rise to the negative emotions as true, and (b) givers cannot tolerate the experience of their own negative emotions. No strategy that attempts to manipulate negative emotion can succeed if either one of these doesn't occur.

There is much, much more that I could say about the Game of Please/No. However, in the interest of time, there's just one more topic I would like to discuss with respect to the Game as it is played in the modern sexual marketplace.

FERRYBOATS AND STOWAWAYS

If you observe the Game of Please/No as it is played down at the docks, certain recognizable strategies begin to emerge across millions of playthroughs. As you might expect, these strategies tend to vary as a function of the players' genders. So before I close this chapter, I'd like to examine the most common gendered strategies in the Game as it is played in the negotiation phase of sexual relationships. Let's start with the men.

The most common strategy for men in the sexual marketplace is to be a *ferryboat captain*. There are several reasons for this. In the first place, men don't enjoy the role optionality that women do. Whereas modern women can either be captains or passengers, modern men can either become captains or languish on the dock. And since it takes a good deal of time, energy, and money to become a full-fledged captain, this situation creates a very high barrier to entry in the sexual marketplace for men. In fact, most people — men and women — will *never* become captains. However, since captains can have more than one passenger, but passengers can only ever be on one ship at a time, an equality in the number of captains and passengers isn't necessary.

In any case, many men attempt to secure their entry into the sexual marketplace more cheaply by coming ferryboat "captains." If you're not familiar, ferryboats are basically floating taxicabs: they take passengers where they want to go. And while some ferries are quite large, they needn't be. A man with a rowboat can take a single passenger around the harbor and consider himself a ferryboat captain. It typically requires fewer resources to build (and less competence to sail) a ferryboat than, say, a three-masted schooner or a transoceanic liner or a nuclear submarine, which is one reason why this can be an attractive option: *it is within the means of more men*.

That said, the men who pilot ferryboats aren't *really* captains, which is why I put the word in quotes in the preceding paragraph. As you'll recall, one of the challenges all captains must overcome is plotting a course, which requires that all those aboard respect their authority to determine the destination and the means of arriving there. However, on ferryboats, the *passengers* are the ones who dictate the route and the destination. We could summarize the business model of most ferryboats as: "I'll take you where *you* want to go."

And this abnegation of authority is a strategy. For whatever reason, some men despair of their ability to successfully compete for passengers against full-fledged captains in the sexual marketplace. They know their ship might not be the most comfortable or the most powerful or the most attractive. So these men attempt to entice passengers aboard by offering something full-fledged captains would never dream of: *the power to determine the destination*. As a consequence, they become passengers on their own boats. These men believe that if they didn't serve their passengers by ferrying them about, their passengers would have no other reason to be on their boats — *and they may be right*.

This is why we see what we see when we walk around the docks of most sexual marketplaces, namely: men standing in front of their boats and asking the women who pass by where *they* want to go. "You want to go to China? I can take you to China. You want to go to Iceland? I can take you to Iceland. You want to go to Australia? I can take you to Australia. For the love of God, *just tell me where you want to go, and I can take you there!*"

Like all common strategies, this one persists because it works. Millions of people use ferryboats and taxicabs every day of their lives. And this offer is a particularly attractive one for many women, as it's the cheapest and easiest way of attaining to their own "captaincies." Think about it: under this arrangement, they functionally get the right to plot the course *without building a ship or learning to sail.* So they succeed in purchasing one of the legitimate privileges of a captain at a fraction of the price. The female "passengers" are getting a discount, and the male "captains" are securing passengers they wouldn't otherwise be able to get. To many men, such a compromise is the cost of doing business.

So while presenting oneself as a ferryboat captain can, in fact, secure passengers (even very desirable passengers), this strategy comes with one significant liability, namely: *a ferry can't ever stop being a ferry*. Think of it like this: imagine you used a ferryboat every day to commute to work. Over the course of ten years, you will have used that ferry thousands of times to take you where you wanted to go. Now imagine that after a decade of this arrangement, the ferry captain were to stop you as you came aboard and say: "Hey, we've been going where *you* want to go for a while now. Do you think maybe you could take me where *I* want to go for a change? Like, do you think we could have some *reciprocity* in this relationship — even if it's just for today?" If he spoke to you in this way, what would you do?

Well, if you're like most people, you would turn around and get off that boat as quickly as you possibly could. After all, that wasn't the relationship you signed up for. In your mind, reciprocity was accomplished by purchasing your ticket — no further action on your part is required. The ferryboat captain never gets to stop being the ferryboat captain. *Ever*. That wasn't the arrangement you both negotiated down at the docks, and violation of that arrangement functionally terminates the relationship.

Unfortunately, whether or not they're aware of it, many men who adopt this strategy hope that maybe one day, further down the line, if they do a good enough job, they might possibly be able to go where *they* want for a change. *But that's not how ferryboats work*. These passengers wouldn't have stepped aboard their boats if they hadn't believed they would have the power to determine the destination, and — to be fair — this is *precisely* how these men advertised their services. So when ferry captains try to reverse the roles in the future, passengers typically experience this as creepy and weird. Once they jump ship, these "captains" are left to lament the cold-hearted nature of passengers who would leave after "everything they've done."

This is why I don't recommend men present themselves as ferryboat captains in the sexual marketplace. Doing so might work to secure a particular female passenger, but it does so at a significant (and perpetual) cost. Attaining to their full captaincies requires men to expend more resources on the front end, but doing so often reduces total costs over a lifetime by avoiding penalties on the back end.

Now let's turn our attention to the women. The most common strategy for women in the sexual marketplace is to be a *stowaway*. There are several reasons for this. In the first place, all other things being equal, passengers want to secure the most affordable passage on the best possible ship — and there's nothing more affordable than free. Basically, if a female passenger can somehow insinuate herself into the ship's ecology, then she might be able to succeed in securing her passage *without actually buying a ticket*. This is good news for her because (a) passengers typically have limited resources with which to transact their passage, and (b) the face value of tickets on the most attractive ships can be quite expensive. Many passengers would be priced out of consideration if they were forced to pay the fair market value of their passages.

The way in which stowaways accomplish this feat is through a strategy called *relationship creep*. In relationship creep, no transaction is explicitly negotiated, but over time, the female passenger slowly comes to occupy more and more space on the ship. One day, she's leaving her toothbrush in the captain's stateroom; the next day, she's remodeling the cabin. In fact, if this strategy isn't resisted, the female stowaway could even come to commandeer the entire vessel over a long enough timeline.

Now you might be wondering why someone without a ticket would be allowed on a ship at all, but this actually happens all the time. There are two ways this typically comes about. As you'll recall, it's one of the prerogatives of the passenger to inspect the ship. So some stowaways are allowed on board under the guise of inspecting the ship — *and just never leave*. They're "not sure" about the vessel but have already settled in by the time they "make up their minds." So that's the first way.

The second way is far more common. In this scenario, the stowaway transacts for a different, cheaper ticket, and attempts to exploit her position on board to attain a more desirable passage. This is like buying a seat in the upper deck to get into the ballpark and then trying to sneak into the premium seats behind the dugout after the game is underway. She's not a complete stowaway — after all, she paid *something* to get on board — she's just a stowaway on the passage she hopes to ultimately enjoy.

And since this way is far more common, let's briefly discuss how this strategy typically operates. Since female passengers attempt to transact their sexual opportunity for resources, stowaways ostensibly negotiate for *a more casual sexual relationship*, which is a fairly inexpensive ticket, while ultimately aspiring to a "serious" committed relationship, which is a much more costly passage. A male captain might enthusiastically invite such a woman on board since, all things being equal, he wants to secure the most sexual opportunity for the least expenditure of resources — only to realize much later (if he realizes at all) that the casual relationship was a Trojan Horse designed to bypass his security. The upshot is that if her strategy is successful, the stowaway succeeds in securing her passage at a fraction of its true cost.

This strategy is risky, but it can be very effective. In fact, it's often the *only way* many female passengers could ever hope to access the passage they want on the ship they would prefer. If done correctly, the male captain *never even notices what has happened*. However, on the off chance the captain happens to catch on, then all she has to do is threaten to leave. This is because — if she's played her cards right — by the time she's found out, she has so thoroughly insinuated herself into the ecology of the ship that it would be extremely difficult, complicated, and expensive to remove her. Couple this with the facts that most men (a) prefer to avoid a loss than to secure a gain, (b) operate with a scarcity mentality, (c) enjoy little to no actual optionality, and (d) resign themselves to the stultifying effects of inertia, and — *voilà* — the stage is set for a renegotiation of terms that highly favors the passenger. At this point, the captain may even gift the stowaway her desired passage (and more), just to keep her on board.

Of course, the risk is that the stowaway is actually dealing with a legitimate captain: that is, someone who (a) prefers to secure a gain than avoid a loss, (b) operates with an abundance mentality, (c) enjoys real optionality, and (d) aligns himself with the motivating effects of momentum. It's risky to attempt this strategy in this case because legitimate captains *have no problem tossing stowaways overboard.* Like the ferryboat passenger described earlier, he'll simply say, "I didn't sign up for this," and remove her from the manifest. And that woman will be out a relationship — maybe after several months, maybe after several years — with potentially little to show for her time. This outcome can be very costly for female passengers. However, it's less likely than the outcome described in the previous paragraph, so it tends to persist as a gendered strategy in the sexual marketplace on the population level.

In this chapter, I introduced the fundamental game of human relationships: the Game of Please/No. Since the universe lives closed, people are forced by necessity to secure their needs and wants from others using a variety of recognizable behavioral strategies, most of which hinge on the manipulation of a human emotion or a feature of human consciousness. The most successful individuals are those who can consistently turn "nos" into "yeses" by listening attentively to the moment-to-moment exchange that characterizes most negotiations. I also discussed the most common gendered strategies in the Game as it is typically played down on the docks of the sexual marketplace.

Although the Game of Please/No can unfold in an infinite variety of ways, the outcome of every game is decided by a *single factor*. In the next chapter, I will discuss what that factor is and how players on both sides can manipulate it in their favor.

If you'd like to further explore the topics presented in this chapter, please scan the QR code to access a curated playlist on the PsycHacks channel on YouTube.

CHAPTER 6
THE MORE POWERFUL PLAYER ALWAYS WINS THE GAME

As we discussed in the previous chapter, the fundamental game of human relationships is the Game of Please/No, in which wanters attempt to secure their needs and desires from givers by manipulating their emotions using a suite of behavioral strategies. The Game is infinitely varied, can last for seconds or lifetimes, and no two games — even between the same two players — are alike. Given the endless plasticity of the Game, you might be forgiven for thinking there is an equally inexhaustible number of ways in which the Game could end. However, this is not the case. In practice, the outcome of the Game depends on a single factor. In every iteration, *it is the more powerful player who wins the Game.*

Many people are uncomfortable discussing power, yet this reticence does not prevent power from permeating every interaction of every relationship on the planet. Power differentials may well be an inescapable dimension of human relationships. This is because *equality* is an abstraction that is neither supported by the evidence of our senses (no two blades of grass are exactly the same) nor conducive to exchange (in which unequal goods of comparable value are transacted). People are equal *only in the abstract* — but this abstraction is useful. It keeps societies from going too far off the rails. However, you need only look at people, and your eyes will perceive that inequality is the rule; listen to them, and your ears will confirm this belief.

In any case, if inequality is the rule among people, then it would be strange if power were somehow exempt from this general principle. If you can concede that no two people in a relationship can enjoy an equal share of power, then you must admit that at any given moment in any given relationship, *one person is more powerful than the other*. Moralizing about (or inveighing against) this logical deduction does nothing to change reality. And just to be clear: the unequal distribution of power is not inherently bad. If an unstoppable force met an immovable object, *nothing would happen*. It is the inequality of power that drives motion and change, and it is the principal means whereby people get what they want (irrespective of their desires). Of course, power can also become tyrannical and corrupt. My point here is merely that power isn't intrinsically evil.

Now, if power is an inescapable dimension of relationships, and if relationships are the media in which people transact for their needs and wants, then people can't *not* interact with power. As a consequence, it is probably in everyone's best interests to accept this reality and learn to navigate power dynamics as effectively as possible. The most powerful players of the Game of Please/No thrive — in the widest possible sense of the word. Those with less power not only do not thrive, but they exist at the tenuous mercy of those with more.

Interestingly, when people object to this conceptualization, *how* they object typically reveals where they understand themselves to reside in the power dynamics within which they habitually operate. For instance, those who rail against power structures — or clamor for an equal distribution of power — generally believe themselves to be the less powerful players in the Game. Morality aside, most people don't have a problem with a game they can consistently win. And if the Game of Please/No is ultimately decided by power, it would stand to reason that those most uncomfortable with power imbalances have not yet learned to be successful players. Their call for equality — while ostensibly principled and idealistic — is ultimately strategic: an equal share of power would be an improvement relative to their current situation. This strategy is neutralized by remembering that equal doesn't always mean fair: a precept that no one seems to forget when it comes time to split a bill at a restaurant.

On the other hand, those who argue that power doesn't really permeate all relationships — that such a position is cynical and Machiavellian, and that (in any case) there are far more important things to discuss — generally believe themselves to be the more powerful players in the Game. One attribute of power is that it can decide what *can't* be discussed. And if power can't be discussed, let alone recognized, then this silencing functions to protect the privilege of the more powerful party. Keep in mind that such people are often legitimately in denial about their own power, as this coping mechanism not only suppresses any guilt reactions with respect to exercising their privilege but also helps to maintain a preferred self-concept. This is because people would generally prefer to believe that their good fortune is more attributable to socially desirable personality attributes — to virtue, say, or a good work ethic — than to power itself.

IT'S ALL IN THE MIND

Now let's get a bit more concrete. If the outcome of the Game of Please/No always hinges on power, then we need to be clear about what it is, what it isn't, and how it actually operates.

My working definition of power is that it is *the ability to get other people to act in the service of your goals*. It's the ability to get other people to do what *you* want. That's power. And while my hunch is that few people would take issue with this definition, my experience is that most people don't understand it. And this misunderstanding is typically due to a conflation of the ability to get people to do what you want — which is real power — with the means you might use to achieve this end.

It may sound strange, but (strictly speaking) power is not wealth or status or physical strength. It may look like it is from the outside, but in reality, it is none of these things. If it were, how could we possibly account for the seemingly endless number of celebrities, moguls, and politicians who have been bested throughout history by those who were weaker, poorer, and more lowly? Those who instigate the fall of such individuals must be the more powerful players. Otherwise, we would be forced to concede that weakness is really strength, poverty is really riches, and abasement is really exaltation. If power inhered in money or muscle or prestige, then those who have more of these things should never lose to those who have less — which is clearly not the case.

The way through this apparent paradox is to appreciate that power is not material: it's psychological. As we'll see, even when material means are used to motivate others, the actual lever that impels them to act is always immaterial: *it is the excitation of a thought or feeling inside the person being moved.* If the means fail to incite the intended experience, then they fail as strategies in the Game and are contextually devoid of power.

For instance, wealth generally succeeds in motivating others to act to the extent that it inflames desire. As such, this strategy is a form of seduction — and it's generally as useful in motivating action in the non-desirous as food is in someone who just ate. Physical strength and status operate through similar mechanisms, namely: the stimulation of fear and awe, respectively. Without the provocation of their respective emotions, these strategies are functionally powerless to achieve their intended ends. Intimidation that fails to elicit fear *isn't intimidating*; status that fails to elicit awe *isn't prestigious*. These strategies only exist retroactively: they are created by their outcomes.

The upshot is that if things like money, status, and physical strength only motivate others to act to the extent that they succeed in exciting certain psychological states, and if it's possible to excite these states without things like money, status, and strength, then we have to conclude that people *do not need to be rich, prestigious, or strong in order to be powerful.*

These things are *power proxies*: they stand in for power in the popular imagination but are not power themselves. And those who have these things often learn too late that their mere possession does little to protect them from those with real power.

The easiest way to approach this idea is to imagine a German shepherd cowering before a Chihuahua. Maybe you've even witnessed such an encounter yourself. In that moment, the shepherd has forgotten its size and strength — forgotten that it could literally bite the smaller dog in half — and the Chihuahua has forgotten *its* size and strength — forgotten its relative physical vulnerability — and the scene plays out as described. This is because the Game is not enacted in material reality but in psychological reality. For whatever reason, that Chihuahua was able to convince that shepherd that it was something to be feared, something to be reckoned with. It was true in the shepherd's mind, so the shepherd perceived it to be true in reality (and responded accordingly). And if the situation were reversed, with the little Chihuahua cringing before the big shepherd, the mechanism of action would have been exactly the same. In this case, at least, size doesn't matter. The dog that is intimidated is not the dog that is smaller: it's the dog that *becomes afraid*.

The same scenario plays out between people. If intimidation operates through the manipulation of fear, then — in order to intimidate — I needn't be bigger or stronger or tougher than you. That could help, but only to the extent that you fear the imagined harm made more possible by those relative advantages. In order to intimidate, I would only need to succeed in *evoking fear in you* — a fear that may be more effectively stimulated with words than with statures.

What's more, being physically strong doesn't make someone impervious to fear. People can be big and afraid, *and* small and afraid. Similarly, being rich and prestigious doesn't make someone immune to seduction and awe. People can be rich and desirous, *and* poor and desirous; lofty and hopeful, *and* lowly and hopeful. This is why these qualities are proxies: not only are they not real power, but they also offer no inherent protection from those who actually possess real power. In this way, those who possess wealth or strength or prestige without possessing the capacity to resist emotional manipulation are functionally living in society with enormous targets on their backs. Once their power proxies attract the envious, their downfall will only be a matter of time.

Fortunately, there is a way to prevent this outcome. As previously discussed, most of the behavioral strategies in the Game of Please/No are emotional manipulation techniques. And this is good news with respect to prevention, as it's technically *not possible to be emotionally manipulated by another person*. On some level, only you can emotionally manipulate *yourself*. And if you deeply understand this reality, then you will never allow anyone to hold power over you again.

To appreciate the truth of this statement, we need to examine the mechanism of emotional manipulation. How does it work? Basically, emotional manipulation occurs when someone — through their words or actions — succeeds in insinuating an idea into your head that, in turn, stimulates an emotion that (for whatever reason) you find difficult to tolerate. You do not like experiencing that emotion. It is painful or distressing to you, even if — as with (unfulfilled) hope or (unsatisfied) desire — the underlying emotion isn't negative. This someone then draws your attention to a behavioral alternative that — in the game of this interaction — is held out to you as the means of escaping that unpreferred emotion. We typically maintain that we've been emotionally manipulated when we act on that alternative as a means of getting away from this unpreferred emotional state.

However, in actuality, we manipulated ourselves. We manipulated ourselves when we validated the insinuated idea, which is what caused the florescence of the distressing emotion. We manipulated ourselves when we narrowed our focus to exclude all other possibilities for action beyond those presented by the other party, which is what limited the effectiveness of our response. And we manipulated ourselves when we refused to tolerate the painful emotion aroused within us, which is what motivated us to surrender to the impulse or consent to the behavioral alternative. If we neither validated the idea nor narrowed our focus nor refused to tolerate the emotion, then the attempt at emotional manipulation *would not have been successful*. It worked because we manipulated ourselves at the suggestion of another.

In reality, we have many opportunities to covertly interrupt an attempted emotional manipulation. Chief among them is the application of *emotional resilience*. If people were able to increasingly tolerate their own negative or distressing emotions, then — even if these feelings were elicited — they would not feel as motivated to escape the experience by means of the manipulator's behavioral alternative. The ability to abide in discomfort without demonstration is inestimably useful.

Indeed, this is the single most important attribute givers can possess in the Game of Please/No. If givers can arrive at a place where they can experience their emotions without taking action — or, even better, where they can disrupt the cognitive chain of events before the emotions even materialize — then they will be impervious to all the emotional manipulation techniques wanters utilize to get what they want. Such givers might not win, but they can never lose.

In any case, I hope I've impressed upon you the importance of appreciating the psychological dimension of power. Wherever it is played, *this* is the stage upon which the outcome of the Game is decided. Will wanters succeed in eliciting the appropriate emotional experiences in givers to get what they desire? Or will givers succeed in resisting the emotional impulses insinuated by wanters to abide without action? Either way, the more powerful player will win the Game.

PRINCIPLES OF POWER

If power is psychological, then how can we recognize the more powerful player? It turns out there are many signs, if we only learn to see them. After watching thousands of playthroughs, I've identified numerous behaviors and attributes that reliably predict the outcome of the Game. However, I'll limit myself here to 10 of the most common signals. I call these *principles of power,* and (all other things being equal) the players who demonstrate more of these principles to a greater extent will win the Game. If it is the wanters, *they will get what they want*; if it is the givers, *they will keep what they have.*

The first principle is that the more powerful person is the one who **moves less**. Since this is overtly apparent, this is one of the easiest signs to identify. Consider a kingdom. In the center of a castle, the king sits unmoving on his throne, while the entire court revolves around him. If people desire an audience, they must come to *him*, and the effort expended in doing so is a testament to his power. The greater the effortful motion, the greater the recognition of the king's power. And since power is the ability to get others to act, it makes sense that the more powerful player would move less (if at all).

The power of a king is easy to see: he is mighty and strong. However, it's important to recognize that power doesn't always look like this. Paradoxically, it is often the weaker player who is the more powerful. The most obvious example of this truth is an infant child, who simply lies there while the rest of the house scurries about to attend to its needs. Albeit through slightly different pathways, expressing weakness is also the basic principle behind the core strategies of pity and victimization discussed in the previous chapter. The weak move to the strong; however, the truly weak stop moving entirely, and become more powerful as a result.

In the game of mating and dating, this relative lack of motion can assume many forms. For instance, the more powerful players are typically the ones who initiate less, are slower to respond, and use fewer words in their communications. If you don't believe me, just compare your emails to your boss with your boss's emails to you on these three dimensions. It is the privilege of the powerful to take their time, dispense with formalities, or forgo responding altogether. However, the same behaviors in the less powerful would read as insubordination.

Another way to consider power is to observe who goes to whom. When dates are planned, for whom are the logistics more convenient? It's assumed that the time of the more powerful is more valuable, so they are less likely to make concessions as to time and place. On the other hand, the less powerful are expected to make a greater effort to accommodate scheduling requests. Again, this is why you go to your boss's office, and your boss doesn't come to yours (or meet you halfway).

Finally, we can appreciate how certain personality traits — like stubbornness or selfishness — can be associated with power. Given the unflattering nature of these traits, their prevalence would be puzzling were it not for their effectiveness. Disadvantaged players can often win the Game by simply refusing to budge — or by being too difficult or irrational to negotiate with. In fact, this is one of the best strategies for more incompetent players, who may not possess much value with which to otherwise transact their relationships. Such individuals can find it difficult to find partners with whom to play, but — once they do — this approach can be extremely effective.

The second principle is that the more powerful person is the one who is **less committed**. This is because the less committed player is more likely to walk away with less provocation, threatening the basis of the relationship itself. In some cases, more competent players are less committed, as they are confident in their ability to get what they need or want elsewhere, if any given partner proves too difficult or inconvenient. However, in most cases, it is less invested players who are less committed. This means they would have less to lose — either materially, emotionally, or both — if the relationship were to end. This increases the likelihood that they will attempt the *takeaway tactic* (i.e., the core strategy of quitting), and it also decreases their susceptibility to the same tactic when it is used against them. Of course, these two attributions are not mutually exclusive: highly competent, less invested players are the least committed of all.

On the other hand, more committed players — either because they are less competent, more invested, or both — exist at the mercy of the less committed as a function of their commitment. This is because the more committed players are more likely to suffer loss — either materially, emotionally, or both — if the relationship were to end. Cognizance of this fact is generally associated with a higher degree of anxiety and relationship insecurity. And since people are much more likely to take action in order to avoid loss than to secure gain, those who are more insecure in a relationship are easier to manipulate and more vulnerable to nearly every one of the Game's core strategies. It is this susceptibility in the more committed partner that makes the less committed partner more powerful.

In reality, only the player who receives more benefit should be threatened by the end of a relationship. If anything, the player who benefits less should feel relieved for being given the opportunity to create space for another (potentially more rewarding) relationship. However, as we've discussed, the Game of Please/No transpires in the minds of the players, and many people who would be well rid of their partners tremble at the thought of losing them. They are shepherds trembling before Chihuahuas. This is why *cultivating insecurity* is one of the perennial tactics of those who provide less value: it obscures the actual nature of the transaction.

In the game of mating and dating, it sometimes proves difficult to determine which partner is more committed. This is because commitment can assume more than one form: it can be emotional (in the sense of devotion and loyalty), and it can be material (in the sense of effort and provision). Occasionally, one partner in a relationship is the more (or less) committed in both senses of the word. However, it is more commonly the case that these two forms of commitment are split between the two parties.

For example, in any given relationship, one partner will generally be higher in emotional commitment and lower in material commitment (and vice versa for the other partner). And this makes sense, as the basis of a relationship is the exchange of unequal goods of comparable value. Of course, this can give rise to disagreements as to the respective values of each form of commitment, with each partner typically arguing that his or her form of commitment is more valuable, needful, and irreplaceable than the other's. Whether or not they're aware of it, these arguments are about power, in that they functionally try to convince the *other party* that he or she derives more benefit from the relationship — and thus should feel more insecure and motivated to acquiesce.

The third principle is that the more powerful player is the one who has **more options**. As previously discussed, competition drives down prices in the commercial marketplace (while monopoly sends them through the roof). The same is true in the sexual marketplace. A wanter who has hundreds of people to ask won't spend much time and energy on any one giver who says "no." On the other hand, a giver who has hundreds of people asking won't even acknowledge any one wanter who is not offering a sufficiently compelling proposal. Playing with more givers drives down the price of the proposed transaction, and playing with more wanters drives up the price. As competition increases, the less important or powerful any one player becomes and the more the partner with more options enjoys an advantage.

As a result, one of the best ways for players to increase their relative power in relationships is to improve their optionality. In the sexual marketplace, the way to do this differs for men and women, as a consequence of the fact that men exchange resources for sexual opportunity, and women exchange sexual opportunity for resources. In general, men increase their optionality by being *visibly competent*, whereas women increase their optionality by being *visibly attractive*. Ideally, the optimal strategy would be to limit your partners' optionality while retaining your own. And since it is (a) typically easier for women to be visibly attractive (by means of technologies like social media) than for men to be visibly competent (which can require years of effort), and (b) most men would entertain a sexual relationship with most women, but most women would not entertain a sexual relationship with most men, women are typically the more powerful players in *sexually exclusive* relationships. This is because women enjoy more passive optionality than men, who (if they are constrained from actively cultivating their optionality) will typically not be able to close the gap.

Keep in mind that this optionality increases players' power irrespective of whether they choose to act on it, which is something else entirely. At least theoretically, it is possible for players with a host of options to remain emotionally loyal to or sexually exclusive with their partners. In practice, however, it is more difficult for the player with more options to be emotionally committed or sexually exclusive for a variety of reasons: chief among them being the relationship between price and competition. Over time, it will be harder for a giver with more options to accept a less desirable offer when more desirable offers are available, and it will be harder for a wanter with more options to pay higher costs when less expensive options are available. These conditions typically increase relationship dissatisfaction over time and make it more likely that smaller problems will exacerbate that discontent.

Among other things, this helps to explain the behavior of men and women on online dating apps. Since men perceive that they have lots of potential options (after all, it seems like it's just him and an endless supply of women), and every woman competes against every other woman, this drives down the price of the proposed transaction. From his perspective, it is apparently a *wanter's market*. As a result, men are increasingly emboldened to transact for the sexual opportunity at the lowest possible price point. However, all judgment aside, we can see that this behavior is entirely rational, given our various assumptions. In that sea of infinite options, there must exist a comparable option who can be acquired more cheaply. So why pay more than you need to?

On the other hand, since women *also* perceive that they have lots of potential options (after all, it seems like it's just her and an endless supply of men), and every man competes against every other man, this drives up the price of the proposed transaction. From her perspective, it is apparently a *giver's market*. As a result, women are increasingly emboldened to transact their sexual opportunity at the highest possible price point. This is why nearly every woman's dating profile explains that she is looking for a "serious, committed relationship" (and that men who are "just looking for sex" should "swipe left"). Such women are attempting to acquire the most resources for the least sexual opportunity. And all judgment aside, we can see that this behavior is also entirely rational, given our various assumptions. In that sea of infinite options, there must exist a comparable option who is willing to pay more. So why settle for less?

And this (at least partly) explains the counterintuitive fact that fewer and fewer people are entering into relationships as online dating becomes more and more prevalent. Since men and women transact for different goods, their perceived optionalities operate in different directions. To men, optionality suggests that sexual opportunity should be *less* expensive. To women, optionality suggests that sexual opportunity should be *more* expensive. This has produced an ever-widening gap between their respective valuations for the same opportunity, making it increasingly difficult (if not impossible) to negotiate a transaction.

The fourth principle is that the more powerful player is the one **more willing to sacrifice**. Since this principle is associated with loss, it is an often unacknowledged source of power. However, as we'll see, this is precisely its opportunity. This is because competition affects the means to power, as well. The more people vie for power in a particular way, the more of that power any given individual will have to acquire in order to benefit from its application. For instance, while it is significantly above average, a six-figure income doesn't mean much in a world that contains billionaires. Since most people are vying for power using the money proxy, they will need to acquire an ever-increasing amount of it in order for that power to be useful. As you might imagine, this doesn't work out the way most people hope. Pursuing power through a method that fewer people utilize is a much more savvy approach. One way to do that is through sacrifice — or at least through the willingness to sacrifice. This looks a little different depending on whether a player is a wanter or a giver. So we'll look at each position in turn.

First, the wanters. One of the best ways to get what you want in life is *to be willing to do whatever it takes to get it*. Note the word *willing*. If a player is willing to do something, actually doing that something often becomes unnecessary. This is because willingness — if properly executed — is not only imbued with a special power derived from conviction, but it also communicates that all rejection and rebuttal will be a useless waste of time — so why even bother? This effectively ends the Game in favor of the wanter.

In the game of mating and dating, the willingness to do *anything* in the service of the beloved is an attribute of romantic love, which, as we'll explore more deeply in chapter 9, is the transmutation of religious impulse. This is why sweeping gestures of romantic love work much better in books and movies than in real life. Most people are uncomfortable being idolized. The willingness to, say, stand outside your beloved's apartment until she recognizes the strength of your conviction (and consequently consents to a relationship) won't earn you love and admiration as much as it will garner contempt and a conversation with the police.

However, many people — especially young men with little real-world experience — continue to be misled by the examples held out by their culture that if they only suffer enough with sufficient persistence (or if they indicate their intent to do so with a grand enough gesture), they will eventually be rewarded with the relationship they seek. While it is possible for wanters to use this principle successfully, it must be done with the utmost tact, firmness, and humility. This is because the willingness to do whatever it takes can't be a bluff, and it generally requires some action in the direction of approximating the sacrifice to communicate its sincerity. Wanters should employ this strategy in the sexual marketplace cautiously, if at all.

Now let's consider givers. As previously discussed, it's not possible to win a Game against a giver who (for whatever reason) has decided never to assent. Such individuals are willing to sacrifice *everything* to defend their position. And if a player is willing to suffer any cost, actually applying that cost often becomes unnecessary. This is because willingness — if properly executed — is not only imbued with a special power derived from conviction, but it also communicates that all coercion and aggression will be a useless waste of time — so why even bother? This effectively ends the Game in favor of the giver.

Many examples of this phenomenon exist in the political sphere. For instance, Diogenes long ago remarked that the only way to be free is *to be content to die*. This is true for several reasons. First, those who are prepared to die typically cannot be coerced into doing something against their will, as the threat of death is the ultimate culmination of all escalating aggression. And only those who never act against their will can be said to be truly free. Second, the willingness to die acts as a significant deterrent. Why expose yourself to the risk inherent in escalating aggression with someone who will never surrender anyway? In most cases, such individuals are allowed to live their lives unmolested, and when they are not, they typically achieve a moral victory in their martyrdom.

In any case, players with a stronger will — as shown by their willingness to sacrifice in the service of their goals — are generally associated with a greater share of power in any relationship. By communicating that they will be neither deterred nor coerced, such individuals become relatively more powerful by rendering their partners' strategies ineffectual and useless. They dominate through the power of their conviction, and often do not have to make the sacrifices they are nonetheless willing to make.

The fifth principle is that the more powerful player is the one **more willing to transgress**. This is not an endorsement of transgressive acts: it's just a fact of reality. Most people are not only bound by the laws of their society, but they are bound (even more rigidly) by social convention and their internal programming, as well. Those who are willing to transgress across a wider field of play — from self-imposed internal rules to externally-enforced social prohibitions — typically gain in power, as they are not limited in the scope of their action to the same degree as rule-followers. This generally affords such individuals a greater arsenal of potential strategies they can implement more forcefully — making them both more flexible and more effective. Of course, successful transgression must be competent — ideally sufficiently competent to evade detection — otherwise, it will be met with as much retributive justice as the forces of accountability can muster. However, competence paired with a willingness to strategically transgress (as, say, a calculated risk) is often more effective than we would collectively care to admit.

One of the many reasons why those who are more willing to transgress are more powerful is that these people are typically better competitors. Imagine trying to win at the highest echelons of any sport *without ever committing a foul*. It wouldn't be possible, as you would be handicapping yourself in a way that none of your competitors were. The amount of additional skill needed to overcome that restriction would be insurmountable at the highest levels of play (where margins of success become increasingly narrow).

Again, without condoning transgression, it's important to understand that *fouling is part of the game*. All games forbid certain behaviors in order to define the scope of play, and they establish clear and explicit penalties for enacting those behaviors. Otherwise, you don't have a game — you have chaos. And given the risks involved, we should expect to find the most masterful play occurring on the border between the allowed and the prohibited — which is precisely what occurs. Those who are willing to risk stepping out of bounds have a larger field of play — both literally and figuratively — relative to those who are not. This willingness makes such individuals more competitive, and their competitiveness makes them more likely to achieve their goals.

Understanding this principle goes a long way toward explaining why those with *dark triad* personality traits — narcissism, Machiavellianism, and psychopathy — often succeed (at least, in the first two phases) in the game of mating and dating. While such individuals are obviously not virtuous, their apparent freedom from the (often self-imposed) limitations to which most people are subject — and their seeming indifference to the consequences of unsuccessful transgression — can be extremely attractive. To those who do not possess the emotional strength to violate social norms, such individuals can seem bold, courageous, confident, exciting, and self-possessed. This mixture of traits can imbue a relationship with a great deal of passion. When it's good, it's great — but when it's bad, it can be absolutely horrible.

This is because those with dark triad personality traits are not, in fact, emotionally strong. Rather, their behavior merely mimics emotional strength. Though some people might be able to produce remarkably convincing simulations of emotion, these individuals are rigidly defended against their own emotional experience. This partial alienation from self allows dark triad individuals to continue past the point where others stop. For better or worse, they are not dissuaded by the emotional pain that others feel for the simple reason that *they don't feel it*. Strength is feeling the pain but tolerating it. Madness is not feeling the pain at all.

Unsurprisingly, relationships with those with dark triad traits are impossible to maintain (phase three). If these people are willing to violate social norms, then it would be lunacy to expect them to respect relationship norms. They also tend to project their own repressed emotions onto their partners, which can be an incredibly frustrating and crazy-making experience. Between the transgressive behavior and the lack of accountability, the relationship becomes untenable. However, by this point, many of these players have already gotten what they wanted, so the termination of the relationship is no great loss. After all, if relationships are the media in which value is transacted, then they become increasingly irrelevant once the transaction has occurred.

The sixth principle is that the more powerful player is the one **more tolerant of emotion**. As previously discussed, most of the core strategies utilized in the Game of Please/No are emotional manipulation techniques, and emotional manipulation can only occur if those being manipulated are complicit in its success. This happens when those being manipulated are sufficiently intolerant of a particular emotion that they assent to the behavioral alternative held out by the manipulator as the means of escaping that emotion. If players were better able to show resilience in the face of their own negative or distressing emotions — that is, to experience their feelings without necessarily taking action — then they would be much more difficult to manipulate.

The benefit of emotional resilience for givers is obvious. If core strategies are emotional manipulation techniques, and if emotional resilience significantly reduces the effectiveness of emotional manipulation, then givers with a high degree of emotional resilience would be functionally immune to the core strategies in the wanter's playbook. This would allow them to keep what they have more easily and effortlessly than otherwise.

However, this is an essential skill for wanters, as well. If the universe lives closed, then wanters must be prepared to experience (and ideally, learn from) a vast amount of rejection. There is no way around this fact of life. Unfortunately, most people have a grossly distorted conceptualization of rejection, namely: that rejection is *painful*, *personal*, and *permanent*. I call this the "Three P" fallacy. In fact, rejection is none of these things. It is simply *information*: feedback from the universe that you haven't yet unlocked the desired outcome. And if players learn to listen, they can also potentially hear the clue in the rejection regarding how they might be able to move in the direction of getting what they want.

This is why emotional resilience is so important for wanters: *experiencing rejection as painful impairs the ability to hear the clue contained therein*. For instance, if wanters under the influence of the fallacy perceive rejection as, say, a personal insult, then they will inevitably experience some degree of anger as a result. And this anger will make it increasingly more difficult to accurately discern the information contained in the rejection as the emotion intensifies. This is not only because all emotions are distortive to some degree but also because it's simply hard to listen *if the listener isn't quiet*. The absence of sound is only the most superficial expression of silence. True quiet comes when the inner state of a person is peaceful and equilibrated. And it is this state — like the face of a serene pond — that is most conducive to a faithful reflection of reality.

Wanters with a high degree of emotional resilience are much more likely to achieve their desired outcomes because they will be better able to persist in rejection long enough to attain their goals and because they will be less likely to distort the information contained in givers' rejections. All other things being equal, this affords emotionally resilient wanters the possibility of securing what they want much more efficiently. And this — in turn — will decrease the total amount of time wanters spend in rejection, creating a virtuous cycle.

One final note. The capacity to tolerate pain is *patience* (which is why we call those who seek help in alleviating their suffering *patients*). Exercising greater patience than your partner can also lead to victory, either because the other will simply give up and leave you alone, or because the other will eventually give you what you want in order to get rid of you (depending on the role). Just keep in mind that employing this strategy often takes far longer than most people anticipate to achieve the desired result.

The seventh principle is that the more powerful player is the one who is **less visible**. This one is a little counterintuitive. Power as a function of visibility is curvilinear. In any given society, both the most powerful and the least powerful members are invisible. For instance, a homeless psychotic could be standing in the middle of the street, waving his arms and shouting at the top of his lungs in broad daylight, and people won't even look at him. They see him, but they don't *see* him. The lowest-status people in society are functionally beneath recognition. Some might lament this fact, but invisibility is also not without its advantages (such as freedom of movement and immunity from certain laws).

On the other hand, the most powerful members of a society are *also* invisible. These people are not the kings or the presidents or the CEOs. They're the ones behind the scenes, pulling the strings. By exerting their influence through the official channels, they retain all of their power without suffering any accountability. What's more, there are far fewer risks associated with acting from the shadows. When things go sideways, it's the king's head on the chopping block — not his advisor's. And it's this invisibility that keeps power secure. After all, how can you get rid of something *you don't even know exists?*

Appreciation of this reality complicates the modern narrative of power, especially as it concerns the historical relationship between men and women. The predominant view in the West today is that since men have traditionally occupied nearly all the visible positions of power in society, women must have been oppressed by patriarchal control.

And while women have been oppressed by men at times throughout history, it is not true that a male-dominated society is necessarily oppressive. Many powerful men throughout history have been controlled by their wives and lovers, who exerted their influence through private channels with little risk and less accountability. Like Shakespeare's Lady Macbeth, these women wielded power through men, which was both safer and more cunning than wielding power directly. And while there may not be statues devoted to these women today, this also means that their effigies won't be burned when the memories of those they represent run afoul of the current historical moment.

In any case, the less visible partner is often the more powerful player in the relationship. This is not only because they are exempt from many of the responsibilities and expectations associated with visibility but also because their relative invisibility increases the effectiveness of certain core strategies (e.g., pity, victimization) and decreases their susceptibility to others (e.g., humiliation). For instance, people have a field day when a tycoon or a politician gets divorced, but they might not even know his former partner's name. Those who have a lot have a lot to lose, which is precisely where the visibly powerful are vulnerable.

The eighth principle is that the more powerful player is the one who is **more flexible**. Though he wasn't the first to put the idea into words, Maslow's maxim remains the pithiest: "If all you have is a hammer, everything looks like a nail." Basically, this means that the fewer strategies wanters possess, the easier it is for givers to keep them at bay. Their limitations make them consistent and predictable, which functionally automates their rejection. However, it's also important to keep in mind that multiple competencies are useless if players are unwilling to use them. A sword rusts in its scabbard. Flexibility is essential because vanishingly few outcomes are achieved on the first attempt. The more strategies wanters have, and the more adaptable they are in their implementation, the more likely they will eventually transform a given "no" into a "yes."

The most successful wanters in the Game are like water: *they flow*. They're not committed to any given strategy, and they're responsive to the feedback they receive in their rejection. While they are firmly committed to their ends, they are extremely flexible with respect to their means. Politicians are often very adept at this, which is one reason why people mistrust them. Politicians are chameleons: they can blend in. They can read the room and quickly grasp the mood of the moment. Their cultivated intuition about what someone wants to hear, coupled with the ability and willingness to radically change tack, if necessary, together make these individuals exceptionally skilled players.

However, this principle isn't only applicable to wanters. Givers also benefit from increased flexibility. This is because givers aren't perpetually on the defensive, simply trying to resist wanters' various attempts at manipulation. In fact, givers can be *just as manipulative* as wanters because they, too, can imbue their communication with various forms of emotional content. Givers move beyond simply being reactive when they want to wrest control of the interaction to serve their own ends or when they want to end play with a particular wanter. For instance, givers can reject so seductively that wanters are subject to forgetting what they wanted in the first place. On the other hand, they can also reject so intimidatingly that wanters don't just give up trying: they regret asking to begin with. So, flexibility in approach can be beneficial to givers, as well.

With respect to the game of mating and dating, this is precisely why players should take anything said during a breakup with (often more than) a grain of salt. Givers can't really quit the Game; all they can do is convince wanters to stop asking. This is why givers' termination strategies generally take one of two forms. In the first form, givers assume all the responsibility for the failure of the relationship (e.g., "It's not you, it's me"). This might seem kinder, but it functionally attempts to manipulate wanters' hope by indicating that no possible strategy (or corrective action) wanters might implement has *any* chance of success. If givers were to concede that wanters were responsible for at least some of the failure of the relationship, then this would create a rational basis for wanters to keep trying. However, if the accepted narrative is that responsibility lies solely with the givers, then there is nothing more to be done. In this scenario, givers end the game by manipulating wanters into believing that further action is *hopeless*.

And in the second form, givers unleash as much vitriol, malice, and spite as they can muster. The idea here is twofold. On the one hand, these givers are trying to induce enough emotional pain in wanters that they are motivated to end the interaction of their own accord to avoid further harm. And on the other hand, they are attempting to destroy any positive regard the wanters might still have for them in order to eliminate the basis for future approaches. This isn't a pleasant strategy, but it can be very effective. If it is successful, wanters experience both diminished motivation to approach and increased motivation to avoid, bringing an indefinite close to the unwanted interaction. In this scenario, givers end the game by manipulating wanters' *desire*.

In both cases, the important thing to understand is that givers aren't really telling the truth when they employ these tactics. Rather, they are saying whatever they believe in the moment will effectively incite the emotional experience that will motivate a wanter to stop asking. And this experience is typically some form of pain, as this is the primary way in which aversion is manipulated in all higher animals. So don't put too much stock in what is said during a breakup: the words were chosen less for their veracity than for their ability to induce a specific emotional state to change your behavior.

The ninth principle is that the more powerful player is the one who is **more knowledgeable about the other**. As the saying goes, "Knowledge is power." Unfortunately, years of academic indoctrination have led most people to misconstrue the knowledge in question to refer to factual knowledge, which is functionally useless. Knowing that Vaduz is the capital of Liechtenstein, or that the Battle of Hastings occurred in 1066, or that the mitochondria are the powerhouses of the cell has never made anyone more powerful. The knowledge this phrase refers to is the knowledge of *how things work*, and it's the knowledge of how people work that is most directly related to the exercise of power.

Books like this can help you understand how people work, in general. However, in the Game of Please/No, this understanding is only useful to a point. This is because it's not possible to play with people in general — only with specific individuals. And these specific individuals have their own desires, preferences, and goals — some of which will deviate significantly from normative (or statistical) expectations. Consequently, wanters only have two choices if they want to be successful: either they must appropriately tailor their approach to the specific giver in question, or they must take massive action to increase the likelihood that their specific approach will find a responsive audience among givers, in general. The two options are mutually exclusive in practice, as it's not possible to scale a custom-tailored approach, given the costs involved.

Wanters' ability to tailor their approach effectively depends on their knowledge of the giver in question. They can glean this knowledge piecemeal by listening attentively to the information contained in a particular giver's rejection. However, the process can be greatly expedited by learning as much as possible about the individual giver, either through careful observation, surreptitious research, or (as a last resort) direct questioning. Learning what a person hates and loves, fears and desires, regrets and hopes is an absolute gold mine, as it reveals the specific pathways through which one can effectively implement the general strategies. After all, it is much easier to, say, seduce, intimidate, or charm if you know what a certain person desires, fears, or hopes, respectively. This is why asking questions is one of the most reliable indicators of interest: the questioner is trying to secure information on how best to go about getting what he or she wants. Without sufficient interest, there is rarely a desire to learn more.

Knowledge about the other player serves both a positive and a negative function — both of which facilitate obtaining a desired outcome. In its positive function, this knowledge may be construed as *knowing what the other person wants*. In general, no one cares what *you* want — and the less acquainted you are, the more indifference they exhibit. This is why going around trying to convince others to give you what you want is a terrible strategy. A much better idea is to determine what other people want and then figure out how to frame the achievement of your goal as a means to the achievement of theirs. If wanters can demonstrate that their goal is a means to their partners' ends, then they stand a much better chance of securing a "yes" from any given giver. And this, of course, is facilitated by accurate knowledge of the other party's desires, hopes, and aspirations.

On the other hand, in its negative function, this knowledge may also be understood as *knowing what the other person doesn't want*. Everyone has a *thumbscrew*: an emotional experience that he or she finds extremely difficult to tolerate. Framing the achievement of your goal as either the means of preventing the application of a thumbscrew or of removing a thumbscrew that has already been applied can be tremendously effective. Indeed, this approach is typically more potent than the one previously described, as people are generally more motivated to avoid pain than to secure pleasure. If wanters can demonstrate that their goal is a means for their partners to avoid or escape pain, then they stand a much better chance of getting what they want. And this, of course, is facilitated by accurate knowledge of the other party's fears, insecurities, and vulnerabilities.

Society typically frowns upon manipulating people's psychology like this. However, it happens every day in socially sanctioned ways. In reality, the most successful contingency management always includes utilizing knowledge in both its positive and its negative functions: the carrot *and* the stick.

People pay taxes because their contributions help fund the infrastructure that makes their lives easier *and* because not paying will land them in prison. People go to work because their labor serves others and generates income *and* because not working will expose them to certain deprivations. People stay married because they want to honor their commitments and enjoy a loving partnership *and* because divorce is a painful and expensive process.

If societies can use contingency management to incentivize some behaviors and inhibit others, then individuals can do the same in their personal relationships. This management becomes more effective when individuals become more knowledgeable about what their partners want and don't want. Ultimately, people don't really have a choice but to exercise this principle, as those who can neither offer benefit nor threaten harm are functionally irrelevant. Relationships with such individuals are simply not possible, as there are no grounds for transaction. The only real choices people have are the degree to which they become knowledgeable about others and the extent to which they apply that knowledge in the service of their goals.

Finally, the tenth principle is that the more powerful player is the one who is the **better communicator**. Words are *magic*. Simply calling something by its proper name affords some measure of control over it, and expressing an intention clearly and articulately is tantamount to casting an enchantment. If successful, words literally conjure ideas and emotions out of thin air.[27] A masterful command of language also enables more nuanced modeling, which allows our conceptualizations

27 The magic word *abracadabra* is derived from Hebrew words that mean *I create as I speak*.

to more closely conform with reality, with all its diversity of experience. The right word is the key that opens many locks.

However, semantic language is only one form of communication. As you'll recall, players are almost completely deprived of this method of expression in the theatrical game of please/no. This restriction forces them to rely more heavily on non-verbal forms of communication — especially tone and facial expression. When words have been stripped away, it becomes even more obvious that effective communication is coherent across as many different levels of expression as possible. What does this mean?

Communication occurs across many different levels of expression simultaneously. Information is contained in semantic meaning, of course, but information is *also* contained in a glance, in a gesture, in a posture, in a movement, in a silence, in a tone. Indeed, in many cases, what isn't said is often more informative than what *is*. Communication becomes coherent to the extent that the *same intention is simultaneously expressed on different levels of expression*. And communication becomes incoherent to the extent that different intentions are simultaneously expressed on different levels of expression. For instance, players attempting to communicate intimidation would most effectively do so by glaring menacingly, standing erect, expanding their chests, crossing their arms, leaning forward, reducing personal distance, snarling (or frowning) their mouths, deepening their pitch, and flaring their nostrils. Words would not be necessary to communicate their intention: everyone in the world would understand what they were trying to convey.

In the game of mating and dating, the concept of communication coherence has two important applications. In the first place, it's generally not possible to get what you want if people don't understand what you want. And it's generally not possible for people to understand what you want if your communication is incoherent. This is why effective communication is a form of power: it increases the likelihood of getting what you want from others for the simple reason that people are more likely *to know what to give you.*

And in the second place, when communication is incoherent — especially between the levels of semantic language and emotional timbre — people will always give more weight to what is expressed non-verbally. Shrilly screaming "I LOVE AND RESPECT YOU!" at the top of your voice with a crazed look on your face will probably not cause others to receive your message as intended. By the same token, purring "You have *some* nerve coming here tonight," while gently stroking your partner with your fingertips will communicate something very different from what your words suggest. Of course, the most common manifestations of incoherence are not mixed messages like these but rather verbal expressions unaccompanied by emotional timbre. The absence of a non-verbal correlate generally undermines the power of semantic language, especially when communicating information about internal states.

So there you have it: 10 principles of power. In any given playthrough, the one who aligns more closely with these principles — in both number and intensity — is the more powerful player and will win the Game. All things being equal, this means that players who move less, are less committed, have more options, are more willing to sacrifice, are more willing to transgress, are more emotionally resilient, are less visible, are more flexible, are more knowledgeable, and are better communicators are much more likely to get what they want in relationships. Moving in the indicated direction on any of these dimensions leads to an increase in power.

This is why sexual relationships — over time — *tend to benefit women more than men.* Since the average woman tends to align with more of these principles than the average man, she is typically the more powerful player in a heterosexual relationship. And since relative value tends to flow from the less powerful to the more powerful, we should expect women in sexual relationships to benefit as they do. Women are able to mate and date for gain because they are more adept at getting what they want from men than men are at getting what they want from women. On the other hand, men must generally mate and date for acceptable loss for the same reason. Ultimately, however, these realities have more to do with power than with biological sex.

In this chapter, I argued that power — the ability to get other people to act in the service of your goals — is the single most decisive factor in the determination of the outcome of any Game of Please/No. Of particular relevance, I noted that most of the attributes that people associate with this factor — like money, status, and physical strength — are proxies of power, while actual power is immaterial, as the lever that compels people to act is always psychological. I then discussed 10 principles of power, which collectively can be used to identify the more powerful player in any given interaction.

These principles are applicable to relationships, in general. However, another dimension of power exists that is especially relevant to sexual relationships, in particular. We'll look at this important factor more closely in the next chapter.

If you'd like to further explore the topics presented in this chapter, please scan the QR code to access a curated playlist on the PsycHacks channel on YouTube.

CHAPTER 7

ATTRACTIVENESS IS THE KEY TO POWER IN SEXUAL RELATIONSHIPS

A special form of power is particularly relevant to sexual relationships: *attractiveness*. In any given sexual relationship (and in many non-sexual relationships), more attractive players are more likely to get more of what they want. They also have a relatively easier time across all three phases of a relationship. They are more likely to stand out from their competition — so they are targeted more quickly and frequently in the attraction phase. They can command more advantageous terms for themselves — so they fare better in the negotiation phase. And they are more likely to retain their relationships (if they so desire) — so they are more secure in the maintenance phase, as well.

This is because attractiveness is a *master key*: it unlocks many of the principles of power discussed in the previous chapter. For example, attractive players can move less because other players are motivated to approach, and they enjoy greater optionality, given their marketplace visibility. They are also often more willing to transgress since they typically experience fewer negative consequences for the same violation relative to less attractive people. And due to the halo effect, attractive partners are also more likely to be perceived as possessing more of the positive traits associated with power (and fewer of the negative ones) than is warranted in reality. This suggests that to optimize their performance in the sexual marketplace, *players should prioritize increasing their attractiveness*. All other things being equal, resources applied in this way will generate the largest possible return on investment.

Since attractiveness is both biologically determined and culturally informed, it's a fairly complex construct and one that is subject to continuous evolution. Consequently, it can be hard to pin down, though people typically "know it when they see it." My working definition is that attractiveness is the degree to which people align with the gendered archetype of beauty that serves as the standard for their normalized sexual marketplace value, in general, and the degree to which they align with the specific interests, preferences, and desires of a given partner that serves as the basis for their perceived sexual marketplace value, in particular. Basically, the higher your nSMV, the more attractive you are to more people, and the higher your pSMV, the more attractive you are to the particular person with whom you are potentially transacting.

Now, attractiveness can be a touchy subject for many people. So before I go any further, I'll share some good news and then some bad news, and then some more good news, to contextualize the following discussion. The good news is that *everyone can be beautiful*. This sounds cliché, but it's true. People are beautiful to the extent that they accept and express their true nature. Most people are not beautiful, not because they can't be but because they spend so much of their lives hiding or trying to be someone else that they can hardly recognize their true nature, let alone express it. However, when people deeply know themselves, accept themselves, and express themselves, then beauty shines out of them like a subtle light, irrespective of their physical appearance. And since self-awareness often increases with time, people can become more beautiful as they age.

The bad news is that *not* everyone can be attractive. In fact, at any given moment, most people will not accord with their respective gender's archetype of beauty. Attractiveness also tends to decrease as a function of time — more quickly for women, less quickly for men — so those fortunate enough to be attractive have a limited time window in which to enjoy the privileges of that condition. It's best to think of attractiveness as a season, like spring. It only exists for a short time relative to the rest of the year, and some springs are lovelier than others. Consequently, since attractive partners are more likely to secure better terms with more desirable partners, it stands to reason that all participants in the sexual marketplace should seek out what they want most aggressively while they are most attractive. Like trust, attractiveness is difficult to regain once it's gone.

Fortunately, the second piece of good news is that *attractiveness can always be increased*. There are always actions men and women can take to bring themselves into greater alignment with their respective gender's archetypal standard of beauty, and there are always behaviors men and women can learn to improve their performances of masculinity and femininity, respectively. Like all ideals, these standards are infinitely receding: they can be approached but never attained. And like the acquisition of any other skill, moving in the direction of the ideal will be associated with diminishing returns on the investment of resources over time. While not everyone can be very attractive, everybody can be more attractive than they currently are. It is foolish to lament the attainment of an ultimate goal when more proximate goals remain unattempted. So, as long as returns exceed expenses, participants in the sexual marketplace should do what they can to increase their attractiveness.

In discussing attraction, all people should understand three very important considerations regarding how this attribute of power operates within sexual relationships. I call these considerations *the laws of attraction*. And in this chapter, I will examine each law in turn.

THE FIRST LAW

The first law is, appropriately enough, *the fundamental law of attraction*. It's simple: **people want what they want, not what wants them**. Many people struggle in the sexual marketplace precisely because they do not adequately appreciate this fundamental law. There are two reasons for this.

In the first place, the behavioral impulse embedded in attraction is to approach the desired object. This is literally the meaning of the word *attract*, which is derived from a Latin word (*attrahere*) meaning *to draw near*. So the natural instinct in attraction — when it is undiluted by fear — is to move toward the attractive object, and this can easily transition into pursuit. This is so often tragic because the natural instinct to being pursued is *to flee*, even when it might be in the pursued's best interests to allow themselves to be caught. The unfortunate upshot is that many people pursue those to whom they are attracted, driving them right out of their lives.

And in the second place, Western culture — permeated as it is with romantic ideology — is saturated with the belief that *love wins in the end*. At the end of the movie, the nice guy gets the girl; at the end of the novel, the billionaire proposes marriage. This obsession with romantic love leads many — especially many young people — to believe that people ultimately end up with the ones who love them the most. This is far from the case. Unfortunately, this belief does not prevent people from thinking that demonstrating a high degree of interest is the best way to secure a desired relationship.

The fact is that you can't get people to want you more *by wanting them more*. The reason this is the case will become clearer once we discuss the second law. For the time being, however, I'd like you to consider that more than material things can be shared between people in a relationship: immaterial things can be shared as well. For instance, people who anxiously worry often allow their partners to worry less. It's almost as though the former are doing the worrying for the entire relationship, making any anxiety on the part of the latter unnecessary. The same can hold true for attraction: people who are highly desirous often allow their partners to desire less. It's almost as though the former are doing the desiring for the entire relationship, making any desire on the part of the latter unnecessary. The upshot is that wanting more doesn't translate into being wanted more. In all likelihood, it will have the opposite effect.

On the other hand, wanting someone less *can* generate greater interest, especially if the other party holds the wanter in positive regard. The reason this is the case will become clearer once we discuss the third law. However, the mechanism just described also applies in this scenario. It's as though a relationship is an organism onto itself, and (like all organisms) it wants to maintain homeostasis. If one partner starts to demonstrate diminished interest and desire, the other often works harder to "make up for" the decrease. The idea is to rekindle the other's flagging desire and prevent the termination of the relationship. Keep in mind this doesn't always work, and — when it does — it typically only does so for a limited amount of time.

In any case, if it's true that people want what they want, not what wants them, then the most effective pathway to being wanted should be clear. Rather than trying to want someone into wanting them, players should focus on becoming *more attractive to the person — or type of person — to whom they are attracted*. The more attractive they are to these people, the more they will be desired by them: no wanting required. And if becoming more attractive to this person — or group of people — means becoming less attractive to others: so be it. In general, it is better to be more desired by fewer people than to be less desired by more. Always a bridesmaid, never a bride.

THE SECOND LAW

Now let's move on to the second law. It's also fairly simple but with far-reaching consequences. In any given relationship,

it's not possible for two people to be equally attracted to each other. This can rub folks the wrong way, but that's the way it is. Like most things in life, inequality is the rule: so why should attraction be any different?

In any case, this inequality gives rise to two essential phenomena: *the balance of attraction* and *the attraction gap*. If it's not possible for two people to be equally attracted to each other, then there must be someone who likes the other person more, and there must be someone who likes the other person less. If the second law is true, this is an inescapable consequence. I call the person who likes the other more *the adorer*, and the person who likes the other less *the adored*. Together, they constitute the balance of attraction, and the discrepancy between the two positions is the attraction gap.

There is much to understand about the balance of attraction. First, it's necessary to appreciate that these roles do not inhere in specific individuals. The same person can be the adorer in one relationship and the adored in another. The same person can even be the adorer and the adored in the same relationship, albeit at different time points. Consequently, it's better to consider the adored and the adorer as places that people can occupy (or roles that people can fulfill) as opposed to attributes of the individuals themselves. And just like other roles that people play as they go about their lives, these roles draw out certain traits and obscure others.

In the second place, it's important to acknowledge that these positions are both gender-neutral and role-independent. Men can be the adored, and women can be the adored; men can be the adorer, and women can be the adorer. Likewise, captains can be the adored, and passengers can be the adored; captains can be the adorer, and passengers can be the adorer.

No moral or ethical obligation dictates that certain people occupy certain places in a relationship. However, as we'll see, some positions are generally better fits for certain roles and genders than others.

And in the third place, we need to understand that one position is not better than the other. People often think that adorers are good and loving, and the adored are bad and selfish. However, this is hardly even a general rule. The adored aren't necessarily taking advantage of those who occupy the place of the adorer (although this can happen), and adorers aren't necessarily kind and sincere (although they can be). And of course, someone *has* to be in the place of the adored for the place of the adorer to even exist, so it's better to think of these as complementary postures. Like two sides of the same coin, they create each other. In fact, both roles are associated with pros and cons, and the balance of benefits and liabilities of each position will naturally align with some people's preferences and temperaments more than others. Accurate self-knowledge — in conjunction with acceptance of some of the realities discussed in this chapter — is extremely useful in determining any given individual's position of best fit.

Now let's look at each role in turn, starting with the adorer. The feature that most distinguishes the place of the adorer is that whoever occupies this position *experiences more feelings more intensely*. This can be either a benefit *or* a liability, depending on one's preferences for emotional experience. On the one hand, **adorers get to be with the ones they love** — which is one of the best feelings in the world. On the other hand, and as a consequence of being with the ones they love, adorers are also subject to experiencing a variety of other, less positive emotions as the relationship runs its course.

Adorers are the ones who anxiously wait by the phone and become flustered when the call finally arrives. They're crestfallen when plans fall through and joyful when invitations are accepted. They can be thrilled by a glance from the adored and positively transported by sexual intimacies. However, they can also be devastated by rejection (even perceived rejection) and inconsolable after a breakup. Adorers find simply being in the presence of the adored to be an inherently valuable experience, which (as we'll see) serves as one of the most reliable metrics for measuring attraction. Finally, adorers may occasionally become exhausted by the roller coaster of emotion associated with this position, but when these feelings have been absent for a time (or when they date someone to whom they're not as attracted), they can grow bored and complain that "something is missing." This last point also indicates another inescapable attribute of the place of the adorer: *a relative lack of power and control.* And this, of course, is to be expected. If attractiveness is the key to power in sexual relationships, then it stands to reason that the person who is more attracted would be less powerful. That's just the way it goes. Furthermore, if you like to experience emotion, then — on some level — you have to surrender control. Roller coasters are exciting precisely *because* you're being taken for a ride. For better or worse, when you strap yourself in, you have chosen to relinquish control over the way things will go, which is both terrifying and exhilarating. Depending on how you feel about assuming responsibility and making decisions, this surrender of control can be either deeply troubling or profoundly relieving.

Again, everyone is different and this diversity is a good thing. However, given the attributes of the place of the adorer already discussed, we can appreciate that this role is generally a better fit for women and passengers. Though it may appear otherwise, most people — men *and* women — want to be the adorer. This is because most people want to feel something in their relationships, and many people believe the absence of feeling to be a sign that the relationship is flawed. If it's not present in the early stages of the courtship, people object that "there's no chemistry." If the experience dwindles as the years go by, they protest that they "don't feel the same way" or that they're "not in love anymore." Many people today believe that these experiences constitute sufficient grounds for ending a relationship — though (as we'll discuss in a future chapter) the importance of this emotional dimension is a recent historical development in the story of relationships.

There are three reasons why women are particularly suited for the adorer role. The first reason is that if most people want to feel something in their relationships, then this is especially true for women, who tend to be more emotionally oriented. As the saying goes, you can make a woman in a relationship feel anything except boredom — at which point, she often starts to look for the door. Relative to men, women are much less likely to entertain a potential relationship (or to remain in a preexisting relationship) if this emotional dimension is missing, even if the relationship in question is (or would otherwise be) beneficial to her. Women are more likely to go to relationships *to feel*, and they often expect the feelings they experience there to be special and unique.

Given the fact that most men would have sex with most women, women often get to experience being desired. As a result, this experience is neither special nor unique to most women, which is part of the reason why many find men's physical desire for them insulting. It's the economic equivalent of being paid in pocket change: low value, high circulation. On the other hand, the experience of being with the one *they* desire is a much more uncommon experience for women. It's also an experience that men typically have to cultivate, as female desire is typically more slowly aroused and less spontaneous than male desire. Consider the differences between pornography and romance novels (and who uses which). In any case, since the adorer role is much more amenable to the experience of all kinds of emotions, it's generally a better fit for women.

The second reason is a consequence of the average woman's superior optionality in the sexual marketplace, which allows them to be more demanding with respect to their potential partners. As optionality increases, the utility of less salient criteria in making decisions increases significantly. If two cars have the exact same make, model, production date, feature package, ownership history, and price point, then you might decide which one to buy based on which color you like more. For many women, sexual selection is not a choice between a partner who can provide benefit and a partner who cannot, but a choice between a partner who can provide benefit (but for whom they feel *less* attraction) and a partner who can provide benefit (and for whom they feel *more* attraction).

As a result of women's optionality, *benefit is a given*. So the decision to enter into any given relationship will depend on other (potentially less important) factors. And because of this, women are also more likely to leave a relationship if this feeling, which may have been the deciding factor for entering into the relationship to begin with, disappears. Men typically do not have this privilege. In general, women get to date who they like, and men get to date who will have them. This is true all the way through marriage ("she said '*yes!*'"). Of course, men can also leave relationships when their feelings change and those who do are typically men who have options. However, they are more likely to stay — and stay longer — out of a sense of duty or obligation, relative to women.

Finally, the third reason is that the adorer role is more consistent with women's fundamental sexual selection principle: *hypergamy*. Both literally and figuratively, women want men they can look up to. However, when a man adores a woman, he puts her on a pedestal. This may be flattering for the woman at first (especially if it comes after playing the adorer in a previous relationship), but it's generally not a sustainable dynamic. This is because if he's looking up at her, then he is functionally forcing her to look down on him. Among other things, a woman who looks down on a man will find it difficult to feel like she's with the one she loves. She cannot respect such a man, and — if she can't respect him — she certainly cannot love him. As a result, relationships in which women are the adored are much more likely to be unstable, contentious, and discontented.

Even if a man satisfies all of a woman's hypergamous criteria on paper (e.g., taller, richer, higher status), pedestalizing her will significantly reduce the likelihood of a successful relationship, as the man is effectively communicating that he, himself, does not believe he is someone she can look up to. As previously noted, when communication is incoherent, people will always give precedence to the non-verbal dimension of that communication. So behaving in this way will often cause women to feel as though their hypergamy hasn't been satisfied, irrespective of the objective reality of the situation.

It's necessary to teach people how to feel about you. If men act like they're not a catch, *women will believe them* — and toss them back in the water.

On the other hand, it should be fairly obvious why passengers are better suited for the adorer role (regardless of gender). They didn't build the boat — they just bought a ticket. In so doing, they implicitly consented to surrender some of their rights, including (but not limited to) some degree of control over the experience. And in exchange for that concession, they are generally relieved of a great deal of the responsibility for making the ship run properly. This is fair. Passengers cannot reasonably demand a greater share of power without taking on more responsibility, and they are less likely to be competent in assuming that responsibility because they did not build the boat, learn to sail, and plot the course. Without having mastered these challenges, it's in everyone's best interests for passengers to stay *as far away from the helm as possible*. And this is why passengers make better adorers: it's the more suitable role for those who already (and appropriately) enjoy less power, control, and responsibility in a given relationship.

Now let's turn our attention to the place of the adored. As might be expected, the experience of the adored is diametrically opposed to that of the adorer. Because they are relatively less attracted to their partners, those in the adored position do not get to be with the ones they love: **they get to be loved by the ones they're with**. And as a consequence of this, their emotional experience in the relationship is significantly dampened. They feel neither the dizzying highs nor the terrifying lows to which adorers have access. And this can be either a benefit *or* a liability, depending on one's preferences for emotional experience. Indeed, since the adored feel less attraction to their partners, they often have a "take it or leave it" attitude with respect to the relationship. Some might find this indifference a profound relief, while others might find it tedious and intolerable. As before, appropriate placement depends on accurate self-knowledge. In lieu of the supreme joy of being with the ones they love, the adored are compensated in a host of other ways. To begin with, the adored command more power and control in any given relationship. And this stands to reason: if attractiveness is the key to power in sexual relationships, then we should expect the partner who is less attracted to be more powerful. As a result, relationships are more likely to exist within the adoreds' frames and to more closely align with their preferences and expectations. The actual operation of the relationship will also be more logistically convenient for the adored, who can functionally dictate where, when, and how the relationship transpires.

If this were the end of the story, nearly everyone would prefer to be the adored. However, wielding more power and control carries with it two significant liabilities. The first is that too much control can drastically *diminish engagement and motivation*. Most people don't want the end of the movie spoiled for them. If it is, they're much less likely to watch the film, and — if they do anyway — they typically need to have a much more compelling reason for doing so than they otherwise would. Most people do not have that reason, nor do they typically possess the self-discipline required to pursue it (if they had it). Similarly, many folks would find it hard to keep living if they knew exactly what life had in store for them. After all, this might be as good as it gets. Ignorance of how things will unfold is a necessary precondition for hope, which is far more important than most people realize.

It may sound strange, but people are generally happier when they are hopefully looking forward to something that may not occur than when they are looking back on something happening that they had once hoped for. Even though many people now enjoy things they once hoped to have, most are not particularly happy. What happiness exists for them is *in hoping for things that they may still yet receive in the future*. And these folks must at least pretend (sometimes convincingly) that these things are not entirely in their control to manifest. Otherwise, how could they explain why they don't already have them?

The upshot is that after the novelty associated with being the more powerful player in a relationship subsides, the adored need to identify an overarching mission toward which that power can be directed — and cultivate the discipline required to execute that purpose — if their lives aren't to go completely off the rails. If they don't, the adored will likely experience a kind of psychological implosion, which they may attempt to stave off with the heedless acquisition of even more power and control. Just consider what fame, which is the experience of being the adored on a grand scale, tends to do to people. The happiest people aren't typically the most powerful: most would rather laugh at the punchline than have to write the jokes.

This dovetails into the second liability associated with power: *responsibility*. Responsibility is a contraction of "response ability," that is: *the ability to respond*. Those who enjoy the power to dictate conditions are generally also those best able to respond to the challenges associated with maintaining those conditions. This is why power and responsibility are so closely connected: those who have the power to respond are the ones responsible. It's also why all cultures everywhere believe that wielding power while abnegating responsibility is corrupt. If you make the call, then you must be held accountable for the consequences.

However, this works both ways. If wielding power with immunity is corrupt, *then so is investing immunity with power*. The same result is produced from either direction: tyranny. For relationships to be healthy and sustainable, the distribution of power must be commensurate with both responsibility and accountability. If this doesn't occur, relationships can only maintain themselves through a measure of force, coercion, or manipulation proportionate to the size of the injustice. In order to justly assume power, people must first divest themselves of any special claims to safety, protection, or provision. Assuming power without renouncing these claims is just as corrupt as using power to exist above the law, and it will require an ever-increasing amount of resources to maintain. One of the costs associated with legitimately occupying the place of the adored is *the willingness to be held accountable*.

Now, given the attributes of the place of the adored already discussed, we can appreciate that this role is generally a better fit for men and captains. The reasons for this are complementary to those given earlier. Men tend to be less emotionally oriented and more tolerant of the muted feeling states associated with the the role of the adored. Men also typically enjoy fewer options in the sexual marketplace and so are less likely to secure the object of their desire (i.e., to be with the one they love). Finally, men who assume the adored role conform to women's hypergamous expectations, increasing the likelihood that women will choose to enter into (and remain in) relationships with them.

Men are also better suited for this position because — despite all our modern, enlightened ideas about gender roles — *they are still expected to make the offer*. This offer can take on many forms — from "You up?" to "Can I take you out to dinner?" to "Will you marry me?" — but the game remains the same. Men say "please," and women say "no" (and occasionally, eventually "yes"). This is an inherently more powerful position for women to occupy. Men can overcome this relative disadvantage either by sufficiently arousing a desire in women that didn't previously exist or by cultivating such an emotionally compelling lifestyle that women forgo their reactive posture and take the initiative. In either case, men who achieve their desired outcome are in the place of the adored — at least at the point of transaction. If men initiate the game (i.e., make the offer) *and* occupy the place of the adorer (i.e., the less powerful position), they are unlikely to overcome their disadvantage: their relative lack of power will not be sufficient to overcome women's relative excess of power. And as previously discussed, the more powerful player always wins the Game.

By the same token, captains are also better served in the place of the adored. After all, they're the ones who invested considerable time, energy, and money into building a boat and learning how to sail. So it makes sense that they should have a greater share of control over the navigation of that vessel and the management of its operations (i.e., sailing and plotting a course). Since captains know their ships inside and out, they're in a much better position to effectively respond to the challenges that will inevitably arise. They are also generally expected to go down with the ship if disaster strikes. Therefore, since captains are willing to assume both greater responsibility and greater accountability, it is reasonable (and legitimate) that they should also possess the privilege of wielding more power. Anything less would be a corruption.

Again, these are general observations. Some men will be better suited for the adorer role, and some women will be better suited to the adored. It's for each couple to figure out what works best for their particular relationship. However, I can also say that a great many of the issues that people are subject to encountering in their relationships are based on *a failure to adequately appreciate the realities of the balance of attraction*. For instance, they want power without accountability — or the feeling of being in love without giving up control. *This is not possible*. Each position in the balance of attraction has its benefits and liabilities. Trying to secure the benefits of both while attempting to avoid the liabilities of either is a fool's errand. That's because the price of power *is* responsibility, and the cost of being in love *is* control. Acceptance of these facts is a precondition to having successful, harmonious relationships.

It's also generally not possible to enter into relationships (or at least relationships free of conflict and drama) with those who have *the same role preference as you*. Complementarity is the secret to sustainability. When two people with the same role preference try to have a relationship, each will typically try — consciously or otherwise — to maneuver the *other* into the unpreferred position, no matter how they duplicate. For example, in its extreme manifestation, two people who both prefer to be adorers will argue over who loves the other more. Both are vying for the privilege of getting what they want, which is to be with the one they love. However, for that to occur, each needs the other to love him or her *less*. It's ridiculous, but it's true. They can accomplish this by either outdoing the other in acts of devotion or (more commonly) behaving in such a way that the other grows less interested. Once the other's ardor has diminished — or he or she has withdrawn to a more comfortable distance — adorers are then free to enjoy their preferred role uncontested.

On the other hand, two people who both prefer to be adored will also find it difficult to traffic with each other. This is because neither will be willing to enter into the other's frame, and neither will be willing to make any concessions for the sake of the relationship. Taken to the extreme, these individuals won't even acknowledge each other — like Disney princesses who, when grouped together, are always drawn to look out at the viewer and never at each other. This makes sense because each one is a ruler in her own little world. If they were all suddenly transported into the same reality, well, which one would be *that* world's princess?

A struggle would ensue to determine the princesses' pecking order. They would all be vying for the power and control derived from being loved by the ones they're with. And for this to occur, each princess would need the others to love her *more*. This is why, when Frodo offers Galadriel the ring of power, she fantasizes that "all shall love [her] and despair." Being loved is a *source of power*, whereas loving is a *disempowering* experience (more on this in chapter 9). In any case, being loved more can be accomplished by either behaving in such a way that the other grows more interested, or (more commonly) underperforming the other in acts of devotion. Once the other's ardor has increased — or by withdrawing to a more comfortable distance — the adored are then free to enjoy their preferred role uncontested.

Either way, it's always easier to maintain a relationship with someone who has a preference for the complementary role in the balance of attraction. However, this begs the question: Didn't I previously note that most people — men *and* women — prefer to be the adorer? If that's true, then how can most men and women enjoy satisfying and harmonious relationships with each other? Won't they both be vying to occupy the same place in the relationship? Most likely, they will — *unless one person concedes the role to the other.*

Since I've argued that, in general, men are better suited to occupy the place of the adored, complementary relationships are often only possible once men consent to make a voluntary sacrifice to surrender their claim to be adorers. It's not possible for two people to occupy the same position in the balance of attraction in any given relationship: one person has to be the adored, and the other person has to be the adorer. If the man insists on being the adorer, then he is functionally forcing the woman to be the adored. To put it another way, if he insists on getting what he wants, then he is basically robbing her of the opportunity to get what she wants: the possibility of being with the one she loves and experiencing the emotions attendant to that place. That's why this is a *sacrifice*. Of course, it's a compensated sacrifice — and one generally conducive to the long-term success of the relationship — but it is a sacrifice, nonetheless. As we'll see, men are actually more romantic than women — so this concession can be painful for many men to make.

MIND THE GAP

The other important consequence of the second law of attraction is the attraction gap: *the interest discrepancy between the adored and the adorer*. So far, I've been speaking of these roles as if they were static entities. This is not the case. In fact, their relative positions are subject to constant fluctuation. At some points, the gap will be large; at other points, it will be functionally nonexistent. The same individuals can even switch places from one moment to the next. However, people tend to settle into established relationship dynamics over time. And the more established the dynamic, the more a significant event — like a birth or a promotion or an affair — is required to radically alter the attraction gap or its polarity.

Just like different people have preferences with respect to their position in the balance of attraction, different people have preferences with respect to the size of the attraction gap in that balance. Some want that gap to be as small as possible. These are people who prefer egalitarian relationships approaching an equal distribution of power. Others are comfortable with larger attraction gaps. These dynamics run the gamut from more traditional arrangements to "lifestyle" relationships characterized by the explicit, consensual enactment of dominance and submission. Most people exist on the continuum between a negligible and a substantial attraction gap.

The reason these preferences exist is that the characteristics that distinguish each role *become more apparent as the size of the attraction gap increases*. Anyone who read the descriptions of the adorer and the adored in the previous section and thought, "That doesn't sound like *my* relationship at all," or,

"He's talking about an <insert negative judgmental adjective here> relationship," isn't necessarily wrong. These reactions typically indicate a strong preference for small attraction gaps. Since it's not possible for two people to be equally attracted to each other, the balance of attraction can never disappear entirely. Look at any relationship closely enough, and you'll see that one person is always the adored and the other is always the adorer at any given moment. However, the two positions *increasingly approximate each other as the attraction gap approaches zero*.

That people have different preferences with respect to both their positions in the balance of attraction and the attraction gap within that balance helps explain one of the more puzzling phenomena of interpersonal relationships, namely: the tendency of some people to repay kindness with hostility. In so many words, kindness is an act of devotion. It indicates a high degree of interest (people generally aren't going out of their way to be indiscriminately kind) and a willingness to expend resources in the service of the other (at least, if the kindness is to be of any real benefit to the recipient). This means that the more you express kindness — either in word or deed — the more you are putting yourself in the place of the adorer and the more you are forcing the other person to occupy the place of the adored.

As previously discussed, this is not where most people prefer to be. Everyone begins to feel uncomfortable when someone is "too nice" to them: they only differ in where they draw the line (and they draw the line at different places with different people). This is because the more care they receive, the more powerful they become vis-à-vis the carer — and power tends to make most people feel awkward. This is part of the reason so many people have trouble accepting compliments, and they rush to repay the praise in kind: they're trying to neutralize a felt power imbalance.

So when your actions threaten to either significantly alter the attraction gap or switch the polarity of the balance entirely — that is, when your actions surpass others' willingness to repay in kind — people will increasingly respond negatively to your expressions of kindness and devotion: from indifference to criticism to contempt. The idea here is to try to prevent the attraction gap from widening (or narrowing) any more than it has by punishing the behavior responsible. Of course, people are not always aware of this intention — and this intention can be executed inelegantly — but that's what's going on. Your kindness is making the other person uncomfortable, as it is affecting the balance of attraction and its underlying power dynamic, and the other person is responding in such a way as to induce a comparable level of discomfort in you in order to get you to stop. As they say: "No good deed goes unpunished." That said, once the kindness stops, generally so, too, does the punishment. This should also help to explain why wanting someone more rarely succeeds in the game of mating and dating: people want what they want, not what wants them.

THE THIRD LAW

Now let's turn our attention to the third law of attraction, which pertains to the *fundamental romantic misunderstanding*. Here it is: **all forms of attraction are functionally indistinguishable**. Another way to say the same thing is that it's not possible to know whether you're attracted to the person or to the circumstances surrounding the person. Everyone thinks they can, but they can't. The two are indistinguishable in the same way that gravity and acceleration are functionally interchangeable under general relativity. Put someone in a closed box, and he won't be able to tell whether he's standing still on the surface of the Earth or being accelerated toward the floor through a featureless void at 9.8 m/s^2. In the absence of additional context, both experiences would feel identical.

Attraction works in the same way. It's not possible to know whether you're attracted to people themselves or to the conditions around those people. Both experiences feel identical, which makes them functionally indistinguishable. This is the origin of the fundamental romantic misunderstanding: *mistaking attraction to features of the relationship for attraction to the individuals themselves*. The two are not the same, but they *feel* the same. And that equivalence of feeling creates a lot of problems in sexual relationships.

Again, most people don't believe this when they first hear it. So I typically have to provide examples of how this operates. The easiest way I've found to demonstrate the truth of this law is to ask people to consider how they felt getting back with an ex. This isn't an experience I typically recommend, but people are going to do what they're going to do. Let's take a look at what typically happens.

It's often the case that folks are indifferent — if not positively relieved — when they end a relationship (or when someone else ends it for them). There were difficulties and problems ("It just wasn't working"), and now they'll never have to deal with the other partner again. They are now free — *free!* — to live life on their own terms: to explore, to expand, to experiment. How wonderful!

However, as the weeks pass, these feelings may start to change. The sexual marketplace often offers a rude awakening: dating can be frustrating and exhausting, and it doesn't seem like there are many good options anyway. The relief subsides, and loneliness and boredom begin to set in. Since most of their friends are in relationships, it becomes increasingly difficult to fill their newfound free time. Then, the *fading effect bias* — the tendency for bad memories to fade more quickly than good ones — starts to kick in. Maybe it wasn't so bad after all?

This reevaluation of the past predictably stimulates curiosity ("I wonder how he's/she's doing these days"), which, in turn, motivates some covert investigation ("I'll just take a peek at their social media"). However, this just exacerbates the problem: despite the breakup, the ex seems to be doing just fine, if not *better*. Life is moving forward for this person, with new experiences and opportunities and "Who is *that??* They sure seem *cozy*. What does my ex see in *him/her?*"

This then can compel people to reach out to their exes. And when the response isn't as warm as it used to be — the reply is delayed, the tone is polite or aloof — it starts to feel as though this person is slipping away from them for good. At this point, many experience a panicked, urgent desire to re-attract their exes. They become positively obsessed with their former partners, ruminating on what they could have done differently and torturing themselves with fantasies of what their exes might be doing right now (and with whom). Some even shell out thousands of dollars on programs, systems, and consultations, which promise to get their exes to come crawling back ("in 30 days or less!"). And the more rejection they experience, the more desperate and despondent they become.

For better or worse, most of these people won't succeed in getting back with their exes. However, a few of them will. And the relief and ecstasy that attend this reunion can hardly be overstated. It's positively rapturous! It's like Simon and Garfunkel's "Cecilia" was written just for them! This glorious suite of emotions goes on and on and on...for a few weeks. At this point, the old dynamic begins to reassert itself, and the problems they never thought they'd have to deal with again start to reemerge. As the curtain falls, a different kind of panic sets in ("What have I done?"), and the players are left to sleep in the beds they have made. *Fin*.

If you've never embarked on this emotional journey, then consider yourself lucky. It's a story that millions have lived and millions more have the dubious pleasure of looking forward to. However, for our intents and purposes, personal experience with this narrative is irrelevant. The important thing to consider here is why the attraction seemed to vacillate so dramatically over the course of the story — from relief and disinterest, to desperation and obsession, to jubilation and gratitude, to frustration and disinterest — in just a few short months. After all, the people involved couldn't have changed all that much in such a short amount of time. They probably weren't much different at the end of the story than they were at the beginning. So they couldn't have become significantly more (or less) attractive across the same time period. What's going on here?

The third law of attraction is the key to solving this mystery. Our hapless protagonists weren't responding to attraction cues in their former partners. They were responding to attraction cues in the circumstances surrounding their former partners — *and they couldn't tell the difference.* People who are relieved or disinterested when a relationship ends are typically in the place of the adored. However, when their partners finally up and leave, they experience a dramatic reversal in the balance of attraction. After all, as indifferent as they were, they still weren't indifferent enough to leave. The actions of their partners indicate that their partners are now less interested in the relationship than they are, which functionally forces them into the place of the adorer.

As time progresses and exes move on with their lives, the attraction gap in the relationship continues to increase. This is precisely when people start to "remember" how special or beautiful or caring or loving their exes *really* were, and they begin to wonder whether they've made a terrible mistake in undervaluing their relationship. However, this upswelling of attraction is not a function of seeing their exes more clearly — if anything, their vision is even more distorted by their surging interest — but a function of their new and unaccustomed position in the balance of attraction. They are responding to the circumstances around their exes.

What's more, this burgeoning attraction was further inflamed by several important *catalysts,* including: rejection, distance, unobtainability, mystery, uncertainty, danger, and jealousy. All these catalysts tend to increase attraction, *whether or not we want them to.* This is just how attraction *works,* and those who think these "games" don't work on them are often most susceptible to their influence. These games work on *everybody,* though some require more catalysts for a reaction to occur than others do. In this way, attraction catalysts are kind of like alcohol: people have different tolerances, but — if you have enough — you'll end up not seeing straight. And like recovering alcoholics, it's only those who continually keep their vulnerability in the forefront of their minds who tend to avoid the distortions entirely. Paradoxically, their acknowledged powerlessness gives them some measure of control over their experience.

In any case, we should now be able to appreciate that the dramatic swings in attraction previously described had nothing to do with any attractiveness cues coming from the exes themselves and had everything to do with the attractiveness cues coming from the conditions around the exes, in particular: the re-polarization of the balance of attraction and the presence of certain attraction catalysts. However, the attraction feels the same to the individuals involved, who fall prey to the fundamental romantic misunderstanding.

We can confirm our hypotheses by observing what happens after we reinstate the original conditions. Once the passion of reconciliation subsides, the attraction fades and the initial disinterest reemerges in force. This is because, after some time, the old relationship dynamic is reinstated, and the adorer once again comes to occupy the place of the adored, which is always associated with a more muted emotionality. Furthermore, all the attraction catalysts that brought this person's desire to a fever pitch just months before will have been removed in the weeks following the reunion, dampening interest even further. Ironically, the reward for successfully re-attracting an ex is *the elimination of all the factors that motivated the effort to do so in the first place*.

This reveals why the fundamental romantic misunderstanding is so dangerous. If you mistake your attraction to the circumstances around people for your attraction to the people themselves, then what happens if you're actually successful in securing the desired object? Well, you may just end up with someone *you're not really attracted to*. And that's a problem because you will either need to constantly manipulate the dynamic to keep the attraction alive, or you will ultimately walk away from a relationship you may not have had any real business being in. Because all forms of attraction are functionally indistinguishable, in the game of mating and dating, things are not always what they seem to be.

THE MEASURE OF THINGS

Before I bring this chapter to a close, I'd like to discuss one final topic. So far, I've spoken extensively on how attractiveness is the key to power in sexual relationships. If that's true, then how can players reliably determine how attracted their partners are at any given point in time? That is, how can people measure attraction? Without some kind of metric, much of what we've discussed here would remain too abstract or conceptual to be useful.

There's a fairly simple way to determine any player's level of attraction. However, the metric differs slightly depending on the gender of the person. This is because there are biologically determined and culturally informed differences with respect to men's and women's behavior in sexual relationships. In either case, those who feel a high degree of attraction consider *simply being in the presence of the other to be an inherently valuable experience*: the greater the attraction, the more valuable mere access to the other becomes. And the more valuable the access, the more the attracted parties will be willing to transact for the opportunity to be close to the attractive other. How does this work?

The easiest way to measure a woman's attraction is to observe *how much she gives*. A highly attracted woman will be very generous, especially with her body. She will do things for the man to whom she is attracted that she wouldn't do for others. Among other things, such a woman will not only make it cheap and easy to access her sexual opportunity, but she will put more services on the menu, as well. This is because the price of that access is inversely proportional to any given woman's interest. And while this may sound cynical, it makes sense. If a woman isn't authentically attracted to a man — and, generally, if she is the adored in the relationship — then she will need to be compensated in other ways in order to stick around since she doesn't find simply being in the presence of the other to be an inherently valuable experience.

A highly attracted woman will show that interest by increasingly relinquishing the privileges afforded to her by her culture, most notably: *passivity* and *hypergamy*. Like flowers, the most attractive women don't have to move. They can stay rooted in one spot and call the world to them. However, a highly attracted woman doesn't just move in the direction of her desires: *she pursues them*. So she yields her passivity. What's more, since women enjoy the privilege of mating and dating for gain, she demonstrates her attraction by forgoing this opportunity. Instead, *she provides value*. And she typically does this by making her partner's life better and easier. This assistance can run the gamut from mundane errands all the way to substantive responsibilities, but — in all cases — she is trying to offset the felt value discrepancy she has incurred by being with the one she loves.

Her behavior is striking because, in general, a woman doesn't have to act this way. It's a reversal of the status quo: most women are not attracted to most men. And this relative lack of attraction is manifest in the way women normally behave in the courtship process: they take less action, they make less effort, and they provide less value. After all, this is precisely what enables women to date hypergamously: if they provided more value, they wouldn't be able to date for gain. So a highly attracted woman will signal this interest by deviating from her standard operating procedure as much as possible: by taking more action, by making more effort, and by providing more value. And she typically does this by doing things for the attractive other that she wouldn't do for anyone else.

On the other hand, the easiest way to measure a man's attraction is to observe *how much he gives up*. Think about it: if women typically mate and date for gain, then they are functionally admitting that they believe men are capable of providing more value than the women themselves are capable of providing. Since *to want* means *to lack*, we can identify women's self-acknowledged, relative deficiencies by considering the qualities of the men they typically want. That is, women's attraction for stronger, richer, higher-status, more accomplished, and more competent men is functionally a confession that they believe *themselves* to be weaker, poorer, lower-status, less accomplished, and less competent by comparison.

The issue is that men typically must earn these attractive attributes — often through decades of hard work — and women have no inherent claim to the fruits of this labor. So in this case, the status quo is that men retain this value themselves until they are motivated to share it with women in relationships. Remember: hypergamy only benefits women *if they can find men willing to part with their resources*. If they can't, the resources remain with their original owners. And keep in mind that the relative success and independence of modern women do nothing to change this: it merely serves to narrow the pool of prospective men with whom they would be willing to transact.

Like women, men demonstrate their attraction by deviating from their standard operating procedure. If their default posture is to retain their resources, then highly attracted men will give up their earned resources to the attractive other. This generally involves the surrender of value in excess of that which they receive in return, hence *giving up* instead of *giving*. As previously stated, if this didn't occur, hypergamy literally wouldn't be possible. And among the various resources a man can surrender — his time, his money, his freedom — the most valuable (especially for highly attractive men) is his *sexual optionality*.

As a general rule, the more attracted a man is, the more he will be willing to forgo other women. Giving up his sexual optionality is one of the surest signs of high attraction in a man. Women aren't like men in this regard. Whereas most women would not have sex with most men, most men would have sex with most women: so men must sacrifice significantly more desire on the altar of exclusivity than women do. Since sexual exclusivity is typically a more painful felt experience for men — and one that is generally more difficult for them to maintain — the surrender of their optionality is one of the most valuable goods they can offer (though it may not always be in their best interests to do so). Of course, as discussed in a previous chapter, this can also be a way of conjuring value out of nothing if the man in question has no real options to speak of. However, it is a cost dearly paid in proportion to a man's actual optionality in the sexual marketplace.

In any case, both men and women reliably signal their attraction by doing things for the attractive other that *they wouldn't ordinarily do for anyone else*. And since men and women are ordinarily expected to do different things, this predictably leads to a different gendered suite of behaviors to indicate interest. A woman's interest can be measured by what she *gives*; a man's interest can be measured by what he *gives up*.

In this chapter, I introduced the most important dimension of power pertaining to sexual relationships: *attraction*. After defining this concept in relation to sexual marketplace value, I argued that — all other things being equal — the more attractive partner is the more powerful player in any sexual relationship. This led to a discussion of the three laws of attraction and several of the constructs to which they give rise, including: the balance of attraction, the attraction gap, and the fundamental romantic misunderstanding. Using these ideas, I was then able to explain a number of otherwise mysterious phenomena and provide a reliable metric for measuring people's levels of attraction.

At this point, I've provided an overview of various aspects of the negotiation phase of relationships. In the next chapter, I'll move on to the maintenance phase so that we may better understand why some relationships go the distance — and others do not.

If you'd like to further explore the topics presented in this chapter, please scan the QR code to access a curated playlist on the PsycHacks channel on YouTube.

CHAPTER 8

THERE IS NO HAPPILY EVER AFTER

Over the previous several chapters, we've examined the first two phases of relationships: attraction and negotiation. As discussed, we can imagine the sexual marketplace to be a bustling dock with crowds of passengers trying to voyage forth on ships of all sizes. A certain vessel might catch a passenger's eye; the captain notices a face in the crowd. That's *attraction*. The passenger then explores the cabin and examines the itinerary; the captain performs a security check and explains the operation of the ship. Both attempt to secure the best possible deal for themselves, and they consent to transact unequal goods of comparable value. That's *negotiation*. If the two reach an agreement, the interaction ends with the passenger climbing aboard and the ship sailing off into the sunset. *The end.*

Of course, not really. If anything, a relationship only begins once it leaves the dock, and there are many dangers that await on the high seas. Unfortunately, the lion's share of dating advice restricts itself to the attraction and negotiation phases of relationships. And while this isn't exactly unexpected — after all, captains and passengers need to have overcome a number of challenges just to arrive at the maintenance phase, which means that fewer people will be found further down the relationship pipeline — it does tend to leave people unprepared for their own success. The truth is that *there is no happily ever after*. When you're out on the open seas, you spend every day staying above water. A ship never gets to not float.

The literary definition of a comedy is any story that ends in marriage. My definition of a tragedy is any story that continues past that point. Indeed, the main difference between these two apparently diametrically opposed genres is where the story *stops*. Consider the ending of that modern masterpiece of dark comedy, Mike Nichols's *The Graduate*. We've just witnessed this incredible display of romantic ardor: Ben interrupts Elaine's wedding, the two fight their way out of the church, then flag down the first passing bus going who knows where. "Who cares? As long as we're together!" In the penultimate shot of the film, the two lovebirds are sitting in the back of the bus, absolutely giddy over what they just did. Can you believe it?? Love wins in the end! What a triumph of passion and hope! Hurray!!

If this film were a straight comedy, it would end at this exact moment so that all the spectators could leave the theater a little lighter for having partaken vicariously in the romantic victory. The genius of the film is that the camera holds this last shot longer than it "should." We see the giddiness fluoresce, wane, and give way to a growing, panicked realization. "What the hell just happened? Where is this bus even going? What are we going to do??" As the bus rolls out of sight — like a ship sailing toward the horizon — we can hardly feel confident in the success of their venture. If they don't end up in paradise, they may just make it to their just deserts. The maintenance phase of any relationship begins as soon as the ship sets sail and lasts as long as it stays afloat. Of the three phases, it receives the least amount of attention in the popular imagination, but it may well be the most important. After all, why bother conquering a kingdom if you can't hold it afterward? Since the maintenance phase typically dwarfs the other two in terms of duration, much could be said about it. In the interest of time, however, I'll resign myself to addressing *the three most significant crises* that folks tend to encounter out on the open seas. And of course, I will discuss how each might be successfully navigated. Let's attend to these crises in the sequence in which they typically present in relationships.

AT THE WATER'S EDGE

The first major crisis of the maintenance phase is what I call the **Crisis of Disillusionment.** This Crisis generally occurs about six months into a burgeoning relationship. If you're the type of person who gets into relationships quickly but has difficulty keeping them past this point, then you're probably floundering on this shoal.

Attraction always precedes negotiation and maintenance because — without attraction — there is significantly less emotional motivation to invest the time, energy, and resources necessary to advance to the other relationship phases. Attraction is *fuel*: you need it to go places. A commitment without attraction is simply an obligation — and people tend to have a difficult time discharging obligation indefinitely. So, at least some degree of attraction (and usually much more than that) seems required for a successful outcome. Unfortunately, attraction is always distortive, and the greater the attraction, the more significant the distortion. Combine this fact with the reality that most people today are dating strangers — people they match with on dating apps, people they pick up as they move through life — and we can easily conclude that, in the vast majority of cases, *attraction is not based on accurate knowledge of the other*. The decision to like someone almost always precedes the rational basis for that liking.

This is why no one can ever explain their attraction. "What do you see in him/her?" Any characteristics you could possibly name — he's tall and strong and handsome; she's cute and sweet and kind — are characteristics shared by literally millions of other human beings: people to whom you are presumably not as strongly attracted. These attempts at explanation are not reasons why someone became attracted as much as they are rationalizations to defend an attraction that already existed. It may not be satisfying, but the most truthful answer to this question is something like: "I like him/her *because I do*."

This confirms what everyone already understands about attraction: that it is not experienced as a choice. Indeed, as we've seen, it's based on certain biologically determined and culturally informed factors over which the individual has little to no control. Furthermore, the idiosyncratic valuation algorithms that calculate the perception of value are largely inaccessible in the unconscious minds of the individuals in question. People can choose whether (and how) to act on that attraction, but they can't choose whether (or how much) they feel that attraction. In fact, most people have even had the experience of feeling attracted to someone to whom — for whatever reason — they didn't *want* to feel attracted. Attraction can be a capricious imp.

In any case, if attraction isn't based on accurate knowledge of the other, then it can't be true (at least in the beginning) that people are attracted to the other person. After all, at this stage, they don't know who the other person is. What people are actually attracted to are certain projected components of their own minds, namely: *idealized fantasies of who they want the other person to be*. This is very important, so allow me to explain it in more detail.

Nature abhors a vacuum. This is as true psychologically as it is physically. Whether or not they want to, people unconsciously fill in the gaps in their knowledge bases with what they expect to find there. And what they expect to find there is largely determined by their current emotional state. For example, when people are afraid, they fill in their knowledge gaps with pessimistic projections and worst-case scenarios. By the same token, when people are attracted, they fill in those same gaps with hopeful projections and positive attributes. This is an example of the *halo effect*, in which people unconsciously attribute positive personality traits to those to whom they are attracted. Statistically speaking, it's unlikely that the beautiful woman you just met is also funny and charming and intelligent and kind. And in any case, you can't possibly have enough data to support those conclusions at this point. It's safer to assume these are projected fantasies generated by your initial attraction. You want her, and so your mind increasingly transforms her *into someone you want to want*. And since seeing what they want to see only increases attraction, people can easily get carried away by the resulting positive feedback loop.

This is why romantic love has (appropriately) been accused of being *narcissistic*. In the myth from which the term is derived, Narcissus falls in love with his own reflection when he sits down to rest at the edge of a pond. When his longing is sufficiently inflamed, he reaches out to embrace the "other" and drowns. Most people incorrectly believe that narcissism is always the aggrandizing love of self as self. In fact, narcissism is more commonly the aggrandizing love of *other* as self. Like Narcissus, the romantic lover tends to fall in love with his or her reflection — except, in this case, the projected surface isn't water: *it's another human being*. These people aren't engaging with another person as much as they are interacting with the reflected projection of their own fantasies. Romantics fall in love with themselves — though this is not how they experience this phenomenon in their own subjectivity.

Of course, just like the myth, this infatuation is both unsustainable and tragic. To paraphrase Ayn Rand, though people can avoid reality, they can't avoid the consequences of avoiding reality. And these consequences tend to build up over time until they reach the point at which the fantasies can no longer support the weight of the disconfirming evidence. Whether this threshold is reached by a single large "betrayal" or an accumulation of many small "disappointments" is irrelevant: over a long enough time line, all lovers eventually arrive at this point. And when they can no longer turn a blind eye to the amassed counterfactual evidence, the fantasy upon which their attraction is largely based shatters and falls apart. This is the Crisis of Disillusionment.

Though their partners are the same people they were yesterday, they will look and feel *completely different*. And how could they not? Reality has sufficiently intruded on their fantasies, which were primarily responsible for their infatuation. It's difficult to keep dreaming when you know you're awake. Even if their partners are wonderful and desirable people in reality, this experience can't fail to lower attraction because — irrespective of how good they are — no one can measure up to the personalized, idealized version of who you want them to be. So those who pass through this Crisis may not only experience significant reductions in their desire and attraction, but they can feel panicked or cheated, as well. They won't quite know what happened, but they definitely won't "feel the same way anymore." They may even believe that they've "fallen out of love."

This experience is particularly devastating for those who are "chasing the spark." Millions of people — especially among the young and inexperienced — use the feeling of "being in love" (or *limerence*) as the primary means of measuring the value of any given relationship. They seek it out, consciously and intentionally. However, since they generally don't understand what this experience is (and how it is created), spark-chasers often navigate the sexual marketplace like particles in Brownian motion, caroming about in apparent randomness. Such individuals can struggle inordinately with the Crisis of Disillusionment. Like addicts, they can bounce from one short-term relationship to the next, looking for their next hit. The high they're chasing doesn't come from a substance. Rather, it's the endogenous chemicals released by their own reward circuitry that are responsible. In its extreme forms, this can become a process addiction akin to gambling or gaming disorders. However, even those who experience a more attenuated Crisis will at least pause at this point of the relationship. To some degree or another, our partners aren't who we thought they were, and we're likely not too committed or invested at this stage of the game. Should we abandon ship before we completely lose sight of the shore? As disappointing as it may feel, this might be the wisest course of action. Or is there enough left in reality to justify and maintain the relationship? Regardless of how long the courtship has progressed, *this* is the moment when the relationship actually begins. Up until this point, both parties were more or less interacting with their own projected fantasies. The collapse of these fantasies is precisely the opportunity to begin engaging with the other in reality. Is this someone I can *actually* love? Do we *really* have what it takes to go the distance? To be useful, these questions must be answered soberly and with accurate self-knowledge.

Since relationships can only be negotiated prudently when attraction is within certain limits — high enough to motivate action but low enough to minimize distortion — it's generally a good idea for people to table any significant decisions regarding commitment and investment until they have successfully resolved this Crisis. This often takes longer than most people would like. However, the cost of impatience can be quite high: a string of unstable relationships characterized by a fair amount of chaos. No one will ever be as good as you want them to be, but — with a little luck — they may be *good enough* for the voyage you have planned.

In general, the Crisis of Disillusionment becomes less disruptive with experience. If you already have a few relationships under your belt, if you've experienced heartbreak (and potentially broken a heart yourself), and if you have a clear idea of who you really are (as opposed to who you think you are or who you should be or who you want to be), then you will likely set sail on any new relationship with tempered expectations. Projection is always an unconscious process, and it may be unavoidable to some degree, but the more fully you understand and accept yourself (and the more firmly you keep your feet on the ground), the less susceptible you will be to this particular enchantment. However, this kind of maturity is usually only gained through time and pain. Can people do anything to minimize the impact of this Crisis *without* going through the wringer? It turns out there are two relatively easy ways to do so.

First, I encourage people *not to date*. I appreciate that this sounds pretty weird on the surface. How else are people going to collect the information they need to make a reality-based decision with respect to a prospective partner? In the absence of dating, wouldn't people just skip straight to commitment? Not necessarily — and I wouldn't recommend that, in any case. What I'm suggesting is that people forgo the activities we typically associate with dating in favor of other types of interactions, which, ideally, *should more closely approximate the actual relationship the players aspire to have*.

Most dating activities fall into two general categories: either they are fun and frivolous (getting drinks, going dancing, playing mini golf), or they are luxurious and romantic (fine dining, sumptuous settings, weekend getaways). Since most dates are planned by men, and since men attempt to exchange resources for sexual opportunity, men select these activities because they presumably increase the likelihood that such an opportunity will arise, albeit through different pathways, namely: playful stimulation on the one hand and resource validation on the other. That these activities are chosen primarily for their ability to induce a sexual encounter can easily be seen by contrasting them with the date many women suggest for an initial interaction: meeting for coffee. Few activities are less likely to lead to a sexual encounter than drinking caffeine in a brightly lit café at 11:00 a.m. — which is precisely why women, who are trying to exchange the most resources for the least amount of sexual opportunity, are so fond of the idea.

So men want to have sex, and they're willing to entertain or impress women in order to make it happen? This is hardly news. In any case, what's the problem with dating in this way? The problem is that if you're like most people, you're *not* spending your free time at the bowling alley or Michelin-star restaurants. The activities that most men choose for dates have almost nothing to do with the lives they actually live when left to their own devices. As a result, they are training their dates to expect a lifestyle that they will be hard-pressed to maintain if and when they succeed in securing a commitment.

In general, whatever someone does to *get* a relationship is what someone must do to *keep* a relationship. Otherwise, players will (justly) feel as though they transacted under false pretenses. While bait-and-switch is a viable strategy for those who want to churn through short-term relationships, it's a terrible idea for those looking to retain partners long-term. This approach to dating also significantly exacerbates the Crisis of Disillusionment, as players are intentionally trying to cultivate a fantasy to facilitate the transaction. To the extent that the fantasy is misaligned with the players' actual lifestyles, it becomes increasingly unnecessary and unsustainable once the transaction has been secured. A relaxation of the effort needed to maintain the fantasy often coincides with an abatement of limerence's positive distortions several months into the courtship, which together create a perfect storm.

Rather than plan activities that have little to do with their actual lives, it's a better idea to date *by inviting people into the structures of their preexisting lifestyles*. This is especially true for whoever is occupying the role of the captain. Since passengers have a right to inspect the ship before getting on board, captains should strive to give them an accurate idea of what might be in store for them out at sea. Among other things, this means that *captains shouldn't go out of their way for passengers*. If captains would otherwise spend the evening at the gym, then they can invite a passenger along for a session. If captains generally make dinner at night, then they can invite a passenger over to help them cook. And if mini golf just so happens to be an important part of captains' lives, then they can invite a passenger out for a round or two. Captains looking for passengers who can successfully acclimate to life on board would do well to invite prospects into their everyday lives and simply go about their business. Doing so will significantly reduce the misalignment between fantasy and reality, which is the primary driver of the Crisis of Disillusionment.

And second, I counsel people *not to hide*. First impressions are important, and it's good advice to play to your strengths and put your best foot forward. Salesmen should have no qualms about presenting their products in the best possible light. By the same token, however, if you have good reason to believe that something about you that you are either unwilling or unable to change — your true age, your religious beliefs, your political affiliation, your drug use, your children by a previous relationship, your sexual preferences — might be a dealbreaker for a non-insignificant portion of the population, then you should find ways to introduce these aspects of yourself into the dynamic fairly early in the process. Many are loath to do this, as it can realistically lead to the end of a relationship. But the alternative is to either hide indefinitely or risk termination after the investment of considerable time, energy, and money. It's a good idea not to lead with this information, as people tend to be more generous and forgiving and considerate to those for whom they feel positive emotions (and it can take time to cultivate this positive regard), but it's probably best to share these parts of yourself in an organic way sooner as opposed to later.

It would be naive to argue that certain behaviors or attributes don't make men and women less attractive in the sexual marketplace. And since attractiveness is the particular form of power most relevant to the outcome of the negotiation phase of sexual relationships, then hiding (or intentionally lying) to increase one's perceived attractiveness will — much like dating to cultivate a fantasy — likely contribute to the other party eventually feeling swindled by the transaction. This will significantly increase the chances they will jump ship (or be thrown overboard).

However, the good news is that no matter what it is that makes you feel less attractive (and, therefore, prone to lie and hide), there are people in the world who don't care about that certain something and those who may even find it desirable. I guarantee it. They may not constitute the majority of people, but the majority of people won't ever be your customers (no matter what business you're running). In general, it's a better idea to be more attractive to a smaller subset of people than to be less attractive to a larger portion of the population. If you market yourself appropriately, then you will not only secure better terms for yourself more easily during the negotiation phase, but you will also retain your relationships with less effort and expense during the maintenance phase. Ultimately, those who neither date to cultivate a fantasy nor hide to avoid dealbreakers are best positioned to successfully navigate the Crisis of Disillusionment.

THE DANGER WITHIN

Let's now move on to the second Crisis. Chronologically speaking, it tends to occur sometime after the Crisis of Disillusionment, anywhere from 12 months to several years into a relationship. Whereas the previous Crisis is precipitated by a shattering of the fantasy cultivated by attraction, this Crisis can only occur once captains — who generally enter into the negotiation phase with a favorable power differential — *have invested considerable resources into a given passenger*. At this point, captains might be emotionally bonded or sexually monogamous or legally married, all of which tend to diminish the relative power of captains and increase the relative power of passengers. This investment — and the shifts in the power dynamic it inevitably produces

— sets the stage for the second Crisis of the maintenance phase: the **Attempted Mutiny**.

Not all passengers attempt a mutiny. However, the temptation to do so increases in all passengers as a function of captains' investment over time. Virtuous passengers of high moral character can resist this temptation for longer periods of time, but even these individuals become increasingly susceptible as conditions favorable to mutiny arise and persist. Indeed, given the various incentives in play, it can be the case that significantly more risk and effort are required *not* to mutiny than are needed to follow through on the attempt.

Attempted mutinies typically occur when the ship has made substantial progress toward its intended destination and is well out of sight of land. Back at the docks, the captain set a course for the ship, which the passenger confirmed by examining the itinerary. Both parties seemed to be on the same page with respect to the journey's ultimate goal when the passenger climbed aboard, and the voyage may have progressed more or less smoothly up until this time. However, at some point, the passenger will show up at the helm and inform the captain that he or she is no longer interested in sailing to the destination they agreed to back at the docks. The passenger would rather go *somewhere else instead*. Attempted mutinies are Crises of power: *Who is really in charge?* Is it the captain, who knows how to pilot the vessel? Or is it the passenger, who knows how to pilot the captain?

Mutinies transpire in the middle of the ocean for obvious reasons. If passengers attempt their hijackings within sight of land, captains could just turn around and return their seditious cargo to the docks at little cost. Conversely, if passengers wait too long to initiate their coup, there might not be sufficient resources left to support a journey to the new destination, even if the mutiny comes off. As a result, these power grabs are most likely to occur when the ship is functionally equidistant from its point of origin, the initial destination, and the new, proposed endpoint. That is, when it is just as costly to retreat or follow through as it is to alter course. In fact, the more passengers can insinuate that maintaining the initial course will be more expensive to captains than altering the destination, the more likely passengers will be able to persuade captains to cede functional control of the helm.

When we remember that every journey is composed of an infinite number of subjourneys (much like a line is composed of an infinite number of points), we can appreciate that mutinies can occur at any scale of the endeavor: from the ultimate destination of the voyage (the Ends) to the route by which they arrive at that destination (the Means). When passengers suddenly confess that having children is *actually* very important to them and that they need a captain willing to start a family immediately, you have a *Mutiny of Ends*. On the other hand, when passengers become sulky or throw a tantrum every time captains go out with their friends, you have a *Mutiny of Means*. In all cases, the principal mechanism of action is the same: to make non-compliance with the passenger's agenda significantly more costly to captains than compliance.

And this is the main reason mutinies can only succeed after significant investment from captains. Without this buy-in — without an emotional bond or a financial entanglement or a functional dependence — most captains would simply cast passengers foolish enough to attempt a coup adrift in a dinghy. Mutinies succeed when captains believe that it is less costly for them to lose power and retain the passenger than it is for them to retain power and lose the passenger.

This is why clever mutineers prefer to assume control of the ship by degrees rather than wrest control of the helm in a sudden, decisive action. When the cost to the captain of making a small deviation in course is dwarfed by the potential cost to the captain of losing the passenger in refusing to do so, then concession seems the rational course of action. Practically speaking, however, this reasoning is generally flawed, as (a) small changes can produce massive deviations over time, and (b) rewarding a behavior significantly increases the likelihood that it will recur in the future. When captains cater to their passengers' rebelliousness, they train their own mutineers.

As stated previously, few passengers can entirely resist the urge to mutiny over a long enough timeline, especially when conditions are ripe for an attempt (as they are when, say, the captain is overleveraged). This is because most people make decisions based on an (often unconscious) analysis of the various incentives under which they are operating, as opposed to recourse to a personally extrapolated moral or ethical code. Even relatively virtuous people can be corrupted "for the right price." However, with this in mind, we can also anticipate that some passengers will be much more prone to mutiny than others. Perhaps counterintuitively, the distribution is bimodal: passengers with few skills and resources are more likely to mutiny, and passengers with a great deal of skills and resources are *also* more likely to mutiny. Why might this be?

Mutineers will always masquerade as legitimate passengers as long as the process of becoming a captain is costly and time-consuming. Attaining a *de facto* captaincy by commandeering a vessel will always require fewer resources than building a ship, learning to sail, and plotting a course. In fact, the tendency toward mutiny would likely prove universal in passengers were it not for the substantial risk inherent in the attempt. This is why — much like real-life criminals of all stripes — passengers will be more disposed to mutiny *the more they have to gain and the less they have to lose.*

This is why the distribution is bimodal. Passengers with few skills and resources are high risk because they may (realistically) despair of ever attaining a captaincy on their own merit or effort. They may lack the training and capacity to responsibly discharge that position, but that often doesn't stop them from wanting the status and prestige associated with the role. For such passengers, a successful mutiny has a nearly unlimited upside and a very attenuated downside.

Captains generally seduce themselves into such a situation by focusing exclusively on the advantages of a widely disproportionate power differential (which are considerable). Unfortunately, this advantage becomes a liability once the differential crosses a certain threshold. A society of people with nothing to lose and everything to gain will be at perpetual risk of revolution. This is why prosperity is a government's best defense against rebellion. Even if life could be much better, people will find a way to endure when they believe they have more to lose than they have to gain.

On the other hand, passengers with a great deal of skills and resources are also high risk because they are much more likely to fall prey to the corrosive force of envy. Envy is a complicated emotion. It can only manifest when there is a perceived deficiency in a personally relevant good with respect to a perceived equal. The more people believe themselves to be equals, the more likely they will perceive any variation in outcome to be unearned and unfair. With respect to our metaphor, this means that passengers who believe themselves to be the captain's equals will find it increasingly difficult to abide in an inferior role. Over time, they may come to resent the captain's authority and express this resentment in escalating displays of disrespect and insubordination. Such passengers are emboldened by the belief (appropriate or not) that they could always use their skills and resources to attain to their *own* captaincies should the mutiny attempt prove unsuccessful. As a result, like their more desperate counterparts, these passengers conclude that they have much to gain and little to lose.

Captains are much more likely to find themselves in this situation the more they subscribe to the strict tenets of *egalitarianism*. Such an attitude toward relationships may come with certain advantages, but one of its most glaring drawbacks is that it provides no rational basis for (often necessary and justified) distinctions in power and authority. And as might be expected, the more equal people are presumed to be, the smaller differences in outcome need to be to stimulate envy. When passengers believe themselves to be just as skilled and competent in the navigation of the ship as captains are, the less likely they will be to content themselves with a subordinate position over time.

In any case, we can now appreciate that one of the best ways captains can defend themselves against an attempted mutiny is through careful passenger selection. As the saying goes, An ounce of prevention is worth a pound of cure. If mutinies are most likely when the power differential is too big or too small, then they are least likely when the power differential is *just right*. That is, passengers should have enough skin in the game to fear the downside of an unsuccessful attempted mutiny but not so much that they begrudge their inferior positions on board the ship. With this in mind, a 70 — 30 split in resource investment between captains and passengers is probably ideal to maintain stability.

That said, any passenger — even one carefully vetted by a captain — can attempt a mutiny when the conditions are sufficiently favorable. So how should captains respond if and when this Crisis occurs? In the vast majority of cases, the most appropriate response to an attempted mutiny is to *call the bluff*. While it might be painful for captains who have become emotionally attached or financially entangled to lose a particular passenger, it is generally much more devastating for a passenger to lose a particular captain. Sailing an understaffed ship is much less dangerous than being abandoned on a deserted island.

A failed hijacking is even problematic for very attractive mutineers. While sufficiently attractive abandoned passengers might be able to flag down a passing ship and secure passage with a new captain (sometimes fairly quickly) — they'll certainly have some explaining to do. And any captain worth his hard tack will take these passengers' stories of being the innocent victims of cruel narcissists with a healthy dose of salt. An attractive passenger languishing on an uninhabited atoll is...suspicious, to say the least. And these circumstances might compromise such a passenger's ability to secure a better arrangement moving forward.

Most passengers are not shareholders in the venture: they don't own equity in the ship. The benefits they accrue depend on their continued attachment to the vessel. As a consequence, many passengers who have been jettisoned following an unsuccessful hijacking have nothing to show for their (often considerable) investment of time. If they choose to start over with a new captain, they potentially do so as older, less attractive versions of themselves. Of course, with a sufficiently lucrative severance package — like those offered in many divorce settlements — *this is much less of a deterrent for passengers*. In fact, removing the painful consequences of a failed mutiny will significantly increase the likelihood that an attempt will occur at some point of the journey. This is why prudent captains not only vet their passengers carefully but craft their agreements with all due caution, as well.

Losing a valued passenger can be bitter, but captains who are threatened with such a loss would do well to remember that it will likely be even more unpleasant for the passenger in question. What's more, small concessions designed to appease upstart passengers only reward rebellious behavior, functionally guaranteeing that captains will have to deal with more aggressive and frequent attempts in the future. In most cases, it will never be easier for captains to resist a hijacking than it is today, with the amount of power they currently enjoy. For these reasons, it is typically the right move for captains facing an attempted mutiny to meet it head-on.

In general, the best way for captains to maintain their relationships is to persist in those behaviors that successfully attracted their passengers down at the docks. Regardless of how passengers might consciously feel, those behaviors *worked*. Otherwise, they wouldn't be passengers on that particular captain's ship. Whether or not they are aware of it, passengers who pull off their mutinies typically only undermine their own rationale for choosing to board that particular vessel in the first place.

This is why captains must also vigorously resist these attempts for the passengers' sake. If these captains allow their passengers to dictate the Means or the Ends, then the captains would be complicit in compromising passenger attraction, subverting the continued basis of the relationship. In the absence of interest or attraction, there is only obligation — and passengers are generally under less obligation than captains. Obligation untempered by positive emotionality is very difficult for most people to maintain over time. So, it is important for captains to hold the line with their passengers, as passengers' continued commitment largely depends on their continued attraction.

How do captains do this? Captains successfully quash attempted mutinies by aligning with the relationship. Responding with too much force — or attacking the mutineering passenger directly — will likely cultivate resentment and prove counterproductive in the long run. An effective response to an attempt could look like this: "For the sake of our relationship, I can't give you control of the helm. If I allow you to dictate where we go and how we get there, then we're going to run ashore somewhere. Maybe not today, maybe not tomorrow — but eventually. And that's because you don't know how to sail: *I do*. If you knew how to sail, *you'd be your own captain*. And if I didn't know what I was doing, *you wouldn't be here*. So for the sake of everyone's safety and well-being, I can't allow you to commandeer this vessel. And if that doesn't work for you, I'd be happy to leave you with a canteen of water on the next island we pass."

Responding in this way will cause most passengers to back down. Once they surrender the attempt, it's important both to reward that behavior and to clarify future consequences. This could look like: "I'm really happy that you've decided to continue on in the spirit in which we've been traveling. I'm glad that you're here, and I hope that we have many, many good years ahead of us. As long as we're together, I'll make sure that you're comfortable and well-provided for. And if you ever try something like that again, *I'll cast you adrift in a rowboat*. There will be no discussion and no questions asked. Do you understand? Don't *ever* do that again."

This is a 30-second conversation. It's possible to move forward from here because it's not important whether captains trust that passengers won't attempt another mutiny in the future — *it's only necessary that passengers trust captains will implement the stated consequence*. If the consequence is sufficiently aversive to passengers and their best interests, they will find a way to keep themselves in line, one way or another. If done correctly, captains should only ever have to put down an attempted mutiny *once*. Repeated attempts suggest the captains have bungled their responses.

A DEAD CALM

We now come to the third Crisis. Chronologically, it occurs even later than an Attempted Mutiny, generally many years into a relationship. Unlike the other two, this Crisis won't feel like a crisis. There is no sudden or jarring precipitating event. This Crisis overtakes the vessel slowly and gradually over time. It often begins imperceptibly and proceeds by such fine degrees that many don't even realize it's occurring until it's too late. This is the crisis of the **Doldrums**, and it affects all relationships over a long enough timeline.

In the real world, the Doldrums are a region around the equator where trade winds converge and cancel each other out, creating a perpetual calm. However, in our metaphor, the Doldrums are the period in a relationship characterized by *a significant decrease in passion and sexual intimacy*. Like their real-world counterparts, these Doldrums might be stable — even tranquil — but they can also be monotonous and suffocating. Like so many other aspects of relationships, it's not possible for two people to want sex at exactly the same frequency: one person will want sex more often, and the other will want it less. How this Crisis is experienced largely depends on where one is situated in this libido imbalance. What may be serene for the partner with the lower libido might be agonizing for the other. Furthermore, whether this Crisis can be resolved depends on the size of the imbalance: the larger the gap in libidos, the more difficult it is to work out.

Couples in the Doldrums are functionally roommates. They may feel a good deal of respect and appreciation — even love — for each other, but the sexual dimension of their relationship may have disappeared long ago. This can be dangerous, as it leads to either (a) a complacency in which one or both parties stop growing and settle into comfort or (b) a sublimation of the libido (most often into work or children) that takes one or both parties further and further away from the primary relationship. Neither of these "solutions" is ideal, and few people would consciously strive for such an end. In fact, many people (understandably) shudder at the prospect of ending up involuntarily celibate in a monogamous relationship. However, if no one seems to want this outcome, *why do so many people end up here?*

To answer this question, it's important to understand that sex is about a lot more than "just" pleasure and reproduction: it serves many different functions in a given relationship. And the more sex remains necessary — that is, the more functions it actually serves — the more likely a relationship will remain sexually active. One primary function of sex in a relationship is to create and maintain *emotional bonding*. On a physiological level, this occurs because certain sexual behaviors are predictably associated with the release and circulation of oxytocin, a hormone that facilitates the formation of emotional attachments. In general, the higher the oxytocin levels, the stronger the emotional bond.

This (in large part) explains why sex is generally so hot and heavy early in the courtship process. At this stage of the relationship, neither party has a legitimate claim on the other, and either person could suddenly disappear with little consequence. However, a partner is much more likely to return for a repeat performance if there is an emotional bond. This is why people typically throw as much sex as possible at those they're interested in seeing again. Whether or not they're aware of it, sex is their way of saying: *"I want you to come back!"*

This strategy tends to work because more sex generally means more oxytocin, more oxytocin generally means a stronger emotional bond, and a stronger emotional bond generally means more frequent interaction. This is pretty much true for everyone. However, women — who typically have much higher levels of circulating oxytocin than men[28] — *tend to bond faster than men*. For better or worse, men are able to compartmentalize sex and emotional connection more effectively than women. That said, even master compartmentalizers aren't immune: with enough iteration, they'll eventually get there too.

However, with time and repetition, the emotional dynamic within the couple begins to transform. Elusiveness and indifference give way to consistency and commitment. No one wonders whether the other is going to come back. If anything, each might now be wondering if the other is *ever going to leave*. In any case, the emotional bond has become firmly established: no one is going anywhere. And to the extent that the other becomes a sure thing, sex — with its ability to facilitate emotional bonding — becomes increasingly unnecessary and irrelevant. Why tie someone up who isn't planning to move anyway? This is one of the main reasons why sex becomes more infrequent in relationships as a function of time.

When it comes to people, it turns out that there are no true solutions, only trade-offs. And while most of the ideals that couples intentionally strive for — like commitment and closeness and communication — might solve some problems, *they absolutely create others*. That said, many people don't know they have a choice about which suite of problems might be more tolerable for them to bear. This lack of awareness is due to our cultural template for long-term, heterosexual

28 Apparently, oxytocin levels have also been positively correlated with generosity. Source: Marazziti, D., Baroni, S., Mucci, F., Piccinni, A., Moroni, I., Giannaccini, G., ... Dell'Osso, L. (2019). Sex-related differences in plasma oxytocin levels in humans. *Clinical Practice and Epidemiology in Mental Health, 15*, 58-63. doi:10.2174/1745017901915010058

relationships that — despite all our modern ideas and values — remains extremely monolithic and inflexible.

The goal of "mature" relationships is to *settle down*. This is how a schoolmarm reprimands her rambunctious students: no more freedom, no more excitement, no more movement. It's time to leave those days behind and become a consistent source of productivity and sacrifice for your family. After all, forgoing your own purpose and happiness for the sake of your partner and children is one of the greatest "gifts" a person could possibly offer in this lifetime. *Did you expect this to be all fun and games? Serious relationships take work. And aren't you a little old to be thinking with that part of your anatomy, anyway? We can talk about this in couples therapy next week. In the meantime, what do you think of this interest rate for the loan we need for our kitchen remodel? I think we should make a decision soon because I hear that granite is getting harder to come by...*

For better or worse, our culture's relationship construct has been optimized for security and generativity. The ideal marriage in the collective imagination is a bourgeois mélange of suburban prosperity, evidence-based parenting, and protestant work ethic. And when the end goal of this ideal is the chaste, companionate togetherness epitomized by a sweet, old couple holding hands in their respective rocking chairs, is it really a surprise that marriages turn sexless over time? The same structures and behaviors that are conducive to stability and commitment are simultaneously detrimental to passion and sexuality. *You can't have it both ways*. Where the former are, the latter are not; maximizing the one functionally minimizes the other.

This understanding is particularly relevant for men, who trade resources for sexual opportunity in the sexual marketplace. While few women would prefer to be in sexless relationships, men who find themselves in such situations tend to feel cheated and swindled. Such men provide more commitment and more resources over time, only to discover that they are "recompensed" with less enthusiastic and less frequent sex. They feel punished for "doing the right thing," which is a surefire way to generate resentment. Unfortunately, many of these men never learn the extent to which they were complicit in cultivating this predicament. The truth is that their relationships aren't sexless in spite of their efforts: they're sexless in large part because of them.

So how can folks successfully escape the Doldrums? Like so many other issues that are subject to arising in relationships, this can be most easily accomplished through prevention. Selecting partners with a deep and abiding commitment to growth and self-development will reduce the likelihood that they will fall prey to the trap of complacency. And secure and independent partners are more likely to have their own lives and less likely to feel threatened by your autonomy. These qualities should make them better able to tolerate the separateness and uncertainty conducive to a robust sex life.

There are also many practical methods to resuscitate a moribund boudoir. However, given what we now understand about trade-offs, we can expect these methods to look very different from those the popular imagination believes to be associated with relationship "success" — and which may (in reality) be more conducive to security than sexuality. For instance, one of the best ways to stimulate passion in a long-term relationship is *to act as though you were having an affair*. Let's briefly consider why this works, as it will help to elucidate the mechanisms by which desire tends to operate.

What would it look like if you were actually having an affair? Well, you would likely become much less available. You would be spending more time out of the house, doing things you don't ordinarily do and going places you don't ordinarily go. You would probably become less communicative, as well. After all, you wouldn't pick up the phone if you were with your lover when your partner called, and you would likely take longer to respond to texts if your hands were otherwise full. Perhaps your fling would motivate you to pay more attention to your appearance. You might start dressing a little nicer or putting more effort into maintaining your figure. Perhaps the spring would return to your step or the sparkle to your eye.

Of course, you wouldn't tell your partner about your little tryst. This means you will have succeeded in carving out a part of your life to which your partner has no access: a part just for you. And while it may be wrong to admit it, the fact that you "shouldn't" be stepping out of your relationship makes it all the more irresistible. After all, there's nothing quite as tempting as the taste of forbidden fruit. And finally, since you would be getting your sexual needs met elsewhere, there would be little reason to seek satisfaction from your partner. So you would likely stop pursuing sex in your primary relationship (who needs *more* rejection and frustration?), and you would feel increasingly unconcerned about your partner's disinterest.

That said, if you were to do all these things, your partner would likely not remain as indifferent as he or she once was. The deviations in your behavior will not have escaped this person's attention, and these changes will have aroused his or her curiosity. And since you were probably not as smooth as you believed yourself to be in executing the affair, this curiosity might have noticed something: a stray hair, an unfamiliar phone number. The shadow of *the other* now lurks on the fringes just out of sight, threatening the comfortable security of the primary relationship. "Is he going to leave me? *What if she doesn't come back?*"

The upshot of all this sneaking around is that — perhaps for the first time in a long time — the relationship will have come to approximate the conditions that organically existed during the courtship phase, characterized by the most frequent and passionate sexuality. And the good news is that *the actual infidelity is not necessary*. It's everything that comes with the infidelity that is conducive to the cultivation of desire.

And what does the infidelity come with? More time apart. Less communication. More spontaneity. Less transparency. More mystery. Less certainty. More attention to one's appearance. Less pressure to have sex in the primary relationship. More risk and uncertainty. Less security and predictability. More competition. Less coziness. More danger. Less safety. More "me." Less "us." None of these require an extramarital affair: they just tend to come with the territory. That said, if you choose not to have an affair, then you must also choose to consciously resist the constant social pressure to prioritize relationship stability above all things — at least if you want to keep the passion alive in your bedroom (and beyond).

Separation (in all its forms) is nonnegotiable. For your partner to miss you, *you first have to leave*. After all, there is no need to use intimacy to reconnect with you if you never disengage from your partner to begin with. For your partner to wonder about you, *you first have to be unknown*. People will ruminate on a riddle for weeks — and never think of it again once they discover the solution. To the extent that you are a completely known entity — a condition you cultivate with constant communication — there is no rational basis to attend to you. Without attention, there can be no curiosity. Without curiosity, there can be no interest. Without interest, there can be no attraction. And without attraction, there can be no desire. If you want to keep the desire alive in your relationship, then you need to protect the upstream sources of desire that feed into that outcome.

Though we often don't like to admit it, it is the threat of loss — more than anything else — that motivates people to make a continual effort. To be sure, too much of a threat can be terrifying and paralyzing. It is not conducive to action. However, most committed relationships suffer from too little threat as opposed to too much. The ability to remove people from their positions as a consequence of incompetence, abuse, or neglect is the only real accountability that exists in this world. Throughout history, the greatest corruptions of power have been perpetrated by those who (for whatever reason) *did not fear they could ever be dismissed*. The threat of loss — a *real* loss that does not offer a soft landing irrespective of performance — is generally necessary to keep people on the straight and narrow and to incentivize their consistent best efforts.

Nurturing the conditions known to stimulate desire is necessary to escape the Doldrums. And one of the best ways to do that is to work to retain (at least some of) the circumstances that existed down at the dock back when the initial attraction was first ignited. Captains should continue to take the actions that succeeded in attracting passengers onto their ships. Passengers should continue to behave as they did when captains were enthusiastic about having them on board. *Neither can relax too much in the performance of their roles*. By cultivating an appreciation for the components of desire, the individuals involved might be able to generate enough movement to break free of the stultifying calm and continue on their journey.

In this chapter, I turned my attention to the third phase that constitutes all relationships: the maintenance phase. In particular, I examined three of the most significant Crises that are subject to occurring once a ship sets sail. In the Crisis of Disillusionment, individuals must decide to whom they are more attracted: their actual partners or their own projected fantasies. Further out at sea, the second Crisis, an Attempted Mutiny, forces both parties to come to terms with issues related to power and frame. Finally, the couple must eventually escape the unwavering Doldrums, the third maintenance Crisis, by nurturing sufficient desire to propagate forward motion. Those who successfully navigate these Crises — either through prudence or cunning — may arrive to enjoy the best that relationships have to offer: a sustained and mutually satisfying intimacy.

Having now discussed all three relationship phases in some detail, we will increasingly abstract from the individual dynamics in which relationships transpire to the larger social and cultural contexts in which they occur. I'll begin by responding to the most common criticism of my economic model of relationships: *the love exception*.

If you'd like to further explore the topics presented in this chapter, please scan the QR code to access a curated playlist on the PsycHacks channel on YouTube.

CHAPTER 9

LOVE HAS NOTHING TO DO WITH RELATIONSHIPS

The goal of this book is to offer a universal theory of relationships: a framework capable of explaining the widest spectrum of phenomena across as many types of relationships as possible. Its fundamental premise is that relationships are the media in which value is transacted. People come together because they want things from others, and they attempt to satisfy these wants by trading unequal things of comparable value. Where this does not occur — for whatever reason — no relationship exists. This is true of all consensual relationships on this planet.[29]

29 Perhaps the most obvious exception to this principle is the relationship between adult parents and their young children. This relationship is *not* primarily transactional, and what goods are exchanged between the two parties are generally of nowhere near comparable value. However, this relationship is also not *consensual*: as far as we know, no child chose to

In this chapter, I'd like to address the most common criticism of my economic model of relationships, namely: *not everything is transactable*. These critics balk that reducing all relationships to a *quid pro quo* exchange cheapens relationships. They argue that the most valuable and precious gifts that can be shared between people are non-transactional and that explicitly emphasizing the transactional dimensions of relationships is precisely what is wrong with the world today. They also maintain that purely transactional relationships cannot explain certain human behaviors — like altruism and compassion — and must, therefore, be (at most) only part of the story.

So how do I respond to this criticism? Leaving aside the judgmental associations that almost always attend these arguments, I agree with the crux of the scruple: not everything *is* transactable. And these goods constitute some of the highest states to which people can obtain. They are often ennobling, encouraging, and enlivening. I call goods like friendship and loyalty and love *non-transactable goods* (or NTGs) because they cannot be bartered for something in return. However, this technically means that these goods are not valuable. Even if the price tag is exorbitant, a valuable good can be bought. On the other hand, NTGs cannot be bought at any price — which makes them *invaluable* (or, what might be the same thing, *valueless*). Like virtue, they must be

---

be born (let alone born to specific parents). This is why I added the modifier to the statement to which this footnote is appended. Of course, as children themselves become adults, they must decide what kind of relationship they would like to have with their parents (if they would like to have a relationship at all), and they would then fall under the general rubric.

their own rewards; otherwise, we would call them by other names.

For example, we don't call serving others for money charity: we call it a job. By the same token, if you *could* buy friends, you wouldn't have friends: you would have an entourage. If the resource with which you transacted the relationship were to run out, so, too, would your "pals" — and there would be limits to what such people would be willing to do in the meantime. Similarly, if you *could* buy loyalty, you wouldn't have loyalty: you would have mercenaries. Such people support your cause as long as they're compensated. Miss a payment, and you may end up with a knife in your back. And finally, if you *could* buy love, you wouldn't have love: you would have escorts. Exchanging resources for the performance of adoration, devotion, and affection is not the basis for an enduring relationship. When the hard times come (and they always do), your "love" will be looking for the door.

These are the transactional surrogates of friendship, loyalty, and love. They often look the same, but their fundamental natures are very different. This is because (unlike transactable goods), NTGs are always given *at the pleasure of the giver* — never in exchange for what the giver might receive in return. Not only is it impossible to exchange these goods for value (because doing so would be tantamount to ascribing a value to an invaluable resource), but it's also impossible to earn them from others in any way.

For instance, you can't do anything to make someone be your friend. You could be the most supportive, amusing, and amicable person in the world, and there will still be (many) people who would not be interested in being your friend.

What's more, at least some of these same people will choose to make critical, boring, and disagreeable people their friends instead. This is because friendship *cannot be earned*. There are no traits or goods or behaviors that you can transact for it. Friendship is always given at the free and spontaneous pleasure of its givers, often for their own inscrutable reasons. And because they are gifts — *true* gifts — given at the pleasure of the givers, they do not come with strings attached and do not need to be repaid. This is true of all NTGs.

The problem with the criticism that not all goods are transactable is not that it doesn't have a point but that its point is irrelevant. It should only take a little effort to understand why. If relationships are the media in which value is transacted, and certain goods are invaluable and non-transactable, then it would follow that *relationships would not be necessary to transmit these goods*. This is exactly what we see when we observe human behavior: non-transactable goods fall outside the purview of relationships. So arguing that the economic model is flawed because it fails to account for goods that it has no business accounting for doesn't make much sense. Let me explain.

If non-transactable goods required relationships, then we should not be able to find evidence of these goods *outside* of relationships — and this is hardly the case. Take loyalty, for instance. At this very moment, millions of people are enacting their loyalty to athletes or entertainers or politicians who have absolutely no idea these particular fans even exist. And this loyalty isn't just the fair-weathered allegiance of bandwagoners. Many have devoted their lives — have killed and been killed — in the service of this loyalty. What's more, these devotees receive nothing in return for their loyalty from their idols, who (again) often do not know these people are even alive.

If such a person were to confide in you that he was "in a relationship" with his idol, you would (correctly) think he is delusional. Such a "relationship" would only exist in his mind, not in reality. Yet he might *actually* be more loyal to this idol than he is to anyone else in his life. His loyalty was given as a free and spontaneous gift at his own pleasure, for his own inscrutable reasons, and with no expectation of reciprocation — no relationship required. If any of these conditions were not met, then he would have been attempting to enter into a transactional relationship. He would be giving to get, and we could no longer call his behavior loyalty. We could only truly understand his actions to be purely loyal if he received absolutely nothing in return — and if he received nothing in return, *he wouldn't be in a relationship*. Comparable examples can be found for all other NTGs.

In fact, the defect in the criticism under discussion is most apparent when we consider the behavior these critics generally believe is most problematic for the economic model, namely: *altruism*. While extremely rare, it seems clear that true altruism does (in fact) exist. And, of course, the most altruistic form of altruism is anonymous altruism, as it absolves those who benefit from it of even the social obligations of recognition and gratitude.

However, this is just a more prosocial variant of the fanatic just described: the altruistic good was given as a free and spontaneous gift at the giver's own pleasure, for his own inscrutable reasons, and with no expectation of reciprocation to someone oblivious to the giver's existence. Obviously, those receiving the anonymous altruism can't be in an actual relationship with someone whose identity they don't even know, and this would compromise our altruistic do-gooder's ability to be in a relationship with them. A unilateral transfer of goods is not sufficient to constitute a relationship *because nothing has been exchanged*. If this were possible, we would also have to accept that unilateral transfers in the other direction — in which goods are taken without providing anything in return — are also legitimate relationships. And this would be problematic, to say the least.

All this is not to say that non-transactable goods cannot be present in relationships. It would be ludicrous to argue that friendship and loyalty and love can't exist between people in actual relationships with each other. My point is that it's a fortunate coincidence when this occurs. It's like the non-transactable goods are superimposed on the transaction that actually constitutes the relationship. This is because nothing that is actually exchanged in the relationship *could possibly merit the non-transactable good*. It is given (or withheld) at the pleasure of the giver and not because the other did anything to earn (or forgo) it. If this were otherwise, the non-transactable good would functionally have been given a value — *which would transform it into a transactable good*.

Correctly understood, non-transactable goods and relationships are independent of each other; however, this doesn't mean they can't co-occur. What it means is that friendship, loyalty, and love are possible *without a relationship*. In fact, you could argue that this is the truest (and surest) test of these virtues. Cultures all over the world have (understandably) venerated instances in which these goods outlast their associated relationships as the highest expressions of these virtues. Only a heart of stone would be unmoved by the story of Hachikō, the dog who continued to wait for his master at the train station every day for nine years following his master's death, or of Samwise Gamgee, who continued to protect Frodo on his quest even after he was unjustly sent away. These characters are indelibly associated with loyalty and friendship, respectively, precisely because the end of their relationships *did nothing to affect the expression of their virtue*. If you only love until the end of a relationship, did you even love at all?

Some people might read this and think, "Orion, why would I love someone I'm not in a relationship with? If all I do is give and give and give, and I get *nothing* in return, why would I waste my time?" And my response to this would be: **exactly**. Why *would* you? Your time and effort and attention would not only be expended for no external benefit, but they also would be squandered in a context in which more externally beneficial arrangements would likely be available. However, if you're not interested in giving your necessarily limited resources to those who either cannot or will not reciprocate in kind, then you're not looking for love as much as you are *looking to do business*. This is because you reasonably expect something in return. And I see nothing wrong with this except the rampant hypocrisy that wants to pretend that's not what it's doing. Behaving in this way functionally means you understand that the fundamental basis of relationships is the transaction of value and that you support my overarching economic model. This does not make you a bad person; it makes you a person. Welcome aboard.

Of course, it's also possible to have a relationship without friendship, loyalty, or love. For better or worse, this happens all the time. For instance, plenty of people are married to people they don't love, and they love people they aren't married to. This may even apply to your own relationship (or that of your parents). And if love can exist without a relationship, and a relationship can exist without love, then we have no choice but to conclude that the two don't have *anything to do with one another*.

This is not jaded or cynical. In fact, it's probably more cold-hearted to insist that people need relationships in order to love, given the reality that so many people *lack them*. Are we to maintain that these people cannot love? If anything, it is more high-minded and idealistic to argue that love can exist independently of a relationship, as it is only in this state that love can be completely divorced from the possibility of reward. In any case, it's clearly not sufficient to explain relationships on the basis of love, as it's obvious that people do not always (or even often) end up with those who love them the most. Conversely, arguing that people enter into relationships at any given time with their perceived best options among those offering sufficient value is enough to functionally explain all consensual relationships.

So while it is true that certain goods cannot be transacted, it is also true that relationships are unnecessary for the transfer of these goods. On the other hand, the exchange of value is necessary and sufficient for a relationship to exist. And with that established, the rest of this chapter will be devoted to an examination of one of the most commonly misunderstood non-transactable goods relevant to sexual relationships: love.

A TRAGIC MISUNDERSTANDING

It is not possible to pour into a full cup. So to understand what love is, we must first understand what love is not. By disabusing ourselves of certain misconceptions, we'll have a better chance of approaching what uniquely constitutes this experience. Within the context of sexual relationships, the most common distortion of love is that it is *romance*.

In fact, most people even use the term *romantic relationship* as a euphemism for *sexual relationship* (which is typically more accurate). However, when we apply the wrong names to things, we tend to (inappropriately) conflate the ideas of those things together in our minds. This creates a chimeric concept that seems perfectly plausible in our imagination but that might not have an analog in reality. And sex is as different and distinct from romance as romance is (in turn) from love.

Romantic love is a fascinating but problematic phenomenon. To understand why, it will be useful to briefly consider its origins. Whereas the experience of being in love has been documented in ancient records in widely divergent cultures, it is generally treated as a negative (i.e., lovesickness). For instance, being shot is not an experience that most people seek out, which is why the Greeks treated those "pierced with Cupid's arrow" with a kind of pitiable indulgence: a feeling akin to what most modern folks extend to the homeless. Most believed it was an unenviable affliction brought about by a combination of personal weakness and circumstances beyond the individual's control.

Love was considered to be a kind of madness, a departure from reason and the senses. Like many mental illnesses, love was sometimes associated with an ability to perceive a "truer" dimension of reality. However, if this adequately compensated those afflicted, then we would expect to see love treated by the ancients as a desirable experience (which we most certainly do not). Love was not a rise but a fall, an idea that is still represented in some of our idioms (e.g., falling in love). Envying those in love for their heightened sensitivities makes about as much sense as envying the homeless for not paying rent: no one actually thinks these people are coming out ahead.

Our contemporary attitudes toward romance and limerence couldn't be more different. These experiences are not only universally considered as positives but also as the fulfillment of life itself. Our culture sings an endless paean to romantic love. We hear it in our music. We see it on our screens. We read it in our books. When people haven't been in love, they wonder if something is "wrong" with them. When relationships don't have a "spark," people complain that "something is missing." When people "fall out of love," they believe it's grounds for divorce.

And why wouldn't they? If romantic love is the best that life has to offer, then why would anyone willingly deny themselves the opportunity to experience it? This is as incomprehensible as the heathen to the missionary. And this, of course, is why every "sane" person today insists on a love marriage. Anything less would be miserable, exploitative, or worse: *transactional*. To the romantic imagination, a transactional relationship is anathema. Like a steward who sits on a king's throne, it is a pale imitation of the real thing. Indeed, those who approach relationships transactionally are now treated like lovers were in olden times: with a pitiable indulgence bordering on contempt. Such people are "sick," and their sickness is caused by and contributes to the problems of modern society: a commodification of the heart corrupted by the abuses of capitalism. What is the world coming to?

Unfortunately, the irony that romantic love has encircled the globe in lockstep with the march of modernity is lost on most people. Without fail, love marriages become more prevalent *after* a society has industrialized.

To my mind, the ancients' conceptualization of romantic love is more accurate. And if this is true, it would also mean that the world has gone mad, which would go a long way toward explaining the current state of relationships. After all, expecting mature and enduring relations with those who are not only suffering a kind of mental illness but who simultaneously believe that this illness is the most precious and compelling aspect of their experience *would itself be a kind of mental illness*. On the other hand, a more sober judgment would expect limerent relationships to be characterized by the attributes of madness: volatility, capriciousness, despondency, mania, obsession, conflict, instability, ephemerality, and (ultimately) tragedy.

Romantic love as we currently understand it — that is, as a positive fulfillment of life's potential — originated in a specific time and place: Southern France in the 12th century AD.[30] Its roots are found among the Cathars, a sect of Christians who (among other things) endorsed chastity and rejected marriage (hence: *Cathar*, from the Greek *kathar*, meaning *clean* or *pure*). This belief (among others) was condemned as a heresy by

30 A comprehensive examination of the origins of romantic love is beyond the scope of this book. However, those who are interested in learning more are referred to Denis de Rougemont's *Love in the Western World* and Robert Johnson's *We*. The first is an academic treatise that supports most of the arguments here with evidence from the scholarly literature. The second is a brief and highly readable psychoanalytic interpretation of the proto-romantic myth, the story of Tristan and Iseult. Sources: De Rougemont, D. (1983). Love in the Western world (M. Belgion, Trans.). Princeton University Press; Johnson, R. (2009). We: Understanding the psychology of romantic love. HarperOne.

the Catholic Church and was violently suppressed by Pope Innocent III in a holy war called the Albigensian Crusade.

However, as is usually the case with religious persecution, the heretical beliefs were not eradicated: they were transfigured into a form ostensibly amenable to the oppressor. We see a similar example in the syncretic religions of the Americas. When those of indigenous faiths were persecuted by Europeans, the natives adapted by imbuing their rituals with enough of the outward forms of Christianity to appease their conquerors while retaining the core of their traditional spirituality. In response to the Crusade, the Cathars made a similar concession, which allowed them to hide their religion in plain sight.

And where did the Cathars hide their religious doctrines? In the secular romantic poetry and the political institution of chivalry that also happened to be predominant in that region at the time. This transfiguration not only ensured the survival of the Cathars' beliefs but also facilitated their popularization far and wide. This is how romantic love came to be venerated as the highest good to which people could aspire and as the badge of noble and respectable men. *It is religious belief masquerading as relationship ideal.* Accepting the truth of this statement explains a whole host of otherwise puzzling phenomena.

For example, it helps explain why people are generally so zealous in their defense of romance. If romantic love is transfigured religion, then any critical examination of romance would functionally amount to an attack on one's faith, which would deserve to be met with either the vigorous condemnation of an offended knight or the smug indulgence of an initiated righteous. It also partially explains why love marriages are still significantly less common in places like East Asia or Sub-Saharan Africa: these regions have only been exposed to the "civilizing" influences of the Christian-infused cultures of Western Europe relatively recently.

It also does much to explain the experience of romantic love on the individual level. Since the transfigured religion is monotheistic, romantics choose one person to elevate above all others as the object of their devotion. This is the origin of *oneitis*, the affliction whereby romantics humble themselves beneath a pedestalized love object of their own creation. Within their imagination, the love object functionally becomes a god, capable of judging the inherent value of its devotee and either blessing the faithful with ecstatic union (heaven) or damning the unworthy with perpetual separation (hell). And the idolized often play their parts as well, acting as jealous gods who will not tolerate the worship of any other. After all, if all good emanates from this "godhead," then what use are other people? What could they possibly offer that the idol could not? This is why romantic love is ultimately *solipsistic*: it is a *folie à deux* in which the practical considerations whereby relationships succeed are despised in favor of an idealized fantasy.

Indeed, the understanding that romantic love is a transfigured religion explains why romantics tend to have a much harder time with relationships. Romance is the conflation of the human and the Divine, and treating people like gods is a surefire way to cultivate chaos and despair. Though we seem to have forgotten this truth, romantic love was never intended to provide a happily ever after. The word *passion* literally means *to suffer*, which helps explain the otherwise baffling appearance of this word in religious contexts (e.g., the passion of the Christ).

And this suffering isn't optional; within the context of romantic love, it's mandatory. Many people believe that when they suffer in love, they are somehow doing something wrong. Quite the contrary: from the perspective of the romantic ideal, their suffering indicates that they are *doing something right*. And to facilitate this suffering, people have a knack for choosing love objects that meet certain criteria. This is because there are rules to passion, and when these rules are not obeyed, the game of romance cannot progress. Allow me to demonstrate.

Of all the criteria associated with the florescence of romantic love, the most important (by far) is **unobtainability**. People burn with passion for those they can't have and are often indifferent to those they could easily obtain. Unobtainability is an artifact of the Cathar (or, really, any) religion. We are finite creatures; God is infinite. The heavenly abode in which the Divine is enthroned exists at an untraversable remove from the Earthly realm. In fact, it is so permanently beyond our reach that it cannot be accessed in this life — and then only through the unfathomable mercy of God (as opposed to our own merits). This is because the Divine is that which has no equal in goodness, and all virtue and sacrifice must be considered trifles by comparison. However, it is precisely this attribute of perfection that provides the pretext for a lifetime of striving in its direction. And this is useful because the hope of attaining is typically much more beneficial to the aspirant than the actual achievement of the goal.

These beliefs were transfigured into *chivalry*, which served as an informal code of conduct for the medieval (Christian) tradition of knighthood. In an act of quasi-religious devotion, a knight would choose a woman to serve as his personal representation of divinity in its feminine aspect, and he would undergo all manner of trials and quests in the name of "his lady fair." However, to ensure that the game of romance could be played for as long as possible, knights would only dedicate their efforts to women *who were married to other men*. This would not only ensure the unobtainability of the objects of their devotion but would also effectively prevent the purity of their love from being "tainted" by the gross and corruptive influence of sexual intimacies.

Though many now complain that chivalry is dead, these notions continue to live on in the romantic imagination of the present day, especially among men. In the West, the "white knight" remains the most dominant archetype for male behavior in romantic relationships. To such a man, no sacrifice is too large (and no request is too small) for his "princess." His efforts are but a small token of his devotion, and he would willingly do more if he could. The knight is also quick to uphold the "honor" of women and to champion their social and political causes. After all, hasn't the damsel experienced *enough* distress historically? What's more, the knight is sure to believe that he's "not like the other guys," who "only" see women as sexual playthings. He is patient and polite and long-suffering — and this is all for the best, as his efforts are rarely rewarded with sex, anyway. In fact, when he finds that his feelings have not been reciprocated, his solution is typically to *try harder*. In some cases, white knights even make sacrifices of their lives, hoping that doing so will finally "prove" the unrivaled extent of their love. When women insist that they can't find men like this anymore, I respond that this is hardly surprising: their lack of attraction makes such men invisible to them.

By the same token, a great many women today are also possessed with a romantic imagination — at least when it comes to their sexual relationships with men. Despite their modern beliefs about gender and power, such women maintain that they are "the prize" and must, therefore, be "won." To do this, they insist (tacitly or otherwise) that a man must either (a) have already successfully competed in the tournament of life or (b) expend considerable resources in the courtship process in order to obtain her. Better still is the man who does both: the victorious knight who dedicates his triumph (and attendant spoils) to her. In her imagination, the expenditure of resources helps to protect her "honor" so that she need not feel as though she is exchanging her sexual opportunity at a discount, like a cheap prostitute. The romantic woman puts *herself* on a pedestal and expects to be treated like the "queen" she believes herself to be. Devotion, loyalty, and obedience are hers by right. Anything less is met with the righteous indignation of offended nobility.

Another important characteristic of romantic love is **tragedy**. By convention, tragedies are works of literature that end in death (whereas comedies are those that end in marriage). It is not a coincidence that every genre-defining romance is actually classified as a tragedy (e.g., *The tragedy of Romeo and Juliet*), as the suffering of passion necessitates that *no romance can have a happy ending*. This is why people had to invent an entirely new category of art — the *romantic comedy* — to cater to their frustrated fantasies. This concept is actually an oxymoron — like "jumbo shrimp" or "platonic marriage" — and cannot be realized in reality. Unfortunately, this does nothing to dissuade millions from attempting to do so every year.

Like unobtainability, tragedy — as an indispensable attribute of romance — can be traced back to the Cathars. As you'll recall, one of the heretical beliefs of the sect was that it didn't believe in marriage.[31] The Cathars argued that all people were more or less flawed, disappointing, and unsatisfying and were therefore unworthy of the devotion required by marriage.[32] Only union with God was desirable, and this was only possible in the next life. Consequently, any commitments (like marriage) that unnecessarily bound the faithful to this life were to be avoided.

This belief was easily transfigured into the themes of *romantic poetry*. The love object isn't a mere person (who must, by definition, be flawed, disappointing, and unsatisfying) but a kind of divinity in whom all perfection inheres. As a result, the romantic is motivated to join with the love object in ecstatic union, but — *alas!* — this is not possible. Even in each other's arms, the romantics are cognizant of an agonizing separateness: they must forever remain one heart in two bodies. Total union is only possible in the next life, where spirits are liberated from their fleshy prisons. To romantics, the consummation of their love is not found in marriage *but in death*. Only in this way can they finally "be with God."

The equivalence of union and death in the romantic imagination might seem a bit far-fetched with respect to

---

31 Surprisingly, marriage only became an official sacrament of the Catholic Church at the Second Council of Lyon in 1274 — likely as a way to create more distance between the Church and the heretical Cathars.

32 Interestingly, the Catholic Church basically believed the same thing but held that people should get married *anyway*, arguing that loving the unworthy (as the faithful, in turn, were loved by God) was a way of becoming more Christ-like and pleasing to the Lord.

modern relationships. Who dies for love anymore? However, this is not the case from a psychological perspective. The tragedy of modern romance is not that the lovers are literally dead at the end — that's a bit too dramatic for contemporary tastes — but that they are figuratively dead, that is: *it doesn't work out*. This is not a flaw of romantic relationships — it's a feature. This is because it is only after a relationship ends that romantics are free to join with the spirit (read, *idea*) of the love object as they always wanted the love object to be. If things were to work out, romantics would — paradoxically — lose the love object. After all, a real relationship would make it increasingly difficult to maintain the fantasy of goodness and perfection on which the romantic "relationship" is based. Union with that ideal is only possible in death: the real must die so the fantasy can exist unopposed.

Remember: romance is not about reality. Like the Cathars, romantics essentially believe that reality is unsatisfying. Romance is about *transcending* reality. This means that romantics (consciously or otherwise) will often do all kinds of things to prevent a relationship from succeeding. This also helps to explain why people tend to romanticize certain exes: they often find their mental constructs more satisfying and attractive than the people they actually represent. After enough time has passed, such individuals are finally free to enjoy their former partners without the unhelpful intrusion of reality. This often leads to the *on-again, off-again cycle* that characterizes many romantic relationships. Lovers are motivated by these solipsistic fantasies to reunite with their exes — only to be disappointed by their partners anew. Many such people eventually content themselves with enshrining such exes as "the ones that got away," and they "keep a candle burning" for them (another religious metaphor) long after the end of the relationship.

Finally, romantic love is always characterized by **obstruction**, which facilitates the experience of unobtainability. This is the source of many of the ironic (and self-sabotaging) features of romantic relationships. It's no coincidence that Romeo and Juliet's families hated each other and vigorously opposed their union. By the same token, it's hardly surprising that Juliet had absolutely no interest in Paris, the handsome, well-connected man endorsed by her parents. People want what they can't have. If an obstruction in the path of that wanting doesn't naturally exist, then romantics will (consciously or otherwise) create an obstruction between them. This will inflame the passion to which the lovers owe their primary allegiance.

Isn't it strange that when people fall in love, they seem to encounter "bad" timing so consistently? A man finds out that his "soulmate" was only here on business and just so happens to live on the other side of the country. After years of waiting alone, a woman discovers her "person" only after settling for a lackluster marriage. A besotted manager realizes he must choose between his career and a relationship with the beautiful new hire. Why did it have to be *here*? Why did it have to be *now*? "In all the gin joints, in all the world..." How peculiar that love so often blossoms in conditions "inhospitable" to its fruition.

Of course, this is by design. Romantic love is never supposed to come to fruition in the sense of marriage and children. It is supposed to be cut off in full bloom before the beauty of the flower is transformed into something nourishing and functional. This is why every romance contains an obstruction: of time or space, status or station, duty or commitment. These not only stimulate the emotions by keeping the lovers tantalizingly out of reach, but they also provide the pretext for love's ultimate victory: the vanquishing of the separating obstacle. After all, if love conquers all things, *it must have things to conquer*. The greater the obstruction, the greater the glory. Unfortunately, "conquering" isn't nearly as exciting as "maintaining" — which is why romantics will launch an unending crusade against fabricated problems to keep the maintenance perpetually at bay.

For our intents and purposes, it's important to keep in mind that these obstructions need not be physical. They are often psychological in nature. This helps explain why people so often seem to fall in love with the "wrong" person. In a world of billions, what "terrible luck" it must be to be smitten with, say, a self-destructive borderline or an emotionally unavailable narcissist. These traits serve as obstructions not only by effectively preventing an enduring relationship but also by simultaneously suggesting the possibility of an enduring relationship if and when the issues are resolved.

This is the promise at the heart of *La belle et la bête*,[33] the archetypal feminine romantic fantasy. The premise that two people — who just happen to be a rich prince and a peasant girl cut off from the world and subject to significant time and space restrictions upheld by a dangerous and tragic curse — would end up falling in love with each other is surely predictable enough, given what we've discussed thus far. The

33 The original fairy tale deviates significantly from the Disney version and is worth a read. Source: de Villeneuve, G. (1740/2011). Beauty and the beast. The Great Books Foundation. http://humanitiesresource.com/ancient/articles/Beauty_and_Beast-Final.pdf

inspired wisdom of this story is that it goes one step further by making the *prince's character* — symbolized by his monstrous appearance — the *real* obstruction to the relationship. If only the prince weren't such a cruel and selfish boor! Then he might be able to have a "real relationship" with the kind and patient woman who can see past his rough exterior — and whose quiet devotion eventually succeeds in transforming him into a proper gentleman.

Of course, there is a reason the story ends here. If Beauty fell in love with the Beast, then how much longer do you think she would remain interested in *the gentleman*? With nothing now obstructing their union, it would only be a matter of time before the two lovers invented some new difficulty to overcome. By the same token, if Beast fell in love with Beauty, then how much longer do you think he would remain interested *once her looks start to fade*? Romantics will do a great deal to keep the complicated conditions under which their attraction was aroused alive. This is because they are ultimately in love with love — that is, the feeling of limerence — as a flight from the reality of their (often) dreary and commonplace lives. Beauty didn't love Beast despite his grotesque nature; she loved him *because* of it. His character was the obstruction that tempted her with the possibility of triumph.

These attributes — unobtainability, tragedy, obstruction — are not only some of the hallmarks of romantic love, but they are also the conditions under which it flourishes. This is what I meant by the *rules of passion*: these things facilitate the play of romance. Violate the rules by, say, being obtainable, satisfying, and available, and play cannot continue. It's one of life's many ironies that we tend to feel little for the decent, emotionally available options who are ready to commit: the ones who confess their feelings and explicitly offer us a relationship. These people *might actually make good partners*, but it's hard to feel excited about "settling" down with them — not while the ecstatic promise of life yet remains unfulfilled.

Romantics are ultimately not happy people. However, this suffering is their badge of honor. They hold on to their melancholy with the pride of wounded martyrs, who (like the Cathars before them) despise this flawed, disappointing, and unsatisfying world in favor of a better, truer, and purer reality that (they believe) must exist *elsewhere*. For most modern romantics, this "elsewhere" is the past, and they bemoan the landscape of the contemporary sexual marketplace. After a series of difficult relationships, romantics too often either end up alone or spend their remaining years resenting their partners for being themselves. It can be an incorrigible disease.

Fortunately, it doesn't have to be. By unraveling the confused conflation of the human and the Divine — and by healing any emotional wounds that leave them vulnerable to such unfulfilling dynamics — romantics can divest themselves of their delusions and learn to enjoy the everyday satisfactions of a peaceful and productive relationship. However, this typically entails replacing the romantic fantasy with an accurate conception of *what love really is*.

NOT A VICTORY MARCH

As stated previously, love has nothing to do with relationships. To understand this in greater detail, let's examine some obvious differences between the two constructs.

To begin with, since relationships are the media in which value is transacted — and people everywhere are (understandably) concerned that they might be cheated out of the value they hope to receive in return for the value they provide — relationships possess a number of "security features." For instance, we expect relationships to have *rules*: what is allowed and what is not allowed. We expect relationships to have *definitions*: what they are and what they aren't. And we expect relationships to have *compromises*: what I get for what I give up. This is because we need rules, definitions, and compromises to do business with each other — which is what we effectively do when we transact value.

However, love has absolutely nothing to do with any of these things. Do you think love only loves where it is allowed? It has a blatant disregard for rules. Do you think love only loves in certain ways? It has contempt for every definition. And do you think love only loves under the condition that it receives something in return? It is insulted by the insinuation. Like all non-transactable goods, love is given at the spontaneous pleasure of the giver — and expects nothing in return. So there is nothing to compromise, even if the lovers are willing to do so. Expecting love to abide within rules and definitions and compromises is not only absurd, *it cheapens love*. It is the emotional equivalent of taking an animal out of its natural habitat and shutting it up in a zoo. And then we wonder why the creature is so listless and dispirited for all the "benefits" of its new arrangement.

A common rebuttal to this line of thinking is to mention the "necessity" of boundaries. Aren't boundaries important? After all, wouldn't relationships quickly become intolerable without their protective influence? And that's precisely my point: "boundaries" is a *relationship* word. It's the softer, therapeutic equivalent of "rules." Boundaries are designed to constrain the behavior of the other so that the relationship can be more pleasant for the one enacting them. This isn't necessarily a bad thing, although people do tend to invest boundaries with a moral connotation that isn't justified. People aren't automatically "bad" just because they don't do what you want. For that to happen, your wanting would have to be perfectly aligned with universal justice, which (let's be honest) probably isn't the case.

Now if a person violates your boundaries, *then just leave the relationship*. Go find someone who will give you more of what you want and less of what you don't. To my mind, there are few good reasons to stay in an unpleasant or unsatisfying relationship, let alone an abusive or exploitative one. The people with whom you enter into relationships should improve the quality of your life. If they don't, you can love them from a distance (if you so desire). However, if you were to stop loving them as a consequence of their behavior, then you probably never really loved them to begin with. Any positive emotion you experienced was likely not love but satisfaction: *the satisfaction of getting what you wanted*. This is why, when you stopped getting what you wanted, the feeling disappeared.

Since love is given freely at the pleasure of the lover, others can do nothing to earn it. However, this also means that others can do nothing to be denied it. Love will go on loving as long as it is the pleasure of the lover to do so — *independent of what the other does or doesn't do*. Only loving those who respect your boundaries is equivalent to only loving those who give you what you want. The upshot is that it's possible to love even those who treat you badly, which is what makes love very, very powerful and very, very dangerous. It is only within this understanding that Jesus's injunction to "love your enemies" makes any sense whatsoever.[34] If loving were contingent on the treatment we received from others, this would simply not be possible. However, loving others irrespective of what we get in return is not only possible but *necessary*. This is also our first real clue that love is not a positive emotion, as only the psychotic could possibly feel good about those who may be trying to kill them.

So what exactly is love? For most people, the experience of love is a complex psychoaffective state. However, love itself is *simple*. And the easiest way to approach this simplicity is to consider that love is what remains *when all the components of that experience that go by other names are removed*. For instance, most people experience desire as a component of their love. However, desire and all its associates (such as attraction, lust, yearning, and craving) have their own names. This means that it should be possible (as it certainly is) to experience desire without love. So while desire might be mixed into the experience most people call "love," it obviously can't be love itself.

By the same token, many people experience liking as a component of their love. However, liking and all its associates (such as preference, appreciation, admiration, and esteem) have their own names. This means that it should be possible (as it certainly is) to experience liking without love. So while liking might be mixed into the experience most people call "love," it obviously can't be love itself either.

---

34 And, of course, if we did so naturally, the commandment would be unnecessary. Source: Matthew 5:44.

Yet again, many people experience kindness as a component of their love. However, kindness and all its associates (such as compassion, mercy, tenderness, and affection) have their own names. This means that it should be possible (as it certainly is) to experience kindness without love. So while kindness might be mixed into the experience most people call "love," it also obviously can't be love itself.

And so on and so on. If we continue this exercise to its logical conclusion, we'll find that there is only one component in the experience most people call "love" that does not have another name: *the bittersweet, ennobling feeling we experience when we sacrifice ourselves for the good of the other*. The more significant the sacrifice (in terms of both cost to self and benefit to other), the more poignant the experience. Love thinks only of the good of the loved one, even if (or rather, especially if) it means a loss of the self. In fact, the less self there is, the more love there can be. This is because love is the humiliated self, triumphant. It is a kind of proud embarrassment or a majestic shamelessness. In any case, it is the component of the experience of love that has no other name. This means that it should not be possible (as it certainly isn't) to experience the triumph of the humiliated self without love. Anyone uplifted by self-sacrifice for the good of the other *loves*. It is the necessary and sufficient condition.

With this in mind, we can appreciate that it's pretty hard to love. Egoic self-interest (understandably) asks, "*What's in it for me?*" This isn't morally evil. If anything, it's probably the natural state of man. Individuals have a right to their own existence, and they enter into relationships with others to satisfy their needs and wants. This is perfectly reasonable. However, the ego (just as understandably) also cannot comprehend that its own diminution might serve to enlarge the higher possibilities of the self. The caterpillar cannot understand that its death might simultaneously be the fulfillment of its specific potential. There would be few butterflies indeed if this transformation were left to the free choice of caterpillars.

That said, love doesn't love for the sake of its own self-transcendence. It can't — as this would be tantamount to hoping to receive something in exchange for loving, which would reduce love to a transactable good. This is a trap comparable to that which ensnares many students of Buddhism, namely: that the desire to be free of desire *is itself a desire* (rooted in the [non-existent] self's preference to avoid suffering, which further reifies that self). So love doesn't love by virtue of what it hopes to receive in return, even if what it hopes to receive in return is as noble and virtuous as self-transcendence. Love loves *because it's love*. Or, to put it another way, it is simply in the nature of love to love. As such, it's not doing anything (more or less) extraordinary by loving than you are doing anything (more or less) extraordinary by existing. This may not be particularly satisfying, but that doesn't mean it isn't true.

We can learn a lot about love by considering The Sun — which is probably the closest representation of love we have in the material universe. The Sun *shines*. Why? It certainly doesn't shine because it expects anything in return. It's not like we could give The Sun anything anyway, even if we wanted to. And The Sun definitely doesn't shine because we deserve it. It's not like it shines on the righteous but not on the unrighteous, or on the grateful but not on the ungrateful. If anything, it seems completely indifferent to how we feel about its light or who benefits from its refulgence. And The Sun clearly doesn't stop shining because we don't deserve it. If that were the case, I imagine it would have stopped shining a long time ago. The Sun shines because *it's a star*. It's in a star's nature to shine. Indeed, it can't *not* shine, which is why we so often take it for granted. After all, what is so miraculous about water flowing downhill?

Love thinks only for the good of the other and nothing of itself. If it had one, its only desire would be *to remain in the presence of the loved one for as long as possible*. After all, this is the only possible "reward" of Heaven: to be allowed to remain eternally in the presence of the Divine. It is the highest possible good, as it (and it alone) perpetually satisfies without condition. Seventy-two virgins and milk and honey are the enticements given to caterpillars *who would never otherwise choose to become butterflies*. They are incentives to begin the transformation, and they become irrelevant long before the process is complete. Love wants only to be with the loved one. However, it is willing to forgo even this if doing so would somehow be in the loved one's best interests (which is why we can say that love is functionally without desire).

We can understand that love has nothing to do with relationships because all the benefits that people enter into relationships to get — children, commitment, sex, lifestyle, passion, security, status, intimacy, adventure, and support — are as nothing compared to the right to remain in the presence of the loved one. If necessary, love forgoes them all in favor of the *right to remain* as easily and as naturally as a merchant forgoes brass in favor of gold. Like The Sun, love doesn't care whether it gives everything and receives nothing in return, precisely because it's not transactional. In fact, the more it gives, the brighter it shines.

This is why love is such a tricky addition to sexual relationships. We would (understandably) call an arrangement in which one party gives everything and receives nothing in return an abusive or exploitative relationship. However, expecting acknowledgment — let alone reciprocity — for your sacrifice is just *transaction disguised as love*. Though we may not like to admit it, love and relationship pull the individual in mutually exclusive directions. They are not only independent; they are *antithetical*. It is not possible to exchange unequal goods of comparable value while *simultaneously* sacrificing yourself for the good of the other. You can do one or the other, but you can't do both at the same time.

This is why love marriages so often fail: *they suffer from an inherent self-contradiction*. The dictates of love and relationship pull the individuals involved in different directions. This gives rise to *vacillation*, which is typically no less bewildering to the one experiencing the vacillation than it is to the one observing it. One moment, someone might be blissfully blind to self in service to the other; the next, she might be wondering if her needs are being met and her boundaries are being respected. One minute, a person may feel as though it's enough simply to be in the loved one's presence; the next, he might be worrying whether he could do better.

Both experiences are perfectly reasonable *within their respective domains*. It's appropriate to be concerned about receiving your fair share in a transaction, and it's befitting to give without any thought of receiving in love. The problems arise when people attempt (or expect) both simultaneously. And since the two are mutually exclusive, people in (or seeking after) love marriages must vacillate between the two conditions. They "just" want someone to love — but not "just" anyone will do. And when this predictably causes misery, people blame each other ("Where have all the good men gone?") or blame themselves ("I'm just a broken person") — but few think to blame what they are pursuing *for not existing*.

Love is exultation by virtue of the humiliated self. It's a victorious defeat in which the humbled self is raised up high for having been brought so low. To the proud, egoic self, this loss is a terrible disgrace. However, to the humble lover, it is *grace itself*. What's more, there is an incomparable liberation in the experience. If you are willing to give all, then what do you have to fear? It is only when people arrive at the willingness to sacrifice everything that they become invulnerable, as they realize *they have nothing left to lose*. The story of Jesus exemplifies the truth that humiliation of the self for the good of the other is a passage into a higher expression of life. His mortification on the Cross was the necessary means to ascend to Heaven.

And this, of course, is another reason love and relationships don't mix: *love is extremely unattractive*. As previously discussed, attractiveness is the particular form of power that most directly influences the outcome of the Game of Please/No in the context of sexual relationships. More attractive players are more likely to get what they want and keep what they have. However, nothing is particularly attractive about people who abase themselves for another. The shameless surrender of prudence and dignity might make for an emotionally compelling climax in a motion picture. But I can assure you: *this doesn't work in real life*. Such behavior is much more likely to arouse disgust and contempt in others than it is to stimulate desire and appreciation. Men who do this don't get the girl; women who act this way terrify men.

This is due to the fact that such players are using the right strategy for the wrong game. If you want to succeed in the game of relationships, it is a good strategy to make yourself as attractive as possible. On the other hand, if you want to advance in the game of spiritual development, then self-sacrifice in the service of others is the way to go. However, humble self-deniers get the relationships they want about as often as attractive people get into Heaven. It's not that it's impossible — it's just not the primary criterion by which the people in question are selected.

At the risk of belaboring the point, let me offer one final argument to support the idea that love has nothing to do with relationships. If love only wants the best for the loved one, then the lover can only reasonably want a relationship with the loved one *if a relationship with the lover is the best possible thing for the loved one*. And let's be honest: *it probably isn't*. In fact, the arrogance of assuming that a relationship with the lover would be the best possible thing for the loved one is antithetical to the notion of love as the humiliated self. In a practical sense, this is why love is a defeat. Out of their concern for the good of the other, lovers surrender *themselves* — including (most notably) their desire (or claim) to remain in the presence of the loved one. "If you love something, set it free."

All true lovers must make this sacrifice. Indeed, they only arrive at love *through* this sacrifice — though the fundamental humility of love might guard them from the awareness of this reality. This is why, for example, Rick Blaine puts the woman he loves on a plane with another man, or Éponine helps the man she loves to woo Cosette. Both characters understand that — paradoxically — they won't be able to get what they want (i.e., the good of the other) *by getting what they want* (i.e., a relationship with the loved one). The prioritization of the former over the latter is both the surest sign of their love and their passage into a higher expression of existence. For Éponine, this secures her place in Heaven; for Rick, it marks the end of his cynicism and the beginning of a "beautiful friendship."

Like all other non-transactable goods, love fundamentally represents "another way to go." Without these goods, the social world would be nothing more than the marketplace of human relationships. The highest good the individual could attain would be his or her own perpetual self-gratification, which is even less fulfilling than it is possible. Nothing is wicked about transacting with others for our needs and wants, but this is hardly life's highest possibility. Qualities like friendship and loyalty and love have the potential to redeem the suffering of life and can prevent existence from becoming unbearably hellacious. They are real, and they are invaluable. Through the cultivation of non-transactable goods, we not only escape the marketplace but also the narcissism of the ego — with its attendant isolation and despair.

A DEAD CAT

An old Zen koan asks: "What is the most valuable thing in the world?" Like all good koans, it's designed to jolt listeners out of their preconceived notions of reality. The answer is: "The head of a dead cat." When the student predictably asks for an explanation, the master replies, "Because no one can name its price."[35]

I understand that much of this chapter might have been difficult to comprehend. It may even have sounded naive or absurd. However, when speaking about love, that confusion might be unavoidable to some degree. Like a koan, this chapter was designed to jostle you out of certain assumptions that may have been limiting your perception — and, like a koan, to point you in the direction of a reality that (while potentially truer) may not be particularly easy to understand.

Non-transactable goods are the heads of dead cats: *both are essentially valueless*. However, we need to appreciate that the word "valueless" has a double meaning: it can mean both "without value" *and* "beyond price." The goods that no one would ever think to buy are just as absent from the marketplace as the goods that cannot be purchased with all the money in the world. Or, to put it another way, the goods that can't be bought are functionally indistinguishable from the goods that can't be sold (at least, from the perspective of the marketplace). What does this mean?

Many people understand love to be valueless — in the sense that it is *beyond price*. This leads people to think of love as a peerless jewel, as a treasure beyond measure. And it *is* these things — it's just not *only* these things. Another (and potentially more helpful) way to understand love is to consider love to be valueless in the sense of being *without value*.

35 Another personal favorite: "Who is dragging this corpse around?" Source: Reps, P. (Ed.). (2009). Writings from the Zen masters. Penguin Books.

From an economic perspective, a functionally inexhaustible resource (like, say, sunlight) cannot be transacted because it is not subject to the law of scarcity. This means that some goods can be valueless as a consequence of being very, very rare or as a consequence of being very, very common. They are either *extraordinary* or *extra-ordinary*. And it may ultimately be more useful for people to think of love as something so abundant and omnipresent that it is functionally invisible than it is to consider it as something so costly and uncommon that only the lucky few can "afford" it.

By appreciating love as a resource of extra-ordinary abundance, we can access love freely at any time. *We don't even need to be in a relationship to do so*. If relationships were necessary for love, then no one outside of a relationship should ever be able to experience it, which is obviously not the case. The "trick" is to learn to get out of our own way more and more so we might experience love to an ever greater extent. The less "space" we take up, the more love can come in.

This is the path of spiritual evolution: the alchemy whereby lead (i.e., egoic self) is transmuted into gold (i.e., purified being). To the extent that love is an attribute of the Divine, the less we are with ourselves, the more we can be with God. And when the egoic self is completely sacrificed, then love can be a permanently abiding state. This is the experience of Heaven: the grace to eternally remain in the presence of the Loved One. It's also why paradise is so sparsely populated. The gate is located where so few people think to look: on the Cross of the annihilated self.

In this chapter, I responded to the most common critique of my economic model of relationships: the exception that not every good is transactable. I agreed with this observation but argued that relationships — as the media in which value is transacted — are not necessary for the transmission of these goods. I then examined the most commonly misunderstood non-transactable good: love. First in the negative sense of what it is not (i.e., romance) and then in the positive sense of what it, in fact, is (i.e., the humiliated self, triumphant). Finally, I asserted that all NTGs are valueless in both senses of the word and suggested that appreciating the abundance of these goods may be more useful than insisting on their scarcity.

Having laid the groundwork for a general theory of relationships, we can now turn our attention to the attributes of *successful* relationships. In the next chapter, I will discuss the most important consideration with respect to such relationships.

If you'd like to further explore the topics presented in this chapter, please scan the QR code to access a curated playlist on the PsycHacks channel on YouTube.

CHAPTER 10
YOU CAN'T HAVE ANY RELATIONSHIP WITH ANYONE

In this chapter, we'll discuss the single most important consideration when it comes to having a successful relationship: *selection*. It may sound obvious, but the best way to avoid an [insert negative modifier] relationship is to avoid getting involved with [insert negative modifier] people. In my opinion, *90% of a successful relationship comes down to selection*. You have to pick the right person for the job. People often say that relationships take work. This isn't technically true. It's more accurate to say the amount of work a relationship requires is inversely proportional to the goodness of fit. It's possible to make water flow uphill, but it takes a great deal of effort and energy to do so — effort and energy that could be more productively expended elsewhere. It's a much better idea to take advantage of the natural tendencies of water so that its organic motion is effortlessly directed toward your goals.

With this in mind, it's essential to understand that *you can't have any relationship with anyone.* You can only have certain relationships with certain people. This is a concept many people fail to adequately appreciate. They just believe that everyone is functionally capable of giving them the relationship they want. So they simply choose their most attractive option and expect this person to conform to their preferred relationship structure. And when this (almost inevitably) creates problems, people blame their issues on other causes: lack of effort, poor communication, failure of understanding, and situational stress. However, the real culprit is none other than this belief: *they should be able to have the relationship they want with the person they want to have it with.*

This is because a relationship — the actual dynamic between two specific individuals — is non-fungible. You can't just swap out the individuals in question for others and expect the relationship to remain unchanged. On the other hand, a relationship structure — the negotiated agreement to which the individuals attempt to conform — *is* fungible. Think of many legal documents: switch out the names on most liability waivers or informed consents, and you're good to go. The belief that you can have any relationship with anyone is a conflation of these two ideas. Sure — you could write in someone's name on, say, an employment contract and expect them to fulfill their side of the bargain. But just how justified is that expectation? Can the person in question actually do the job? That's a firmer foundation on which to base such an expectation than the mere fact that they were hired (or signed up) for a position.

For instance, *not everyone is capable of a peaceful, loving, committed relationship*. Look around you: it might be truer to say that most people are not capable of such a feat. This may sound like the "bare minimum" to a lot of people; after all, it's "just" three things. However, it's a *very high bar*. "Just" wanting an (a) peaceful, (b) loving, and (c) committed relationship is functionally equivalent to "just" wanting an (a) high-paying, (b) low-stress job that (c) you're passionate about. How many people do you personally know who have that kind of arrangement? In work and in relationships, most people get one thing, some people get two, and only a "lucky" few get all three.

So how do you become one of the chosen few? In the first case, it's important to *develop yourself*. How can you have, say, a peaceful, loving, committed relationship if *you* are not yet peaceful or loving or committed? Keep in mind that if you need to qualify any of these attributes (e.g., "I'm peaceful *but not if...*," or "I could *only* love someone *if...*"), then you don't yet possess them. This doesn't necessarily make you a bad person, but it might mean you need to adjust your expectations for the time being. After all, if you want a high-paying job, you need to be able to offer a high-value skill. The same is comparably true for relationships.

In the second case, it's a good idea to *resist the urge to fit the person to the relationship*. There's a Greek fable about a sadistic innkeeper named Procrustes who boasted that his beds were always the perfect fit for his guests. And why wouldn't they be? If the guests were too short, he stretched them on the rack until they filled the space, and if the guests were too tall, he lopped off their legs until they fit nice and snug. Fitting the person to the relationship is a Procrustean solution because it generally requires some measure of violence and control to accomplish and maintain. This is another reason why I generally advise women against leading with their desire for a "serious relationship" (and why I counsel men that this is a red flag). The likelihood that any man will naturally fit into the relationship structure a woman independently conceived before their first interaction is slim to none. Some "adjustments" will almost certainly be required, and they likely won't be to her preconceived notions.

Finally, in the third case, it's essential that people approach selection through the lens of *accurate self-knowledge*. Everyone starts with a superficial understanding of themselves. This is because you can't really learn who you are through introspection but rather through the choices you make as you move through life, and it takes time to collect this information. This is also why people generally begin their search in the sexual marketplace for someone who approximates their culture's archetype of attractiveness. To put it another way, they just attempt to secure a relationship with the person with the highest normalized sexual marketplace value among their available options. Men want a sexy, young woman; women want a popular, successful man. And there's nothing wrong with such desires; they just aren't particularly personal. They're almost entirely determined by social and evolutionary forces much larger than the individual.

As people begin to better understand who they are — not who they think they are, not who they want to be, not who they believe they should be, but who they *actually* are — they increasingly come to appreciate that certain attributes in a partner are much more important to them as specific individuals. These might include qualities like a sense of humor or an easygoing nature or a growth-oriented mindset: traits that, if they are absent, make it either difficult to accommodate a relationship to the preferred structure or unpleasant to conform to the structure suggested by a revealed dynamic, even if the person in question were otherwise "perfect." People generally discover these essential traits by entering into relationships *with people who lack them*. Wisdom is pain plus insight. In any case, accurate self-knowledge facilitates the selection process by replacing the standard cultural template with a personally relevant ideal.

Keep in mind that "and" is expensive. People have a right to be as picky as they like regarding their relationship partners. Men can want a beautiful *and* intelligent woman who is family-oriented *and* sexually adventurous *and* emotionally supportive. Women can want a rich *and* handsome man who is funny *and* chivalrous *and* socially connected. However, this pickiness can prevent people from finding a satisfying relationship in reality. And despite any protestations to the contrary, this might ultimately be the function of such selectivity: *it's a way of eschewing relationships in a socially acceptable way*.

There are two senses in which "and" is expensive in the sexual marketplace. First, it's simply harder to find someone who satisfies a longer list of criteria, which means that more time, effort, and money will likely need to be allocated to the search. Given the nature of probabilities, the odds of encountering an acceptable option drop precipitously with the inclusion of each additional "and." For instance, let's say you're a woman looking to marry a rich *and* attractive man. To make the numbers easy, let's assume that you believe one in 20 men is attractive and the top 10% of earners are rich. With just these two restrictions in place, the probability that you'll encounter a man who is both rich and attractive is one in 200. In a city like New York, with a population of eight million people, this means that *only 40,000 men satisfy these two criteria.* And how many of these men are going to be single? And how many of these single men are going to want to marry *you*?

This segues nicely into the second sense in which "and" is expensive. Since people attempt to transact for their needs and wants in relationships by exchanging unequal goods of comparable value, the more you hope to receive, the more you must be prepared to give. This means, for example, that a woman could only reasonably hope to secure a rich, handsome man if she were prepared to offer something of equal rarity that is also of interest to the other party — like, say, beauty and loyalty. This means that one specific woman would need to be *both* more beautiful *and* more loyal than 199 other randomly selected women. Look around: most women (by definition) aren't even the most beautiful person *in the room they're currently in*. And the likelihood that any exceptionally beautiful woman is also exceptionally loyal is low, indeed. However, if these conditions aren't met, then the transaction for a rich, attractive man becomes increasingly unlikely, which forestalls the possibility of a relationship.

It's also important to remember that the transactions negotiated in the sexual marketplace do not occur in a vacuum: they are subject to marketplace forces. To continue my hypothetical example, it's probably not unfair to say that most women are looking for a rich, handsome man. However, this means that, in a city like New York, about two million single women might have their sights set on 40,000 men (who may or may *not* be single), which is a ratio of 50-to-1.[36] This imbalance gives rise to an absolutely insane amount of intrasexual competition, driving the cost of transaction with such men even higher. "Just" offering beauty and loyalty *might not be good enough in this market*. So we can say that the more you want what other people want, the more you must be prepared to give — sometimes over and above the value comparable to what you hope to receive in return. The cost of winning is overpaying.

This is why it is so important to be clear about what actually matters to you. If each additional "and" makes the entire process significantly more expensive, then you want to keep those "ands" to the smallest possible number that still ensures a successful relationship. Insisting on unnecessary criteria is *the most common way people price themselves out of the marketplace*. And this is due to a deficit in self-knowledge, both in terms of what they really need and in terms of what they really offer.

IT'S JUST BUSINESS

Now let's turn our attention to how to appropriately vet someone for a potential relationship. The fundamental premise of this book is that we can apply the principles of behavioral economics to the game of mating and dating — and relationship selection is no exception. In reality, dating is *a hiring process*. Sometimes people are hired on sight ("Let's get out of here"), and sometimes people go through a seemingly

36 I appreciate that the actual calculation is more nuanced than this, but I'm using nice, round numbers to facilitate understanding. What I'm saying remains essentially true, even if the actual ratio isn't quite as horrendous.

endless sequence of interviews that stretches on for years. However, in general, it's a good idea to correlate the length of the hiring process with the duration of the proposed relationship: the more long-term the desired relationship, the longer the hiring process should be.

The amount of discernment expended here depends on one's "business model." For instance, many low-paying jobs and highly competitive industries expect a good deal of turnover in their workforce, given the high rates of attrition and burnout. These positions often have very low barriers to entry (e.g., consent and a pulse) and may not even begin to consider investing in employee development until the worker has survived what is — in essence — a prolonged hazing period. This is how people who prioritize short-term sexual relationships and people who enjoy an inordinate amount of optionality tend to behave. In such cases, the selection process is either negligible or deferred, as the expectation is that most will self-select out of the process before too long. Investing too much too soon would be a wasteful expenditure of (necessarily limited) resources.

On the other hand, some positions afford their occupants so much power and security that the selection process is both extremely protracted and subject to radically different kinds of evaluative procedures. For example, law firm partners and tenured university professors typically must pass through a professional crucible that lasts at least a decade before they are offered their positions. They are subject to constant assessment from many different superiors and are expected to generate a certain amount of value for the organization in order to justify their continued employment. Those on the tenure or partner track must consistently demonstrate a high degree of competence in a demanding work environment for years without any guarantee of success. And they do so because the potential rewards on the other side of these efforts are so substantial.

However, for all their enviable benefits, such placements only last for the duration of one's career. Some appointments are so permanent that they last for a lifetime. For instance, popes and supreme court justices are wedded to their positions "until death do they part." For this reason, they are subject to the most exacting selection processes of them all. These individuals must spend decades ascending their respective hierarchies, and their promotions must be approved by an entire regulatory body convened for that specific purpose. And of course, this level of screening is prudent given how difficult it is to remove them from their positions after the fact and how damaging poor choices can be to the mission and credibility of the overarching organization.

With respect to the game of mating and dating, it's important to appreciate that "spouse" is *a lifetime appointment* (at least, in theory). In terms of the security it affords and the consequences associated with choosing poorly, it is the relationship equivalent of "pope" or "supreme court justice." As such, there is absolutely no hurry in the selection process. Anyone looking to speed things along should be approached with the caution appropriate to the politically ambitious. After all, what's several years in the context of the rest of one's life? As long as judges must undergo a selection process before they can dissolve a marriage that significantly exceeds the selection process most people undergo before they enter into one, we will continue to see a high number of broken unions and unsatisfying relationships.

When vetting for a long-term relationship, it's generally a good idea to take a page from human resources: *hire slow and fire fast*. This is true for several reasons. As previously discussed, the first of the three principal crises through which most couples must pass is the Crisis of Disillusionment, in which each party's projected fantasies are shattered by the impinging reality of the actual other. Since the honeymoon period in which these fantasies are predominant can typically last up to a year, it is wise to hold off making a life-changing commitment to someone until you're in a position to accurately perceive the person to whom you are committing. That said, it can still take time after the Crisis has passed in order to determine whether or not sufficient compatibility is present to justify a lifetime appointment. This is why, in most cases, a reasonable minimum due diligence period for a spouse or co-parent is *at least several years*. Those who would collapse this timeline are likely putting their own ambitious designs ahead of the good of the organization. This is hire slow.

By the same token, it is also a good idea to aggressively terminate the selection process for a long-term relationship as soon as the other party demonstrates that he or she is not sufficiently qualified or compatible. In most cases, failing to do so does not prevent a breakup: it only postpones it. As difficult as it is to end a relationship, it will generally never be easier to do so than it is today. With the passage of time, couples typically only become more emotionally invested and logistically entangled with each other — not less. Procrastinating a potentially painful decision due to misplaced hope or relational inertia only makes the eventual decision even more painful.

Most people only get a few good shots at a successful long-term relationship in their entire lives. This is true for both men and women, *but it's especially true for women*. Given her reproductive window, a woman who wants to have her own biological children basically has 20 years to find her partner. At 20 years old, this can feel like a lifetime because, well, it *is* a lifetime to a 20-year-old. However, it's not very long in reality, and this time is reduced even further by certain psychological factors.

Breaking up with someone in whom you've invested a good deal of time and energy is not easy to do. People's hearts are not made of Teflon. They generally can't emotionally move on from such an experience immediately. If it looks like they can, it's typically because they actually broke up with their partners a while ago and *failed to inform the other party*. They stopped emotionally investing in the other, grieved the future that would not happen, and reprioritized their attractiveness for reentry into the sexual marketplace — all without leaving the relationship. In either case, the expended resource is the same: *time*. This means that in addition to the time most people must spend searching for a qualified candidate, they must also factor in the time spent recovering from their previous relationship, as appropriate.

Combine this with the two-to-three-year (minimum) due diligence period that should precede a lifetime commitment, and we can conclude that most women only get three or four good chances at starting a family in their lives. And you can halve this number if the woman in question is uninterested in pursuing such a relationship in her 20s. For better or worse, men have a bit longer to figure this out — which is good, as they typically don't become good "husband material" until their 30s — but they might only get twice as many chances as women do. Their opportunity is limited less by their biological constraints than by their emotional resilience.

The upshot here is that if you only get a few chances at such a relationship, you should be careful not to waste them. There is little point in giving someone one of your few good opportunities, and the years of significant investment that such an opportunity represents, if you already encounter difficulties or perceive incompatibilities early in the courtship process. The earlier in the selection process you are, the more appropriate it is to err on the side of rejection. After all, most people won't be the person with whom you start a family, so this is the safer bet, statistically speaking. Just remember that it is never technically someone else's responsibility not to waste your time: *it's yours*. So make sure you guard your time wisely. This is fire fast.

Rejecting others is not something most people do well. Some people reject far too quickly, and others don't reject quickly enough. All other things being equal, the speed at which people tend to reject others is directly related to their *perceived optionality*. A woman who believes (accurately or not) that she could get another, better man in a heartbeat will reject a qualified man for a trifle. On the other hand, a man who believes (accurately or not) that no one else would want him will fight to keep a toxic woman in his life. This is one of the least-appreciated reasons why being attractive is important: increasing optionality affords people a better opportunity to avoid having to choose between their sexual and emotional needs and their dignity and self-respect. That said, having an uncommon amount of optionality can turn people into petty tyrants, so it's important to temper this privilege with humility. Finally, to the extent that optionality is associated with attractiveness, most women should never be pickier — and most men should never be less picky — than they are today.

One of the most useful concepts in deciding whether to reject a dating prospect is the *deal breaker*. People are entitled to their deal breakers: they can have as few or as many as they would like. That said, the more deal breakers people have, the harder it is for them to find a qualified partner. Basically, a deal breaker is a trait or behavior in a potential partner that — if it never changed or stopped — would undermine your willingness to enthusiastically remain in the relationship, *even if everything else were ideal*.

For instance, one of the most commonly accepted deal breakers is addiction. It's not really possible to have a committed relationship with an addict because an addict is already in a committed relationship with his or her drug of choice. As the disease progresses, it typically creates so much chaos and suffering in and around the relationship that it becomes functionally impossible to have a stable, loving relationship with the individual in question. Roads only go where they go. Unchecked, the road of addiction only goes to discord, heartbreak, and worse. *So why bother walking all the way to the end?* If you're already in a relationship with an addict, you can give this person a chance to decide between a relationship with you and a relationship with his or her drug of choice. And if you're not already in a relationship, just take a different path at the next turnoff. Either way, it's important to adequately appreciate that certain types of relationships are just not possible with people in their active addictions.

That said, not all deal breakers are as flagrant as addiction. Many of them simply indicate a fundamental incompatibility. For instance, it can be emotionally exhausting for an introvert to be in a relationship with an extrovert, or extremely frustrating for a person with a high libido to exclusively commit to a person who has a low interest in sex. Opposites might attract — *but they generally don't stay together.* If neither person ever changed with respect to this mismatch, then the incompatibility would likely undermine the aggrieved party's willingness to enthusiastically remain in the relationship. In most cases, these kinds of trait differences are deal breakers and would be justified grounds for rejection.

Some might protest that such incompatibilities can be overcome with enough trust, communication, and mutual understanding. However, this is usually only true to an extent, and the costs associated with even these compromised outcomes can be quite high. This is because incompatible relationships require more resources (such as time, attention, patience, and creativity) than relationships without such differences — resources that might be better spent in the service of what the relationship was designed to accomplish (as opposed to simply maintaining the relationship itself). Such objections are generally heard from those who (for whatever reason) allowed themselves to become emotionally attached to someone before appropriately vetting the relationship. They never doubted that they could have the type of relationship they wanted with the person they wanted to have it with, and now the square peg must be "finessed" into the round hole.

While it's possible to train potential applicants in a professional context, it's generally a better idea to simply hire those who already have the traits and skills necessary to do the job — a rule of thumb that becomes increasingly more applicable the more "senior" the position. Choosing someone who is already a good fit for the role is always a safer bet than gambling on the potential that the other could possibly be a good fit some time in the future. While nobody is perfect, the same qualities can be an asset in one context and a liability in another. In long-term relationships, it's important to pick the person whose faults you can live with. Demanding that he or she change after the fact is the relationship equivalent of buyer's remorse.

Of course, much of the foregoing is most applicable to long-term relationships. People who situationally prioritize casual relationships — or captains who want to maximize the number of non-terrible passengers on their ships — needn't be as discerning, as the potential risks associated with choosing poorly aren't quite so high. In fact, those who are interested in maintaining more casual relationships should reject *as slowly as possible*. Since they functionally already have what they want, no change is necessary.

This advice might rankle those (usually women) who lingered in relationships in which they were not afforded the level of commitment they would have preferred. However, simply wanting something is not sufficient grounds for receiving it. Think of it this way: many people want to be the CEO of a company, but the vast majority of them will be disappointed in this ambition. In most cases, it is not the responsibility of the employer to *explicitly and proactively disabuse these people of their desires*. In fact, from the perspective of the employer, these desires are extremely useful, as they typically motivate employees to invest more effort into their work than they otherwise would. That said, it's underhanded for an employer to actively cultivate the hope of advancement in someone he never intends to promote.

However, just because management believes a given employee isn't "officer potential" doesn't mean that it has a problem with her discharging her current role *for as long as she is willing to occupy the position*. In fact, such an employee would likely only be removed for a serious offense, like gross negligence or incompetence (*fire slow*). This is because any manager who prioritizes the self-interest of a specific employee ("I want a promotion") over and above the best interests of the company ("The most qualified applicant gets the job") will quickly find that he is no longer in charge.

This is not unfair to the employee. After all, she received a paycheck every two weeks for the position for which she was hired — *otherwise, she wouldn't have kept showing up*. She was compensated for the work she performed under the terms of her agreement. The hope of future gain might keep people hanging on, but it isn't nearly as motivating as the reality of value provided. What's more, in most cases, that particular employee accepted that position because she believed it to be her most attractive overall offer — *otherwise, she would have been working at a different company*. So abiding in the role for which she was hired should be considered no great hardship.

The upshot to all this is that how people select (and reject) generally depends on their role in the sexual marketplace and their preferred relationship structure. With this in mind, we can now take a closer look at the specific process involved.

GOODNESS OF FIT

Sexual relationships exist on a continuum in which the principal axis represents *investment*. I'm using the term "investment" here in the broadest possible sense, which includes (but is not limited to) things like time, energy, money, sex, emotional intimacy, relational commitment, and lifestyle integration. Every position along this axis is associated with a specific combination of trade-offs (i.e., certain areas will be better for certain relationships and worse for others), and the whole continuum is technically value-neutral: particular points on the line aren't inherently "better" than others.

We can divide this continuum into three general sections: casual, serious, and dating. *Casual* is a low-investment relationship structure that exists at one end of the continuum, *serious* is a high-investment relationship structure that exists at the other, and *dating* is a structure that more or less occupies the space in the middle. By definition, all sexual relationships can be sorted into one of these three categories. Conceptualizing sexual relationships in this way is useful as it facilitates selection. This is because different suites of traits and skills are more aligned with different relationship structures. Assigning a particular prospect to an appropriate position on the investment axis is most people's best possible chance of securing goodness of fit in their relationships.

If dating is a hiring process, then it may be helpful to consider how companies go about doing this. A company doesn't hire someone just because it would be nice to have that person around. This is because taking on an employee is an (often considerable) expense, so employers are justifiably concerned about getting their money's worth. Indeed, the most fundamental consideration here is that employees *produce more than they consume*. There are only two ways employees do this: either by generating revenue in excess of their compensation or by eliminating expenses in excess of their compensation. If neither of these conditions is met, then the company is operating in a non-sustainable fashion, and its days are likely numbered.

Basically, a company hires in order to either create significant value or solve an important problem. Otherwise, it's probably best for everyone involved to make do with the current headcount. Sexual relationships aren't much different. Taking one on is always associated with some degree of expense — so it's important for people to consider whether they're "getting their money's worth." They can do this by clearly *defining their need* — that is, by identifying what positive they hope to acquire or what negative they hope to eliminate — and *calculating the cost* they are willing to incur to satisfy that need. Doing both will help prevent people from being exploited in the sexual marketplace. Keep in mind that the more you need, the more you must be willing to offer in return.

By clearly defining the role they wish a prospective partner to play in their lives, people can then reverse engineer the traits, skills, and attributes qualified candidates would need to possess to successfully discharge their responsibilities. In general, it's a better idea to consider the ideal characteristics associated with a specific role than to contemplate the ideal characteristics associated with a specific person. Doing so significantly increases people's chances of getting what they want from a wider range of candidates. We can call these qualities the *criteria set* for a particular relationship. Ideally, this is completed before the dating process even begins. Otherwise, each new prospect might seem just as good as the last, and the whole process will be skewed in favor of the candidate.

While it is useful for women to consider what they're looking for in a man before setting out for the sexual marketplace (keeping in mind that "and" is expensive), it is essential that men define what they're looking for in a woman before doing so. This is because — in the professional analogy we've been using — *men are the employers*. As the gatekeepers of commitment, they are expected to make the offer to women — not the other way around. Women can choose to decline an offer, but they cannot hire themselves. Of course, men cannot hire women without their consent: a woman must first accept a given man's proposal. However, in the sexual marketplace, the real power of women lies not in creating relationship opportunities but in choosing her most compelling opportunity when it is her pleasure to do so.

Women sometimes rankle at this comparison. However, this aligns with the intentions of most women in the sexual marketplace. Remember: women mate and date for gain (because they can). As a result, resources generally flow from the man to the woman in heterosexual relationships. And in every culture that has ever existed on this planet, *it is the servant (i.e., the employee) who takes the money*. Women's role as employees in the sexual marketplace is not the vestige of oppressive patriarchal social structures: it is a necessary consequence of their hypergamous tendencies. Women can be the employers *or* they can get a paycheck, *but they can't have it both ways* (though many women certainly try). And any man who abdicates the privileges of the employer role but not the responsibilities is complicit in his own exploitation.

In any case, it's important for men to carefully consider the skills and attributes a woman would need to possess in order to successfully occupy a given position in his life before entering the sexual marketplace. This will provide some metric by which to evaluate various candidates for the position. Failure to do so functionally means that men will be selecting primarily (or exclusively) based on their physical attraction — which does little to guarantee a peaceful or satisfying relationship. It also means that these men will be more easily influenced by women's preferences, as women typically have a more defined idea of what they want from a relationship than men do. Remember: if you don't have a plan, it means that you're part of *someone else's*. And the more thought men put into appropriate selection, the easier the entire dating process becomes for everybody.

People can't get everything they want. So if you're having trouble finding anyone who satisfies your criteria, then the marketplace is giving you feedback that either (a) your price point is too high (i.e., you're being too picky) or (b) your negotiation posture is dubious (i.e., you're not offering enough relative to what you want). If you want to seal the deal, you may need to either (a) bring down your asking price (i.e., relax your satisfaction thresholds) or (b) improve your value proposition (i.e., offer more of what other people want). That said, if you're going to be in a relationship with any given person instead of literally anyone else, then you should be getting *most* of what you want. Otherwise, what's the point? Life is short. If a relationship doesn't make your life better, then just move on.

Men and women generally approach locating a prospective candidate on the relationship continuum very differently. Women tend to have significant overlap across the criteria sets associated with relationship categories. For instance, many women won't have casual sex with a man with whom they wouldn't at least consider having a more committed relationship. This is not to say that women do not often seek out short-term relationships (they do) but that they typically won't enter into a casual arrangement unless the man in question also appears to be an attractive reproductive option (irrespective of their relationship intentions with him). This is due (at least in part) to the fact that sex is riskier for women than it is for men, as they disproportionately assume the vulnerabilities and responsibilities of pregnancy. As a result, they are more likely to sexually select men who are able to protect and provide (i.e., good genes, high status) — even if there is no need for either in a strictly casual affair. The result is that women often set the bar for a casual relationship as high as they do for a serious relationship — which is why most women won't have sex with most men.

On the other hand, men often have enormous differences across these same criteria sets. Since they are more removed from the realities of pregnancy, they are more able to compartmentalize sex from commitment. From a purely evolutionary perspective, men can often ensure that at least some of their offspring will survive until sexual maturity if they reproduce with many different (and many different kinds of) women — a strategy that would be greatly facilitated by such a compartmentalization. This tendency also helps explain other observed differences in gendered sexuality, like the Coolidge effect.[37] As a consequence, men generally set the bar for a casual relationship very low, which is why most men will have sex with most women, and the bar for a serious relationship very high, as commitment is relatively more costly for them than it is for women.

A lack of appreciation for these differences can lead to fairly predictable failures in intersex understanding. For instance, women can conflate a man's sexual interest for his willingness to commit *because this is how they themselves tend to navigate selection*. In this way, some women can devote years of their youth to men who have no real intention of "moving things forward." Of course, from the perspective of these men, no change is necessary because the relationship is already where they want it to be — and, in any case, not everyone can be the CEO. A better understanding of how men actually select for serious relationships will improve women's chances of securing them.

The idea is for both men and women to enter the sexual marketplace intentionally. This transforms the courtship process into an opportunity to covertly evaluate the extent

37 The "effect" in question gets its name from an anecdote involving former President Calvin Coolidge. One day, the president and his wife visited a farm, and the two were given individual tours around the property by the farmer. When Mrs. Coolidge passed the chicken coop and noticed a rooster vigorously copulating with a hen, she asked the farmer whether this was a frequent occurrence. The farmer insisted that it was and informed the First Lady that it wasn't uncommon for the rooster in question to ruffle some feathers seven or eight times a day. Delighted by his response, Mrs. Coolidge asked the farmer to pass this fact along to the president. Later that day, when Mr. Coolidge passed by the same coop, the farmer made good on his promise. The president thought for a moment and asked whether the rooster always copulated with the same hen. The farmer laughed at the insinuation and assured Mr. Coolidge that the cock had the run of the hen house. Satisfied with his response, the president asked the farmer to pass this fact along to his wife.

to which a given candidate conforms to the criteria set associated with a particular relationship structure. The key word here is "covertly." In most cases, the information needed to evaluate a potential candidate must be obtained indirectly. Just because a person is dating *intentionally* doesn't mean he or she should be dating *obviously*: some measure of strategy will likely still be required.

Factors like poor insight, social desirability bias, and flat-out deception make it difficult (if not impossible) to simply ask whether a given prospect possesses the desired criteria. Ask, "Are you trustworthy?" and both the honest and the dishonest candidate will reply, "Yes." This is why it's useless (and boring) to conduct dates like structured interviews. Think about it: have you ever told a potential employer the whole truth before you were offered a job? In dating as in work, people are generally going to say what they think they need to say in order to get what they want. Expecting otherwise is to assume that most people will place an abstract principle (e.g., "People should always be fully and completely transparent") ahead of their own self-interest — an assumption that is hardly justified by reality.

This is why smart companies don't hire using structured interviews (at least, not exclusively). Instead, they utilize many different methods to indirectly collect the information they need. For instance, companies might ask candidates to complete lateral thinking puzzles or submit professional work samples or attend a dinner party with the acting partners. They'll give many stakeholders the opportunity to observe the applicant throughout the hiring process, and they'll reach out to references for independent corroboration.

People might not tell you who they are, but they will show you who they are — *if you give them the opportunity.*

By extension, it's a good idea to approach data collection for sexual relationships indirectly, especially when vetting for a long-term relationship. Conduct surreptitious research before you interact with the person in question. Create opportunities to observe the prospect in radically different contexts and carefully examine the life around the person of interest. If appropriate, gradually introduce the candidate to your friends and family, and be willing to listen to their honest feedback. Traveling together can also provide a glimpse into how the two of you respond to situational stressors and near-constant togetherness. And, of course, allow enough time to progress for the distortion created by your attraction to (mostly) resolve itself.

That said, I *strongly discourage* people from using cohabitation as a means of evaluating their relationships. This is because living together is *already* a serious relationship. At this point, the test drive is over: you've already bought the car. The more you integrate your life with someone, the more difficult it becomes to extricate yourself (both emotionally and logistically) from the relationship — which defeats the whole purpose of a diligence period. The conveniences of such an arrangement are typically not offset by the liabilities. So if you're not yet ready, then don't sign the lease (or the marriage license). Either continue to date or go your separate ways.

LISTEN TO YOURSELF

Criteria sets are useful tools with which to navigate the sexual marketplace. Clarifying the qualities and attributes associated with various relationship structures ahead of time will prime your attention and make the presence (or absence) of these qualities in potential candidates much more noticeable. And treating the initial courtship as an opportunity to conduct covert due diligence will help prevent you from committing to a poor match prematurely, especially if you're vetting for a long-term relationship. All these strategies are designed to leverage your rational mind against your attraction, which simply *wants what it wants* — irrespective of the consequences.

However, this is not the whole story. If it were, then the sexual marketplace could basically function like an enormous matching service, similar to how medical students are placed in their internships. After defining the role, organizations accept applications from students "declaring their intentions" and conduct several rounds of interviews with the most compelling candidates. Both the students and the organizations rank order each other, and applicants are generally matched with the organization they most want that also wants them. It's all very rational and utilitarian, as it's designed to ensure the most good for the most people on a very large scale. The idea is to "move things along" as quickly and reliably as possible to the business the match intends to accomplish — rather than to prolong the match as an end in itself.

Interestingly, this model isn't all that different from the way courtship operated in the past: back when sex was on the other side of commitment, marriage was brokered between men (i.e., the male suitor and the woman's father), and the paradox that is the love marriage was not yet predominant. We can see it operating today in traditional cultures that still practice arranged marriages. However, for better or worse, we are unlikely to return to this paradigm anytime soon. So expecting modern men and women to approach the sexual marketplace rationally and objectively would be ludicrous. The strategies we discussed in the previous section are practical, but they need to be tempered with more emotional considerations to be palatable to a contemporary audience.

Selection via criteria set has two big liabilities. First, it can happen that people end up with someone who "looks good on paper" but for whom they don't feel much of anything. And committing to a sexually exclusive relationship with someone to whom you aren't very attracted — especially in a social moment that promises near-limitless optionality — is a bridge too far for many people. Physical attraction is *not* superficial. It can be extremely useful for a relationship, as it's one of the primary drivers of sacrifice, service, and respect. Whether or not it's merited, people tend to treat those they are attracted to better than those to whom they are not. Entering into a relationship with someone who is attracted to you increases the likelihood that you will get more of what you want, and entering into a relationship with someone to whom you are attracted often brings out a better version of yourself. Mutual, sustained sexual attraction is one of the most underappreciated keys to a successful relationship. This is why it is odd that we collectively do all that we can to sacrifice this attraction on the altar of security in our long-term relationships.

And second, overly relying on criteria can facilitate indecision. This is because *the mind cannot decide*. If we carefully examine the mind in its decision-making capacity, we find that it's kind of like a complicated odds calculator. Given a certain model of reality and a certain set of data and a certain set of assumptions, all the mind can really do is predict the likelihood that certain events will occur with a certain degree of confidence. For instance, the mind can predict — given its model, data, and assumptions — with 90% confidence that there is a 62% chance that outcome *A* will occur and a 31% chance that outcome *B* will occur, and so on. If we're being intellectually honest, that's the best the analytical mind can do. It can't tell you *what you should do* or whether something *will be worth doing*. It can only crunch the numbers according to the parameters defined by your experience and intention.

As a result, actually deciding to enter into a relationship can never be a purely analytical deduction. Decision is ultimately *an act of the will* — which, as such, makes it closer to an emotion since its function is to motivate action. This is why "impulsive" people who make decisions quickly are typically much more emotional than their "indecisive" peers. Expecting your mind to tell you who you should commit to is as useless as expecting it to tell you why you should commit to them. This is because the "reason" to commit is always the same: you move forward with a relationship (or not) because it is your will to do so (or not). Given our incomplete data and inaccurate models, every prediction under the sun is a roll of the dice. And all the diligence and circumspection in the world will neither insist on a particular action nor guarantee a specific outcome.

By the same token, we certainly can't let emotions run the show. It might take *chutzpah* to put our chips on the felt, but that doesn't mean we should throw our money away because we feel like it. If decisions are fundamentally a form of gambling, then primarily using our emotions as a guide to relationship selection makes about as much sense as betting on a given horse because we "like its pretty spots." People who operate like this won't last too long at the track. So how can we appropriately use our emotions to make good choices in the sexual marketplace? By asking our hearts two important questions.

The first question is: *"Do I like this person?"* Note: *like,* not *love*. In my experience, liking someone is more associated with relationship success than loving someone. This is true for several reasons. As we discussed in the previous chapter, limerence — which is a form of madness based on attraction — is often mistaken for love, and limerence is unsustainable. The passionate intensity of the experience either undermines the stability of the relationship, or the limerence on which the relationship is based fades over time. Either way, it's foolish to make a short-term experience the primary criterion for a long-term relationship.

It's also generally easier to get along with someone you like than with someone you love. Which relationships are more subject to conflict, judgment, and frustration: those with your friends or those with your family? For most people, it's the latter. But why might this be? Your friends are hardly perfect people. They have their quirks and foibles and failings, and they're probably not any more virtuous than your family. However, for whatever reason, you've decided to *like* them — and your liking makes allowance for those negatives. What's more, you probably don't feel as threatened by their disapproval, as irritated by their differences, and as upset by their absence as you do with your family. This is hardly surprising. Since people have strong beliefs pertaining to how a family is supposed to be, violations of these (often unjustified) expectations can elicit outrage and despair.

On the other hand, people often find it much more difficult to tolerate the flaws and idiosyncrasies of those they love (like family members). They expect so much more of these people, who (after all) probably aren't any better or worse than anyone else. As a result, those we love are much more likely to disappoint us than those we like. But whose fault is that? It's not anyone else's responsibility to live up to the ideal of who we would like them to be — even if conforming to that ideal would be "objectively" better for the person in question. A thistle has no obligation to be a rose. Rather, it is our responsibility to temper our ideals with reality — at least, if we want to make the best use of the opportunities we've been given. In the words of one of my mentors, the key to relationships is having high hopes and low expectations. Liking someone makes it easier to do this.

Finally, this particular question (*"Do I like this person?"*) is extremely important for men to ask. While it's probably fair to say that most men don't like most people, we've already discussed how most men will have sex with most women. These two statements together make it far more likely that a man will find himself in a sexual relationship *with a woman he doesn't even like* than it is for a woman to find herself in a comparable situation. To clarify his feelings for any particular woman, a man can find it helpful to consider whether he would actually want to spend time with her *even if sex were off the table.* And since this is difficult to approach in the hypothetical, most men can collect this data by examining their feelings for a given woman immediately after orgasm. Shameful regret or the impulse to get away as quickly as possible are not good signs. Men can use this fleeting moment of clarity to gauge their level of interest independent of their sexual attraction. So that's the first question.

The second question is: *"Do I like myself when I'm with this person?"* This might be the most important criterion for a successful relationship. Different people elicit different versions of ourselves. When we engage with a particular person, some facets of our personality are naturally pulled to the forefront while others recede into the background. As a result, our experience of self can change significantly based on where we are, who we're with, and what we're doing. This is why relationships are so important to personal development, and it's why those who stay isolated so often become stilted and weird. One of the primary ways we learn about ourselves is through the process of relating to others.

So if different people elicit different versions of yourself, and you're thinking of entering into a serious relationship with someone with whom you are likely to spend a significant portion of your conscious life, then it is extremely important *that you like the version of yourself that you become in this person's presence*. When evaluating a relationship, this means that how you feel about yourself is at least as significant as how you feel about the other person. For better or worse, you only accompany someone else, but you cannot avoid the experience of yourself.

Check in with yourself when you're in the presence of this other person. How do you tend to feel? When vetting for a long-term relationship, this shouldn't be a single data point from a particular situation but the dominant mood of the emotional dynamic. Keep in mind that you don't necessarily need to analyze this feeling. If you notice that you tend to feel anxious or sad or irritable in the company of someone else, it can be interesting to conduct a bit of self-inquiry into why that might be the case, but it may be even more useful to simply move forward with a different relationship. Not everything needs to be understood, and not everything can be changed. And a long-standing, unconscious, co-created emotional dynamic can be very difficult to alter after it has been established, even if both parties are interested in doing so. In many cases, it is a better idea to invest your limited resources elsewhere, which, of course, will be easier to do if you refrained from making an emotional commitment too quickly because you hired slow.

Ultimately, you'll want to keep someone around for the long term who *facilitates a positive experience of yourself*. This could mean feeling confident or peaceful or content in the presence of that person. More intense positive emotions are likely the artifacts of limerence, and you should interpret them with caution. More than anything else, a serious relationship should support you in being the person you want to be — or (perhaps more accurately) in growing into the person you would like to become. This is an extremely valuable service — one of the most valuable a relationship can offer — and anything less probably isn't worth the cost of admission.

In this chapter, I discussed the importance of selection in successful relationships. By approaching dating as an extended hiring process, people can significantly increase the likelihood of getting what they want by prioritizing goodness of fit. By hiring slow (and firing fast), men and women can avoid most of the problems known to plague sexual relationships. And by using a combination of reasoned consideration and emotional intelligence, people can minimize risk and maximize reward across time.

At this point, we're well-positioned to discuss how men and women can increase the chances of securing their desired outcomes in the game of mating and dating. In the next chapter, I will examine these optimal, gendered strategies for navigating the sexual marketplace.

If you'd like to further explore the topics presented in this chapter, please scan the QR code to access a curated playlist on the PsycHacks channel on YouTube.

CHAPTER 11

THERE IS ALWAYS A BETTER MOVE

A game is anything with rules and a goal. Within this definition, we can understand that the sexual marketplace is full of games, many of which are nested within each other and all of which are variants of the Game of Please/No. One aspect that makes the game of mating and dating so endlessly fascinating is that it is constantly evolving. Some of the rules are more or less constant, and some exist only for a fleeting moment. However, the game is always in the process of becoming what it is.

Some may find this maddening and would prefer to bind the game into a static progression. However, connected as it is to life — the same wild and amoral force that governs the natural world "red in tooth and claw" — this will never be entirely possible. The game cannot be "won" for good and all. And this, of course, might very well be for the best, as it offers life *the best possible chance of continuing on for as long as possible*. This, if anything, is the object of life: it is a game whose goal is to continue to play. A constantly evolving game also provides its players with a constant opportunity to evolve — which, if the players must act within that game to secure their outcomes, represents their best possible chance of getting what they want.

If we deeply understand the rules in effect and we clearly perceive the pieces on the board, then it should always be possible to make better choices. Indeed, at any given moment in a game, there is always an optimal move — though it might be beyond our ability to identify. That said, it may be useful to presume that such a move exists, as it provides a standard against which to measure our efforts in successive approximation. And if an optimal move exists beyond our recognition, then we can also assume that *a better move must always be possible* — though it may be necessary to believe it to see it.

In any game, a player's best possible chance of winning lies in *consistently making good moves without blundering*. Of these two components of success, it is far more important to learn how to avoid blundering than it is to learn how to make better moves. This is due to the asymmetry between creation and destruction. A structure that took a hundred years to build can be leveled in a few seconds of controlled demolition. Whether this is "fair" is irrelevant. It is what it is. In the context of the game, this means that a single mistake can undo the advantage created by a long, successive sequence of good moves. So to improve your performance, first learn to avoid disastrous moves, and then learn to recognize advantageous ones.

The remainder of this chapter will be devoted to examining the optimal move sets for men and women within the game of mating and dating as it is played in the contemporary sexual marketplace. I appreciate that this can be a contentious topic. The important thing to keep in mind here is that none of these strategies constitutes a moral exhortation for men or women to behave in certain ways. People are going to do what they're going to do anyway. Whether these strategies are put into practice is exclusively the business of the individuals in question. And those who choose to do so will be able to verify the effectiveness of these strategies for themselves. There is no need to take anything on faith.

As you'll see, these optimal strategies are extremely gendered: a man's best possible move is hardly ever a woman's, and vice versa. This is because the game of mating and dating as played between men and women is not like checkers or chess, games in which both sides have the same pieces in equivalent positions at the outset. This setup minimizes the advantage afforded any given player from position and increases the proportion of the outcome attributable to skill. In such games, the "better" player wins more often.

On the other hand, when the game of mating and dating begins in earnest, there is no symmetry on the board between the two players. The fact is that women enjoy a significant advantage over men at the start of play, and they retain that advantage for quite some time (though not indefinitely). In this way, the game of mating and dating is more akin to Axis & Allies, a board game simulation of World War II. At the outset, the Axis powers have both initiative and a more powerful military. As a result, the overarching strategy of most Axis players is *to win the game as quickly as possible* —

which is precisely what the actual Axis powers attempted to do in reality with their unprovoked invasions and *blitzkrieg* tactics. Morality aside, this is a rational strategy: attack when the enemy is weak and exploit one's advantage as fully as possible.

And the Allies *are* weak at the start of the game. They are unprepared and vulnerable, relying on countermeasures designed to defend against a method of warfare that no longer exists. As a consequence, the overarching strategy of most Allied players is *to prolong the game as long as possible* — which is precisely what the actual Allied powers attempted to do in reality. Read Churchill's speeches to Parliament[38] (which collectively — and deservedly — earned him a Nobel Prize in Literature): it took years for the British war machine to match Germany's materiel output. What's more, the UK had to accomplish this feat while fending off invasion and supersonic rockets. And this is *also* a rational strategy: defend when the enemy is strong and wait for an opportunity to turn the tide. In most cases, this opportunity is when the enemy — in its hubris — overextends its power, leaving itself vulnerable to a counteroffensive on its weakest front.

If we can ignore the connotations we might associate with the various belligerents in this historical conflict, then this situation — in terms of the significant imbalance in power, value, and initiative at the start of the game — more or less maps onto the state of affairs men and women encounter when they first enter into the sexual marketplace. And this is why the optimal move sets of men and women are so

38 "I have nothing to offer but blood, toil, tears, and sweat." Source: Churchill, W. (2010). We will all go down fighting to the end. Penguin Books.

different. All other things being equal, it is in most women's best interests *to push for victory as hard and fast as possible,* as this strategy allows them to exploit their initial advantage in the marketplace. Conversely, it is in most men's best interests *to avoid defeat for as long as possible,* as this strategy affords them time to muster an equivalent (or superior) force.

What follows is a description of what this might look like. Let's start with the women.

A BEAUTIFUL SEASON

Take a look at this graph.

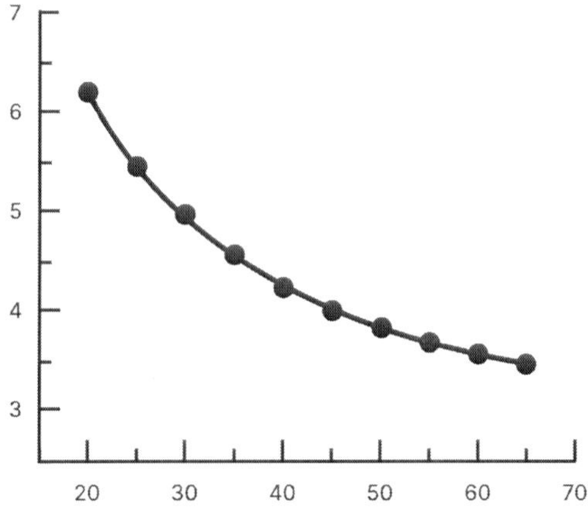

Imagine this was presented to you by your financial advisor. After the usual proviso that past outcomes are no guarantee of future performance, he tells you that the graph represents the average value of thousands and thousands of stocks in a particular sector over the 40 years following their initial public offerings. As you can plainly see, this value only decreases as a function of time. He then explains to you that, through no particular fault or merit of your own, you were recently bequeathed a large portfolio consisting of a new stock in this sector by a long-lost relative. And as your advisor, he would like to know what you plan to do with this windfall.

In light of the given information, if you had any sense in your head whatsoever, you would tell your advisor to immediately liquidate your portfolio — today, if possible. As should be obvious, this is because the longer you wait, the less valuable your stock will likely become. So procrastination here is functionally allowing your future self to be robbed. Of course, your particular holding might be the exception to the general rule — after all, the graph represents the average value of stocks in the sector — and you may be tempted to retain your portfolio for a while in order to determine whether it has "the right stuff." However, this will be a poor strategy in most cases.

We can use simplified math to understand why. Let's assume that it takes about 10 years to run the experiment on any particular stock. Over that time, we might expect 1% of stocks in this sector to see a significant increase in their value (say, by 5x), 25% to see a modest increase in their value (say, by 1.5x), and the remainder to see their value decreased by half. Given these payouts and odds ratios, we would expect any portfolio subjected to this experiment to be worth about 80% of its initial value 10 years later. Or, to put it another way, *the experiment isn't free*. On average, it costs about 20% of the value of the holding to run — which is a non-insignificant amount. It also maps fairly well onto the presented data.

Now for the big (and, hopefully, unsurprising) reveal. The prior graph does not, in fact, reflect the value of a hypothetical stock portfolio over time: it is the visual representation of women's normalized sexual marketplace value over a 40-year time period.[39] On average, women's nSMV is highest at 18 years old, and it only decreases with time. This suggests that, in most cases, there will never be a better time for a woman to secure the relationship she wants with the man she wants to have it with than today. As her attractiveness declines, so, too, does her ability to secure more favorable terms for herself across all three relationship phases. As I explained in chapter 4, the default mode of women is *to act*.

Why is this the case? The main premise of this book is that people enter into relationships to exchange unequal things of comparable value. If you want a lot, you must not only be prepared to offer a lot in return but to offer a lot of *what the other party wants, as well*. And if it's also true that women generally seek to exchange sexual opportunity for resources in the sexual marketplace, then we should reasonably expect better sexual opportunities to command higher exchange rates. And to the extent that the quality of a sexual opportunity — *as reckoned by men* — is related to the fertility, purity, and physical attractiveness of the woman offering it, then we should also expect the value of such an opportunity to be highest among younger women, all other things being equal. These women are the ones most likely to beat out their intrasexual competition for the most desirable men.

---

39 This graph was taken from a study that (among other things) examined female desirability through the lens of the revealed preferences of men on dating apps. Citation: Bruch, E., & Newman M. (2018). Aspirational pursuit of mates in online dating markets. *Science Advances, 4*(8). doi:10.1126/sciadv.aap9815

Under the rules currently governing the sexual marketplace, this means that the window in which most women are best able to secure a lifetime commitment with a high-value man is between the ages of 18 and 25. This is not a large window by any means, but it should be enough time to achieve the desired outcome *if this goal is prioritized.* For better or worse, however, modern women have found it increasingly difficult to prioritize this goal and exploit the relative advantage of their positions. This is true for several reasons — two of which are highly significant.

In the first case, the majority of people in the West are inundated with the tenets of ideological feminism from a young age. In the case of girls, this often takes the guise of disincentivizing behavior that conforms with traditional gender roles and encouraging behavior that aligns with postmodern social mores. Femininity — one of the few goods that men cannot secure more cheaply and easily from other men, which makes it a trait that men highly value in women in the sexual marketplace — has increasingly been considered a shameful relic of a benighted past. This shaping is often subtle and well beyond the capacities of children to appreciate. And this is insidious since most of these women won't even possess the cognitive capacity to recognize this ideology as such until their brains fully mature — right around the time they start to lose their competitive advantage in the sexual marketplace.

The outcome of being exposed to this conditioning over the first two decades of life is fairly predictable: fewer and fewer young women are even remotely considering the prospect of marriage and children. Many believe they won't *ever* want to start a family — and, in any case, they have "plenty of time" to change their minds. When these women turn 18 years old, they roughly fall into one of two camps: either they prioritize short-term relationships and "having fun," or they heavily invest in their education and career. Either way, women often inadvertently squander a propitious moment. If a married woman feels as though she has missed out on the experience of selling her labor on the open market, she can always become an employee in her 30s. However, if a working woman feels as though she has missed out on the experience of having children, she might encounter (often unexpected) difficulties in starting a family later in life.

This segues into the second significant obstacle faced by modern women: the decline of the role of the father in the mate selection process. If most young women are either in school or having fun during their years of peak attractiveness, then they will largely be surrounded by young men who are doing the same. Unfortunately, due to factors that we'll discuss later in this chapter, most men don't become "husband material" until their 30s, at least. As a result, many young women are simply not exposed to qualified bachelors: stable, successful men who are prepared to start a family and offer a suitable lifestyle. This means that women must either wait until they themselves are sufficiently successful to enter into the circles of such men — by which time, they have not only lost their relative advantage in the sexual marketplace but are now operating at a relative disadvantage — or take a gamble on the untested fortunes of a promising young man.[40]

40 I call this strategy "betting on the dark horse," and it's particularly useful for women who — even during their peak years of attractiveness — consistently fail to beat out their intrasexual competition. It also explains why women typically place such a high value on trait attributes such as ambition, drive, and industriousness in their mate selection criteria: they

This issue was largely avoided for several reasons when fathers played an active role in their daughters' courtship process. First, fathers could leverage their social networks to bring their daughters into contact with competent, successful men who were looking to settle down. This was the function of events like debutante balls, wherein young women were officially introduced to "society," and interested parties could be appropriately vetted after making their intentions known. Second, fathers could dissuade non-serious suitors for their daughters' affections from active pursuit. "What are your intentions with my daughter?" was a question that most young men would have needed to be prepared to answer back in the day. Nowadays, many women only seem to learn the value of such gatekeeping much later in life (e.g., "What are you looking for on this app?"), precisely when it would be more effective to relax their filtering processes than to tighten them.

And finally, fathers would be better able to negotiate on behalf of their daughters with the men in their social circles for more favorable terms across a longer time horizon. It should go without saying, but here it is: most young people (men and women) are not only stupid, but they are also willfully convicted in their stupidity. This isn't entirely their fault, but without sufficient guidance on the one hand (and appropriate obedience on the other), it can lead to poor outcomes, nonetheless. In fact, the relative absence of fathers in the modern courtship process is one of the primary drivers behind raising the age of consent, since even younger women would be completely outmatched in the sexual

---

signal the possibility that a younger, low-value man has a decent chance of becoming an older, high-value man with the passage of time.

marketplace if they were expected to act on their own behalf.[41] Unfortunately, unless we are collectively interested in raising the age of consent to 25 — when most people's brains have fully matured — we must continue to expect some degree of immaturity in the mating and dating decisions of young women.

Some women might balk at the suggestion that their fathers become more involved in their courtship, fearing a return to a time when women were married off against their wishes by their male relatives for personal gain. And while I'm sure this did happen, I'm also sure that — in the vast majority of cases — a young woman's father would be significantly more invested in her happiness and success than a random man she meets at a party (or on a dating app) would be. While not all women can count on such support from their male relatives, most young women will find their fathers (and brothers) to be the men in their lives most committed to their long-term outcomes. In many cases, they want more for their daughters (and sisters) than these women want for themselves.

Being older men, fathers are in a much better position to negotiate with other men on their daughters' behalf. This is because, as men, they are both more likely to understand what other men value when transacting for long-term relationships and less likely to be bamboozled by superficially attractive offers (potentially because they've been bamboozlers themselves in the past). And as older men, they have seen the

41 Contrast this with traditional cultures in which menarche was generally considered a girl's entry into womanhood. This did not typically arouse the panic and outrage it would in "civilized" society because the young woman would also not be expected to act as her own agent in the sexual marketplace since her relations would be vouchsafed by her male relatives.

decline symbolized by the graph presented at the beginning of this section with their own eyes. They understand that female attractiveness is a flower: it blooms for a season and then is gone. Fathers are much more likely to appreciate the deceptiveness of time: that season will be over before their daughters know it. However, what these women will have to show for that passage of time is increasingly anyone's guess.

The opening line of *Pride and Prejudice*[42] has truth in it: when men are sufficiently successful and established, they tend to turn their attention toward securing their legacy through marriage and children. And since successful, established men looking for commitment are not only the men most attractive to women but also the men most able to beat out their own intrasexual competition for these women, such men bring a great deal of value to the sexual marketplace. And since relationships are predicated on the transaction of unequal goods of comparable value, we would reasonably expect the highest-value men to select the highest-value women to whom they are allowed access.

This is why women are most able to secure long-term relationships with the most eligible bachelors when they are young and fertile, all other things being equal. The involvement of a woman's male relatives would not only make such a pairing more likely, but it would also increase the likelihood of her securing more favorable terms in the relationship. This is because it's improbable that she would possess an accurate estimation of her own nSMV — both currently and over time — without actually participating in

42 The line is: "It is a truth universally acknowledged, that a single man in possession of a good fortune, must be in want of a wife." Source: Austen, J. (1813/2002). *Pride and prejudice*. Penguin Classics.

the sexual marketplace. Among other benefits, male relatives provide a proxy for the male gaze of potential suitors. Women who emphatically insist that they do not care what men want are likely to be as successful in the sexual marketplace as job applicants who profess to be indifferent to what employers are looking for in the commercial marketplace.

In any case, modern women will probably not be asking their fathers and brothers to broker their relationships anytime soon. So in the absence of this resource, it is essential to a woman's reproductive success *to act as her own father*. This has two key components. The first component is *socializing with the high-value men she would most like to mate and date*. The men at nightclubs and house parties are not looking for wives. So young women who are serious about finding husbands may need to break away from their peer cohorts and pursue different activities. This could take on many forms, from working as a paralegal in a top-tier law firm, to regularly appearing at happy hours frequented by successful professionals, to using social networks to attend prestigious cultural events. The women who complain that there are no "good men" around are often the same women who do not situate themselves among "good men." Leveraging their social and professional connections is the first way women can act as their own fathers. However, this only solves the problem of access. Successfully attracting (and retaining) the men in whom they are most interested requires a different set of skills.

This segues into the second component of how women can act more effectively on their own behalf: *gatekeeping their sexual opportunity more strategically*. For better or worse, this can no longer be accomplished (as it has for generations) by simply insisting that commitment precede sex. "Why buy the cow when you can get the milk for free?" assumes a marketplace in which milk is *generally purchased*. However, in a marketplace where milk is distributed *freely*, the question becomes, "Why buy the cow when you have to pay for the milk?" In such a situation, providing milk no longer motivates a sale since milk is common to almost all transactions; however, withholding milk jeopardizes a sale since withholding milk makes a transaction more expensive among comparable goods.

Insisting that commitment precede sex is no longer a viable strategy for most women. In today's sexual marketplace, this would be tantamount to trying to sell a car without wheels. The presence of wheels does little to motivate action (since the vast majority of cars come with wheels), but the absence of wheels significantly demotivates action (since the actual cost of the car to the buyer — in terms of time, energy, and money — will be much higher than the listed price). Just like the only viable way to sell a car without wheels on the open market would be to significantly reduce the sticker price so that the overall cost to the buyer were less than (or comparable to) the costs he would have incurred had he purchased a fully functional car, the only viable way to sell commitment without sex in today's sexual marketplace would be to simultaneously offer something of value to men that would offset the higher relative cost of the proposed transaction but would not be available from women who did not attempt this strategy, namely: *chastity*.

Men selectively value chastity. It is a frustrating liability in a lover and a highly desired virtue in a wife. Unfortunately, given the fact that most women lose their virginity as teenagers,[43] young women often miss out on the opportunity to leverage their chastity — largely because they are transacting in the wrong markets. A woman's virginity might be an interesting detail of a sexual conquest, *or* it could be the determining factor in the decision to marry. Like the "newness" of a car, virginity can only be transacted *once,* and — once transacted — leads to significant reductions in subsequent valuations.

Consequently, it makes sense for women to insist on commitment prior to sex while they are still virgins and to shift their gatekeeping strategically if and when this does not produce the desired outcome. In most cases, continuing to insist on commitment prior to sex after becoming sexually active is unlikely to prove effective since the woman has already demonstrated that she is willing to transact her sexual opportunity at a lower price point. No one is enthusiastic about paying more for the same good that others have acquired more cheaply, and most people would only be willing to do so if some conditions of duress motivated their decision. Since these women won't be able to offer a compensatory good (i.e., chastity) in exchange for commitment prior to sex, and since most of their (similarly non-virgin) intrasexual competition will be offering sex prior to commitment, a non-virgin who pursued this strategy would likely be priced out of the market.

With this in mind, we can see that women's best strategy in today's sexual marketplace is to offer sex prior to commitment (especially if they are no longer virgins)

43 In the US, both men and women lose their virginity at 17 on average. Source: https://worldpopulationreview.com/state-rankings/average-age-to-lose-virginity-by-state

— not because it will facilitate commitment but because it will prevent ineligibility. Now that the availability of milk is a given, women must transact *other goods that are of interest to men in order to secure their commitment*. Unfortunately, many of the goods with which modern women attempt to secure that commitment — higher education, professional accomplishment, and personal lifestyle — do not meet this criterion. They are not of much interest to men, who (often to their downfall) are monomaniacally focused on women's sexual opportunities and reproductive cues. What's more, male captains already have these goods in abundance, so the marginal utility of a woman who can provide additional accomplishment is negligible.

However, the marketplace expectation that sex precede commitment creates two new opportunities for women to beat out their intrasexual competition for the most desirable men. In general, the cost of winning is the willingness (and ability) to do what your competition won't (or can't). In the context of the sexual marketplace, women secure relationships with the men they want by being willing (and able) to do what their intrasexual competition won't (or can't). This can still be done with respect to a good that men value highly — namely, women's sexual opportunity — in two significant ways: by providing more desirable sexual opportunities and by facilitating more numerous sexual opportunities. Quality and quantity.

Not all milk is the same. There's everything from flavorless skim milk to rich heavy cream. In a marketplace in which milk is freely distributed, women can differentiate themselves *by offering the richest, creamiest milk available*. People used to say that the way to a man's heart was through his stomach. This isn't true: the passage is actually a few inches lower. Men will go to incredible lengths to secure and retain women who offer sexual experiences they cannot find elsewhere — even against their better judgment. And they are often more loyal and dedicated to women who provide such opportunities since it's hard to go back to skim once you've had a taste of cream.

Every month, I work with men who have fallen in love with escorts. Even though they are paying for the experience, and even though they often know very little about the woman in question (including, in some cases, her real name), and even though they appreciate that they're likely being hoodwinked by a person of questionable morals, they fall in love anyway. Why? Because these women provide these men with *unparalleled sexual experiences*, both in terms of what they do and how they do it. They not only perform sexual acts that other women won't, but they provide them with enthusiasm and gusto while conveying their rapturous appreciation for the man's cocksmanship, as well. Such women cater to men's fantasies and are often richly compensated for doing so.

The male ego is highly susceptible to flattery. A woman who can make a man believe that he is the best she's ever had is a *smart woman*. Doing so will inspire a corresponding suite of traditionally masculine behavior in the man in question: confidence, provision, and protectiveness. Men are also aware that a woman will do more things more quickly with a man to whom she is more attracted, so they use a woman's sexual behavior as a gauge of her interest. And it is her willingness (and ability) to go above and beyond in the bedroom that helps her secure a desired relationship.

If women are proactive in this department, they can secure a *de facto* exclusivity from any given man, as he will be significantly less likely to go through the trouble of securing additional sexual opportunities in a state of perpetual satiety. He will also endure worse conditions for longer before terminating the relationship since it would prove more difficult to find a replacement with a comparable skill set or work ethic on the open market. In general, women accrue many positives for themselves when they provide high-quality sexual experiences for the men with whom they are interested in having relationships. It is the "hook" with which they "catch" men.

The other way in which women can beat out their intrasexual competition in a marketplace in which sex precedes commitment is *by relaxing their strictures with respect to sexual exclusivity*. Commitment and sexual exclusivity are not the same thing. Whereas *commitment* is the willingness to invest in a relationship — in terms of time, energy, money, and resources — *sexual exclusivity* is the agreement not to have sex with other people. Some people are committed to those with whom they are not sexually exclusive, and others are sexually exclusive with those to whom they are not particularly committed. So the two constructs are independent of each other.

While they value sexual exclusivity in men, many women often value it less for its own sake than for the "savings" it provides. If men exchange resources for sexual opportunity, then additional opportunities represent a potential diversion of emotional and material investment away from the primary relationship. And any man who willingly forgoes these opportunities relieves a woman of the necessity of defending her relationship by continuing to invest in her own ability to overcome her intrasexual competition. Such women get more (because they can enjoy the entirety of a man's undiverted investment) for less (because they no longer incur expenses to secure their relationship against competition).

However, much like any other transaction, a savings to one party typically constitutes an expense to the other — and this is no exception. In point of fact, sexual exclusivity is *extremely expensive to men* (as it runs counter to their fundamental reproductive imperative), and it is expensive in direct proportion to a given man's optionality. As previously discussed, men without optionality will be quick to offer commitment, as it constitutes a way for them to conjure value out of nothing. On the other hand, men with a great deal of optionality — the relatively few high-value men with whom the majority of women desire a relationship — often find exchanging that optionality for an exclusive relationship with any one woman a remarkably expensive proposition. Consequently, any woman who insists on strict monogamy from such a man might find herself priced out of contention.

This is because — irrespective of her virtues or assets — no woman can compete with the hundreds (or thousands) of novel sexual opportunities a high-value man enjoys (both now and in the indefinite future). Believing that anyone could is a romantic fantasy. The cost associated with forgoing all other sexual opportunities is — far and away — *the single greatest source of commitment hesitancy in men*. And just like any other sale, women must find a way to resolve this hesitancy if they want to seal the deal. Traditionally, this was done through a socially condoned manipulation of shame (e.g., "A real man wouldn't act like this..." or "You need to grow up...") that attempted to punish men who refused to commit exclusively. However, this strategy, associated as it is with traditional gender roles, has become increasingly ineffective in an age in which relationships of all kinds are in decline.

A woman who does not force a man to choose between a relationship with her and the sexual opportunity of every other woman on the planet is a *smart woman*. This is particularly true of high-value men since even a portion of their provision is likely to be significantly more valuable than the undiverted entirety of lower-value men. Most women would rather occasionally share a Porsche than own a Honda. A willingness to tolerate a man's extra-partner liaisons — especially if such liaisons are discreet, responsible, and do not detrimentally affect resource provision in the primary relationship — is one of the most effective tactics available to women in securing relationships from desirable men, as it is the simplest way of bypassing their commitment hesitancy.

The enormous advantage that women enjoy over men in the sexual marketplace is that most men will have sex with most women (but not the other way around). This functionally allows women to target specific men in a dating approach I call *hunting*. By reconnoitering the men to whom they have access through their social and professional networks prior to an actual interaction, women can strategically gatekeep their sexual opportunity by enforcing high barriers to entry for all but their chosen targets. Women can then engage these men in such a way as to indicate their attraction and to suggest that — should they take action — these men would be assured of a high-quality, no-commitment sexual experience. Few men would be able to pass up such an offer. By providing a more desirable opportunity at a lower cost, women can beat out their intrasexual competition and secure relationships with the most desirable men to whom they have access. This is the Trojan Horse that allows women to pass through the gates of the city.

Following this advice is a woman's best chance of securing intimate access to the man of her choosing. However, while access is a necessary precondition of a committed relationship, it is not (in itself) sufficient to secure commitment. A woman does this by *becoming useful to the man*. Through her research, observation, and interaction, a woman who has secured a sexual relationship with a man is in a privileged position to know how to improve his quality of life or further his overarching mission. Providing instrumental value in this way affords a woman the opportunity to slowly insinuate herself into a man's day-to-day life.

The idea is to willingly and enthusiastically provide a man with more and more assistance to the point that her efforts become essential to the operation of his lifestyle. The *provision of value* is what allows a woman to move beyond being the mere pastime of a man who could easily replace her. A woman secures *de facto* commitment from a man once it becomes prohibitively expensive to extricate her from his life. Couple this strategy with consistent, frequent, proactive, passionate sex, and a woman stands her best possible chance of both accessing the high-value man of her choosing and securing him against her intrasexual competition.

This is enough to make most men commit. However, if this strategy is still insufficient, then it nevertheless positions a woman to make effective use of *the takeaway*. Take a page from the modern marketplace: Why do so many people have subscriptions to streaming services? It's certainly not because these companies demand that people purchase a subscription before sampling their content. The reason why people end up paying for a streaming service is because it (a) initially minimizes barriers to entry, (b) provides high-quality, emotionally compelling shows that "hook" viewers on content they can't find elsewhere, and then (c) threatens to remove access. A service that either threatens to revoke access before the hook is firmly in place or provides a service that can be more easily and cheaply secured elsewhere is unlikely to secure a commitment. While somewhat nefarious, any company that succeeds in making a product that would create a bigger problem for its users if discontinued than the problem they initially started using its product to solve can be assured of a dedicated customer base for many years to come.

While no guarantees exist in the game of mating and dating, the foregoing strategies collectively constitute women's best possible chance of securing a long-term relationship with the high-value men they desire, given the current state of the sexual marketplace.

EVENING THE ODDS

Now let's turn our attention to the men. Since my thinly veiled subterfuge has already been compromised, I'll dispense with any further attempts at deception. Here's a graph of men's normalized sexual marketplace value over the same 40-year period.

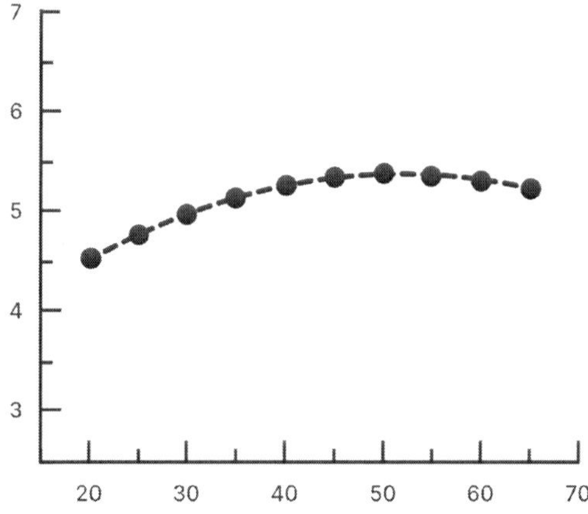

As you can see, men's nSMV is lowest when they first enter the sexual marketplace at 18 years old. It steadily climbs as men approach 40 and then more or less holds constant for a good 20 years before gently declining in old age. For most of their lives, most men will never be in a more disadvantaged position in the sexual marketplace than they are today. This is why their default mode is *to wait*: all other things being equal, men are generally able to secure relationships on more favorable terms with more desirable women as a function of time.

Though largely unacknowledged by society, it is actually extremely difficult to be a young man. Women don't want them because they don't yet have the goods that rank highly in women's selection criteria (like resources, prestige, lifestyle, or emotional maturity). By the same token, other men don't need them because they don't yet have the goods that make them a valuable teammate (like experience, competence, knowledge, or good judgment). Such men are expendable. They exist at the bottom of most status hierarchies, and they receive little to no assistance, sympathy, or support. Relative to young women, young men engage in significantly riskier behavior, as they resort to increasingly more desperate strategies to escape marginalization and irrelevance. For men, being low-status can have life-and-death consequences.

For better or worse, men's quality of life largely depends on *their ability to successfully compete in the game of life.* Those who succeed in this game are rewarded with money, status, honors, and sexual opportunities; those who do not are passed over without a second thought. It is what it is. Despite the fact that society is becoming increasingly uncomfortable with competition — likely due to the social influence of women, who tend to prefer more egalitarian dynamics — this will never change. This is because — ironically — these same women rely on competitive status hierarchies as one of the principal means of evaluating men for relationships. In today's day and age, competition might be frowned upon, but it cannot be dispensed with entirely, as that would frustrate many women's sexual selection strategies. Men who fail to understand this make it easier for other men to compete.

To successfully compete in the game of life, a man must develop a suite of skills and competencies that enable him to provide value to others. The more people to whom he provides more value, the more success he will enjoy. A man who has found his place in the world is not necessarily a good man or a wise man or a virtuous man: *he is a man from whom people want things.* A man who has nothing other people want is invisible to others. He is useless and blamed for his own uselessness. Consequently, the key to having a decent life as a man is to secure and maintain *possession of that which other people value*. More than anything else, this will ensure abundant relationship opportunities for him (with both men and women). Other people will not only have to transact with him, but — in some cases — they will even compete with each other for the privilege of doing so.

We can now begin to understand how men can optimize for success in the sexual marketplace. Like women, men must adapt their strategies as a function of time. However, given the diametrically opposed starting positions of men and women, it should come as little surprise that their respective strategies are essentially inversions of each other. Whereas women are typically most able to secure more resources from higher-value men when they are younger — and so blunder when they postpone action — men are typically most able to secure better sexual opportunities from highly desirable women when they are older — and so blunder when they act prematurely. Instead of prioritizing sexual relationships, men are better served by devoting their young adulthood to the development of valued skills and the acquisition of desirable resources. Doing this is their best chance at increasing their wealth and elevating their status — both of which will enable them to create more emotionally compelling lifestyles that will be more attractive to more women.

In light of this, it is in most men's best interests *to avoid making a long-term commitment to any one woman for as long as possible*. Men typically acquire more wealth, status, and prestige with each passing year, which — if they avoid blundering — they can leverage on the sexual marketplace for more desirable sexual opportunities. This is true regardless of whether men want to secure a long-term partnership or to pursue a plethora of short-term experiences because (as previously discussed) there is a great deal of overlap in women's sexual selection criteria across relationship structures. Even if it is not their preference to do so, most women will consider entering into a more casual arrangement with a man if they are interested in mating with him. In fact, the less women are interested in mating with a given man, the less willing they will be to consider a casual relationship. This is because they (reasonably) demand more resources to compensate them for the costs associated with foreclosing on a less desirable reproductive opportunity. When it comes to sexual relationships, a man must pay — but the more a woman likes him, *the greater the discount*.

In any case, it is for men — who are the gatekeepers of commitment — to determine the relationship structure they wish to have with any particular woman. And they will increase their ability to secure any type of relationship with more (and more desirable) women if they spend their 20s accumulating valuable skills and resources, building emotionally compelling lifestyles, and generally ascending to their captaincies. It is through effort, patience, and sacrifice that men eventually "even the odds" across the grossly imbalanced starting positions in the sexual marketplace. However, to succeed in this, men must resist the internal urge (and the social pressure) to commit prematurely.

And this social pressure will be considerable. Superimposing the two graphs we've previously discussed will reveal why this is the case.

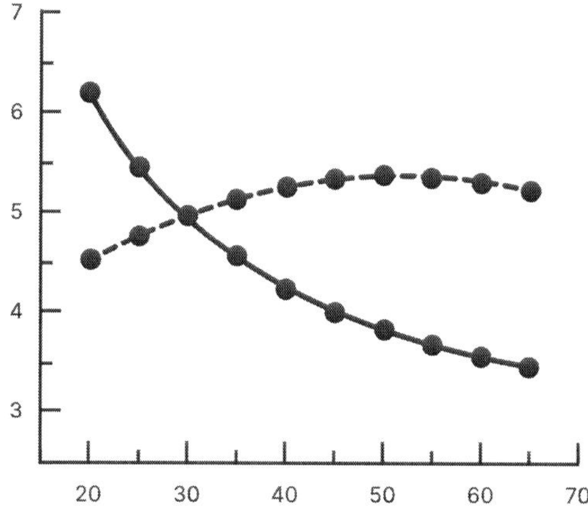

As you can see, the age of 30 is a significant moment in the lives of both men and women. It's the moment when the average man's normalized sexual marketplace value exceeds the average woman's normalized sexual marketplace value for the very first time — a shift in the relative balance of power that persists for the rest of their respective lives. In my warfare analogy, the age of 30 is like the culmination of the Battle of Stalingrad: a long and painful siege that ultimately emerged as the turning point of World War II. The Soviets were able to draw out the conflict as long as they could, and the Axis Powers never again enjoyed an advantage for the remainder of the war.

It should, therefore, come as little surprise that the average age at first marriage in the United States is 29 years old.[44] To

44 On average, men are 30 years old and women are 28 years old. Source: www.bgsu.edu/content/dam/BGSU/college-of-arts-and-sciences/NCFMR/documents/FP/julian-median-age-first-marriage-2021-fp-22-15.pdf

put it in other terms, marriage typically occurs at the very last moment when women enjoy a relative advantage over men in the sexual marketplace. Securing a lifetime commitment while the desirability gap still favors them is clearly in women's best interests, as it will become increasingly harder for them to do so with men of comparable quality as time goes on. Indeed, they may be unable to secure the same level of commitment from the same man in just another few years. Marriage allows women to offset their own depreciation in the sexual marketplace by binding their fortunes to those of a man who will likely continue to appreciate for decades.

It should go without saying, but this is *not a rational or attractive proposition for men*. This is why it's generally only possible for women to secure such an arrangement while they enjoy a relative power advantage and can, therefore, dictate more favorable terms for themselves. As a consequence, an enormous amount of pressure — from family, community, and culture — is brought to bear on men to "do the right thing." Of course, if this "thing" were right for *men*, social coercion would hardly be necessary: men would enthusiastically pursue this outcome of their own accord. Couple this with the fact that — in their late 20s — most men are still naive to the privileges associated with a favorable desirability gap, and it's no wonder marriage typically occurs at this time.

The economic model of relationships also explains why marriage rates are plummeting (more on this in the next chapter).[45] Since women are increasingly prioritizing short-term relationships and career advancement in their 20s —

45 In the US, marriage rates have fallen nearly 40% since 1990. Source: https://www.statista.com/statistics/195951/marriage-rate-in-the-united-states-since-1990/

that is, since they are increasingly blundering their relative advantage in the sexual marketplace by hesitating — more and more women are only considering long-term commitments in their 30s. So why do we see marriage rates falling *instead of the average age of marriage rising?*[46]

The answer is simple: after 30, the proposition is a loss to men at the point of transaction. In contrast, while marriage may have always been a net loss to men over a lifetime, this arrangement has historically been offset by front-end compensation. That is, men could hope to enjoy 10 or 15 years of youth and fertility in exchange for a lifetime of protection and provision. Under these conditions, men benefit from marriage at the point of transaction, which has proven to be a sufficiently attractive offer for many young men, most of whom enjoy little social support and sexual optionality.

On the other hand, marriage after 30 (at least, to a *woman over 30*) is typically *already* a loss to men that will only increase with time. Couple this with the fact that men enjoy a relative power advantage at this point and can dictate more favorable terms for themselves — in conjunction with the fact that men also become increasingly aware of the privileges associated with the favorable desirability gap enjoyed by women since their entry into the sexual marketplace — and it's no wonder that marriage is less likely to occur at this time. Without an appreciation of the value transaction that lies at the heart of

46 To be fair, the average age of marriage has *also* been rising. In the US, the median age of first marriage has risen around 16% since 1990 to peak at 30 years old. Therefore, the question is not why the average age of marriage isn't increasing absolutely, but why it isn't increasing past this point. Source: https://www.census.gov/content/dam/Census/library/visualizations/time-series/demo/families-and-households/ms-2.pdf

relationships, this phenomenon would be difficult to explain (at least, not without recourse to judgmental invectives).

My point is that many of the advantages young women enjoy in the game of mating and dating — the attention, the power, the optionality — do not actually inhere in women. They are associated with *occupying a position of relative advantage in the sexual marketplace*. And this position is gender-neutral. A famous, wealthy, high-status man enjoys advantages comparable to those of a young and beautiful woman. Believing that these benefits inhere in women (as opposed to the position of relative advantage) leads to sub-optimal outcomes for both men and women. This is because, on the one hand, this belief deceives women into thinking they can hesitate without cost, and, on the other hand, it tricks men into foreclosing commitment prematurely.

Most men never experience abundant optionality in the sexual marketplace *because they commit too soon*. And this commitment is costly: time, energy, and money that could be invested into increasing their wealth and status and influence — all of which significantly improve men's positioning in the sexual marketplace — are instead diverted into a relationship. For a man, arriving at the point at which he might (finally) reap the benefits associated with occupying a position of relative advantage in the sexual marketplace is hardly a certain venture. Not only must he succeed in sufficiently elevating his fortunes over time to create such an advantage, but he must remain at liberty to enjoy the benefits of this advantage, as well. Securing the advantage without the freedom to enjoy it is a torturous proposition to many successful men, a sizable proportion of whom will choose to liberate themselves in a process that is dismissively understood as a "mid-life crisis."

The upshot is that the longer men avoid commitment, the better they typically fare in the game of mating and dating.

That said, young men should not avoid the sexual marketplace entirely. A 40-year-old male virgin is hardly an attractive prospect to women, irrespective of whatever wealth and influence he has succeeded in accumulating. This is because women want what other women want. In fact, the easiest way for a man to secure the sexual opportunity of a highly desirable woman is to have access to the sexual opportunities of *other* highly desirable women. The more he has, the more he gets. This is the Matthew principle applied to the sexual marketplace,[47] and it is true for at least two reasons.

The first reason is that women use other women *to vet men*. Down at the dock, this is equivalent to using the size of the crowd standing in front of a ship as an approximation of that vessel's desirability. For better or worse, high-value men aren't as immediately recognizable as attractive women are. Not only does it take time to appropriately evaluate a man for a relationship, but men also often actively frustrate women's assessment attempts through the use of deception. Since highly attractive women are assumed to have significant optionality, and women select men who represent their best overall options, men who enjoy access to such women are widely considered to be very high-value. Indeed, the presence of an attractive woman in a man's life is one of the most reliable signals as to his status. On the other hand, a man who has no women in his life is presumed to have nothing

47 "For whosoever hath, to him shall be given, and he shall have more abundance: but whosoever hath not, from him shall be taken away even that he hath." Matthew 25:29.

that women value. Otherwise, *why would he be alone?* The same man is more attractive to women when he is in a relationship than when he is single — and he becomes even more attractive in direct proportion to the attractiveness of the women to whom he has access.

The second reason is that women use men *to improve their positioning within their own intrasex hierarchies*. A woman who succeeds in securing access to a man known to associate with highly attractive women receives social validation that she herself is highly attractive. This attribution allows her to negotiate better terms for herself in any given relationship and secure the attention of other men willing to provide more attractive offers. We might call this the "Playboy principle." If only the most attractive women are generally reputed to be Playboy "bunnies," then there will always be women interested in becoming bunnies — irrespective of the possibility that they are being objectified or exploited. By the same token, there will always be men interested in securing access to bunnies — as the latter's attractiveness serves to provide social validation of the former's status. In any case, women who associate with men known to associate with attractive women increase their attractiveness by proxy, which improves *their* status relative to their intrasexual competition even more.

The Catch-22 is that men generally need to have access to desirable women in order to get access to desirable women. The same is not true of women. An attractive woman perched on a barstool by herself will not long be without company (whether she desires it or not), while a commitment-minded male neurosurgeon will likely drink alone all night long. And should our doctor have the "good fortune" to find himself sitting next to a gorgeous woman all by her lonesome, will he be able to take advantage of such a chance if he is unpracticed in seduction? And should he succeed in seducing her, will he be able to maintain a relationship with her if he has never before held frame with a beautiful woman? Opportunity is wasted on the unprepared. Men who simply wait for their ideal woman to appear in their lives are unlikely to secure access to her sexual opportunity if and when she does make an entrance — and even less likely to retain that access even if they are somehow able to secure it.

The potentially uncomfortable implication of all this is that in order for men to secure relationships with the women they *really* want, they need to practice seducing and dating the women they *don't*. Learning to seduce from a book is like learning to swim on dry land: understanding the theory will only take you so far. And no one can truly say they know how to swim if they've never been in the water. Women might (understandably) rankle at this conclusion, as it brings them into conscious contact with a suspicion that lurks at the heart of any given sexual encounter (i.e., "I'm being used"). However, until women begin to prefer inexperienced men over experienced men, timid men over confident men, and incompetent men over capable men, this cannot be helped. It is not possible to become experienced, confident, and capable without successful practice. Despite any protestations to the contrary, women functionally create men's need to practice with their sexual selection criteria. This understanding also provides a practical explanation for the sexual double standard to complement the economic rationale discussed in chapter 3.

Men can develop their abilities with women in two ways: sequentially and simultaneously. When men practice *sequentially*, they learn the skills associated with acquisition: approach, emotional engagement, fearless seduction, and sexual confidence. This is "game," broadly defined. Such men typically waste no time in escalating the interaction toward a sexual encounter and are often just as quick to terminate the relationship once the opportunity has been consummated. On the other hand, when men practice *simultaneously*, they learn the skills associated with retention: pacing, role complementarity, experience management, and the maintenance of attraction. This is "frame," broadly defined. The two approaches are not mutually exclusive: men can pursue some women sequentially and other women simultaneously.

Moral or ethical considerations notwithstanding, these approaches are force multipliers of men's effectiveness in the sexual marketplace. A man who simultaneously dates five women a year can cultivate 50 years of relationship experience (with potentially 50 different women) in the span of a decade. And while simultaneously dating five women for a year might not generate precisely the same experience as sequentially dating five women for a year, it is mostly the same — and the compression of greater quantity and diversity of experience into the same time period may more than offset any presumptive liabilities.

The point is that men who pursue more short-term relationships with more women sequentially or more long-term relationships with more women simultaneously dramatically accelerate the acquisition of skills essential to the acquisition and retention of women. This affords such men a sizable advantage relative to their intrasexual competition. Most men eventually face the bitter truth that being "good" does not secure them the relationships or sexual opportunities they desire. This is because women do not go around rewarding goodness with relationships or sexual opportunities. For better or worse, both are awarded *to the men who can get them* — independent of what virtues they may (or may not) possess.

The accumulation of relationships or sexual opportunity as the means of securing even more desirable relationships and sexual opportunities is an essential strategy for men (and not necessarily for women) for another important reason: *it increases men's optionality*. Women do not typically need to pursue active strategies to increase their optionality because they already enjoy passive optionality. Even a moderately attractive 18-year-old woman who does nothing to advertise her presence in the sexual marketplace will receive interest and attention not only from her 18-year-old male classmates but from her classmates' older brothers and fathers and grandfathers, as well. Men never stop desiring young women. And all women must contend with the awareness of this desire in men, one way or another.

The upshot is that most young women benefit from the reality that most men would be willing to enter into a sexual relationship with them — a benefit that most young women enjoy simply by *existing*. They do not need to actively generate optionality. By virtue of this optionality, young women accrue even more power to themselves, over and above the power they already enjoy as a consequence of a favorable desirability gap. Greater relative power enables these women to secure access to more desirable partners, negotiate more favorable terms for themselves, and protect themselves from the costs associated with breaking up. Indeed, a favorable power differential — created in no small part by an advantage in optionality — is one main reason women end relationships more often than men do.

For men, actively generating optionality is a practical necessity for successfully dealing with women across all three phases of a relationship: attraction, negotiation, and maintenance. This is because *it serves to neutralize the power advantage women passively enjoy in the sexual marketplace*. It is a form of deterrence in the sexual arms race. To stabilize a relationship, men must make an effort to actively cultivate optionality for themselves that is comparable to the passive optionality enjoyed by the women with whom they transact. Failure to do this means women retain their power advantage throughout the course of the relationship. This does not bode well for the long-term success of any given relationship, as such an arrangement runs counter to women's hypergamous tendencies.

Keep in mind that this does not necessarily mean that men must consummate their sexual opportunities in order to cultivate optionality (though many will, undoubtedly, consider that to be an irresistible perk). What it does mean is that a man must make an effort to remain sufficiently attractive to enough women for him to be able to effortlessly exercise that optionality if and when he sees fit — *even (or especially) if he is in a committed relationship*. And while women advertise their desirability (and, thus, increase their optionality) by being visibly attractive, men do the same by being visibly competent.

Visible competence is one reason women love a man in uniform, whether it's the dress whites of a Marine Corps officer or the Versace suit of a power broker or the ceremonial attire of a tribal headman. In conjunction with various decorations — like ribbons, brands, or ornaments — a uniform constantly communicates a man's role, status, and accomplishments. It is a culturally sanctioned way for men to broadcast their value without overtly boasting. Men have collectively dispensed with these signifiers to their overall detriment — especially considering that men's fashion today generally fails to transmit useful or reliable information about their social standing. Indeed, most men are wallpaper in the sense that their visual presentation does not allow them to functionally distinguish themselves as focus amid the field of undifferentiated men.

In any case, men today must find other ways to publicize their competence, and (like women) they can do this effectively using social media. By visibly demonstrating their excellence, men can attract (and retain) the interest of others, which will increase their optionality in the sexual marketplace — *irrespective of whether those attracted are men or women.* Obviously, if the demonstrated excellence is of interest to women, men can directly increase their optionality. However, even if the demonstrated excellence is only of interest to other men, men can still increase their optionality indirectly. This is because the praise, respect, and admiration of other men signal the recipient's high status among his intrasexual competition. And status *is* of interest to women, over and above their interest in the competency that created it.

Visible competence and the public demonstration of excellence cultivate *renown,* which is instrumental to men's success in the sexual marketplace for two reasons. In the first place, a man who differentiates himself from other men is easier to "see," which dramatically increases the likelihood that he will be targeted by women's "hunting" attempts. Women will go out of their way to put themselves in his ambit and will give subtle (or not so subtle) signals that they would be positively disposed to his sexual advances. A man increases his optionality when he is the "target" of many women.

And in the second place, a man who has achieved some measure of fame casts a wide "net," which significantly increases the likelihood that he will succeed in catching *something*. This is a dating approach I call *fishing*, as the strategy is to cultivate a superabundance of options from which the most attractive option (or options) can be selected. Renown increases the surface area of a man's "net," allowing him to generate greater optionality for himself without taking direct action.

All other things being equal, men achieve more success in the sexual marketplace by fishing, and women achieve more success by hunting. This is because any given woman is far more likely to reject (than accept) any given man's sexual advances. So if the success rate of any one attempt is low, men can only even the odds *by concentrating less of their effort on more attempts*. This increases the probability of the desired outcome in aggregate. Men succeed by actively accumulating optionality, and they do this most effectively by cultivating renown through visible competence.

On the other hand, any given man is far more likely to accept (than reject) any given woman's sexual advances. If the success rate of any one attempt is high, women exploit their advantage *by concentrating more of their effort on fewer attempts*. This increases the probability of the desired outcome in particular. Women succeed by passively leveraging optionality, and they do this most effectively by offering their targets privileges enjoyed by no other men.

In this chapter, I examined how the asymmetrical outset of the game of mating and dating — in conjunction with the rules currently in force in the contemporary sexual marketplace — gives rise to different optimal strategies for men and women. I argued that women are most able to secure long-term relationships with high-value men when they are younger, and I encouraged them to strategically gatekeep their sexual opportunity in order to "hook" the men they have targeted for commitment. Conversely, I explained why men are most able to secure all kinds of relationships with more desirable women when they are older, and I motivated them to increase their optionality by cultivating wealth, status, and prestige. As the game continues to evolve, so, too, will the strategies associated with the highest likelihood of success.

In the next (and final) chapter, I'll turn my attention to the current state of the sexual marketplace, investigate the forces behind the ongoing relationship crisis, and make a few predictions about the future of mating and dating.

If you'd like to further explore the topics presented in this chapter, please scan the QR code to access a curated playlist on the PsycHacks channel on YouTube.

CHAPTER 12

PEOPLE DON'T REALLY WANT RELATIONSHIPS

After reading through an entire book dedicated to discussing why people enter into relationships and under what conditions, this chapter title may come as a shock. However, to the extent that you're surprised by this claim, you haven't been paying attention. I said as much in the first pages when I defined relationships as the media in which value is transacted. People rarely form even temporary relationships out of the simple joy of connecting with others — and when they do, they are still transacting the value of connection (which, by definition, requires a relationship). Where there is no transacted value, a relationship neither exists nor can it exist.

The only rational conclusion from all this is that what people really want is *value* — not relationships, *per se*. For many people, entering into relationships constitutes their best possible chance of securing that value. As previously discussed, it is a common strategy for dealing with the problem of other people. However, it is only one such strategy. If people can secure the same good more cheaply, more easily, and more safely in other ways, then they will predictably (and understandably) do so.

Suggesting that this isn't true (or only conditionally true) is not only illogical, it runs counter to both the evidence of our senses and what we know about human beings. Arguing that people "should" enter into relationships that require greater expense, difficulty, and risk because it is virtuous to do so — or conducive to self-development, or essential to social cohesion, or somehow necessary for a given moral or ethical framework — is akin to arguing that people "should" undergo hard, physical exercise for the same reasons. Irrespective of whether the argument is true, it doesn't work, which is why the Western world has an obesity epidemic. Continuing to insist on some religious or philosophical imperative to behave in certain ways is not only likely to alienate those who (in the arguer's mind) would benefit most from the message but is tantamount to refusing to understand why people make the decisions they do, as well. It is posturing for the converted.

For instance, the obesity epidemic is occurring (at least in part) because — until very recently — it was more expensive, difficult, and risky for most people to pursue leisure than productive labor (which typically involved hard, physical exercise). Lazing about when there were crops to tend was expensive because allowing key moments to lapse would decrease overall yield. It was difficult because living closer to subsistence was marked by hardships and deprivations. And it was risky because people may have been purchasing today's comfort at the cost of tomorrow's starvation. By the same token — until very recently — it was more expensive, difficult, and risky to consume processed foodstuffs than organic, whole foods. Processing foods through industrial processes when farm-grown food was readily available was expensive because startup and maintenance costs were much higher. It was difficult because it required knowledge and skills that were non-intuitive and not easily transmissible through folk wisdom. And it was risky because people were functionally trying to earn money to procure food (instead of merely procuring food directly).

My point is that — throughout most of human history — people have undertaken hard, physical labor not because they were the salt of the earth, not because they believed doing so conferred virtue or fostered self-development, not because it was good for society, and certainly not because labor was more expensive, difficult, or risky than any other alternatives. They did this because — throughout most of human history — hard, physical labor represented most people's *best possible chance of improving the conditions of their lives and staving off misery*. If they could do these things more cheaply, more easily, and more safely using means other than hard, physical labor, they absolutely would have done so.

My conviction here derives from the fact that human beings — as biopsychosocial organisms — have not significantly changed in recent history. How people make decisions today — through the covert calculus of value discussed in chapter 1 — is how people made decisions 100 (or 100 thousand) years ago. The numbers may differ, but the math remains the same. This is because the valuation process is as hardwired into our neurology as the principles of logic (which do not vary across culture or time).

So what we are collectively dealing with today are the predictable social consequences of making productive labor and organic food more expensive, difficult, and risky than leisure and processed foodstuffs. The current generation is not especially weak or stupid or vulnerable — at least, it's not any weaker or stupider or more vulnerable than any other. We're dealing with these problems not due to a moral lapse, a failure of character, or a culture of narcissism (though there's plenty of that to go around) but *because our technologies have sufficiently evolved to significantly alter the perception of value in a critical mass of people.*

Advancing moral arguments will do little to influence this critical mass. On the other hand, if physical labor and organic food were suddenly and sustainably to become cheaper, easier, and safer than leisure and processed foodstuffs, then the obesity epidemic would resolve itself fairly quickly and without any moralizing. That said, the problem (or the threat of the problem) will never disappear entirely because a preference for fats, salts, and sugars is so deeply encoded in our biological substrate as a consequence of our nutrient-poor evolution that it cannot possibly be controlled for all people at all times. We can alter the availability — or desirability — of certain options *only to a point*. Anything past that point generally requires more expense than is justified by the return on investment.

For better or worse, comfort and convenience are not going anywhere anytime soon. So what's to be done? Campaigns of shame generally don't work in diverse, pluralistic societies because it's difficult to implement the social penalties that actually make shame effective in a consistent and unified manner. Furthermore, expecting people to "voluntarily" select the more expensive, difficult, and risky option (when cheap, easy, and safe alternatives are known to exist and have already been integrated into society) would either require an increasingly tyrannical system of control to keep certain technologies out of the hands of the general public (and a tireless propaganda machine to justify this control) or a war or catastrophe of such unimaginable scale that the recalibration of value accurately reflected the new reality. Suffice it to say: neither of these possibilities is particularly attractive, and the costs and risks associated with either likely far outweigh the costs and risks of the status quo. Consequently, it may be best to accept that certain features of society are likely to remain with us for the foreseeable future, leverage change interventions where they are most likely to be effective, and seek out new advantages and opportunities afforded by the current state of affairs.

All this has a clear analog to the sexual marketplace. As difficult as it may be to believe, people have entered into relationships for largely the same reasons they have historically undergone hard, physical labor: both have represented *the best available solution to certain critical problems of living for the majority of people*. And just as we could predict a decrease in physical labor as this solution became increasingly expensive, unsafe, and risky relative to other available options, we can predict a decrease in all kinds of relationships for the same reason. Or rather, we *could* predict it if we needed to. In reality, the relationship decline foretold by these conditions is already upon us.

AN UNINTENDED CONSEQUENCE

People are not entering into relationships as often as they used to. The number of Americans who report not having a single close friend has quadrupled over the past 20 years.[48] In the United States, marriage rates are half of what they were in 1970 and are currently the lowest they have ever been in history.[49] People around the world are also decoupling more frequently, as reflected in a doubling of the global divorce rate across the same time period.[50] Women today have half as many children as they did just 75 years ago, and half of the population of the world currently lives in countries that exist below self-replacement rates.[51] Much of the "civilized" world is skirting on the fringes of population collapse, as social structures that have been preserved for centuries are disintegrating in real time. How did this happen?

The confluence of variables that has given rise to this situation is extremely complex. No explanation can hope to include every contributing factor. That said, I believe two specific technological changes are principally responsible for the contemporary decline in relationships, and I will briefly discuss each in turn.

48 The "loneliness epidemic" has also disproportionately affected men for several reasons. Source: https://www.americansurveycenter.org/research/the-state-of-american-friendship-change-challenges-and-loss/

49 As we'll see, this is largely due to the fact that American women are marrying later (if at all). In countries where women's average age at first marriage has not significantly increased (like Bangladesh), marriage rates are even higher today. Source: https://ourworldindata.org/marriages-and-divorces

50 The United States continues to have a divorce rate that is around *50% higher* than its closest rival for this dubious honor: South Korea. Source: *ibid.*

51 A rate of 2.1 births per woman is necessary to replace the population. Source: https://ifstudies.org/blog/half-the-worlds-population-is-reaching-below-replacement-fertility

Note that the emphasis here is on technological changes — not ideological ones. For instance, the ideology of feminism is often maligned as the force behind the destabilization of the contemporary sexual marketplace. However, this is implausible since feminism existed as a social movement for over 100 years before the onset of the precipitous decline in relationships. This is not to say that feminism (especially fourth-wave feminism) is not contributing to the issues we are currently facing (it is) but to assert that it is not the principal cause of this state of affairs.

The uncomfortable reality is that certain ideologies are only feasible with sufficiently advanced technologies. Insisting that any ideology is realizable given any set of material conditions is to abide in an idealism divorced from reality. For instance, capitalism could only be fully realized with the machinery of the industrial revolution. Even hunter-gatherer societies exploit the productivity advantage inherent in the division of labor and store up goods in excess of their needs to exchange with other tribes. The fundamental tenets of capitalism are quite old: they just couldn't be realized at scale without the enabling technology.

By the same token, the modern feminist movement can be traced back to the 18th century — and we certainly haven't been flirting with population collapse for the past 250 years. This is because many tenets of feminism remained partially (or entirely) unrealizable until a certain technology was developed, namely: *cheap, effective birth control*. Birth control is what makes feminism possible in the practical sense. Without birth control, feminism would have remained a relatively inconsequential social philosophy, and women would not enjoy many of the freedoms they do today.

For instance, it's not wrong to assert that — without their own economic power — women could never truly become a social and political force that men would need to take seriously. However, any truth in this statement was rendered functionally irrelevant when women were pregnant for the better part of their adulthoods and saddled with childcare responsibilities that only they could discharge. The advent of birth control is what allowed a critical mass of women to step out of the domestic sphere, to develop social identities independent of their reproductive capabilities, and to secure an unprecedented amount of freedom and autonomy for themselves. It was approved by the Food and Drug Administration in 1960, immediately preceding the rapid changes in relationships just described.

Personally, I don't have a problem with any of this. To be honest, it would be morally precarious to argue in favor of less freedom and self-determination for any particular demographic of human beings. These goods are not the issue. The issue is precisely the slowly dawning realization that these goods are inseparable from certain consequences for the sexual marketplace — consequences that reverberate all the way to the core of civilization. They are two sides of the same coin: try as you like, you cannot have one without the other.

Several consequences of the proliferation of birth control are of particular note to us here. The first is that it has *irrevocably reversed the order of sex and commitment in the courtship process*. Throughout most of recorded history, a man was expected to offer a woman commitment in order to access her sexual opportunity. And though it may have masqueraded as such, this requirement was not enforced due to a concern for female "virtue" or a preoccupation with religious morality or a fondness for the institution of marriage — all of which continue to exist (at least to some extent) today. It was enforced because it would have been extremely difficult for a single mother and offspring to survive without the resources of a provisioning man (or a social program that served that function). The stakes associated with pregnancy outside the context of a committed relationship were significantly higher for women when they could neither earn their own money nor rely on social welfare for support. As a result, women were (understandably) much less likely to consent to sex prior to commitment, and this reticence was protected by a powerful social stigma that was grounded less in the righteous morality of the majority and more in the awareness that destitute women and children would be *their* problem if the man in question could not be persuaded to commit.

All this changed with the widespread use of birth control, which functionally separated sex from reproduction. By reducing the likelihood of pregnancy to a negligible possibility, the rational necessity for commitment prior to sex was eliminated. What's more, given the fact that women can (and do) earn their own money, that fathers are legally obligated to provide financial support to their children's mothers (even if they never explicitly consented to such an arrangement), and that heavily funded social welfare programs exist to subsidize single mothers, the stakes associated with pregnancy outside the context of a committed relationship are now significantly lower for women.

Finally, although sex generally involves the active participation of two consenting adults, women have been given the unilateral power to choose whether they become mothers — irrespective of the desires or preferences of the men involved. And since women have been empowered with the formal right to choose whether they become mothers, it should come as little surprise that men have increasingly decided they have the informal right to choose whether they become fathers — in the sense of being an active co-parent in the lives of their children. Indeed, who could possibly have predicted that giving women a cheap and effective way to reduce the likelihood of pregnancy would have resulted in an enormous increase in the number of single mothers?[52]

In the context of sexual relationships, male commitment has been downgraded from a practical necessity to a personal preference, and the rational basis for securing commitment prior to sex has been completely eroded with birth control. In the absence of a necessity for male commitment, all the moral exhortations in the world to return to the previous arrangement — and why it would be "good" for children and parents and society to do so — will not be sufficient in light of these economic realities. Again, it's not that such arguments aren't true. It's that they don't work. Such arguments will only hold sway in certain corners of society among the already converted.

Since men are the gatekeepers of commitment, and the rates of committed relationships have dropped precipitously over the past 60 years, the logical deduction is that men's covert calculus associated with the value of commitment

52 However, this is exactly what has occurred in the US across all racial demographics. For example, whereas unwed White women accounted for only 2% of all those who gave birth in 1960, they constitute nearly 30% of all those who give birth in that demographic today. In Black and American Indian populations, that figure is as high as 70%. Source: https://reasonwithoutrestraint.com/trends-in-marriage-and-fertility-by-race-in-the-united-states/

must have shifted dramatically over that period. And this is precisely what has happened. Let's be honest: a lifetime of protection and provision is an *extremely high price to pay for sex* — especially considering the lack of an enforceable guarantee that sex will be particularly forthcoming *after* commitment. Many of the relationships we are prone to romanticize from our grandparents' generation were actually hastily formed unions between horny teenagers who would have gotten divorced decades ago had the option been available to them. The price that men have historically paid for sex has been incredibly high. However, the male sex drive is so deep and powerful and irrefutable that men have been willing to do incredible things to satisfy it — provided no reasonable alternatives were open to them with a decent likelihood of success.

Birth control significantly decreased the costs associated with sex for both men and women in gender-specific ways. On the one hand, it greatly reduced the likelihood that a woman would incur the expenses associated with single motherhood (against her will). And on the other hand, it materially reduced the possibility that a man would misinvest his resources in an unrewarding partnership by eliminating the rational necessity for doing so prior to the sexual encounter. By functionally eliminating each gender's two biggest fears in one fell swoop, birth control made sex safe.

It also made sex cheap. From commanding a market rate of a lifetime of commitment, protection, and provision (a valuation that, in retrospect, might now seem "too good to last"), the price of sex has fallen to a couple of drinks at the local bar. This is unlikely to change any time soon. Once a critical mass of women was willing to have sex prior to commitment, the remainder were functionally forced to do so as well in order to stay competitive. This is because no one will pay more than they need to for a comparable good — and a woman who continued to insist on commitment up front (without offering a compensatory good for the additional expense) would be pricing herself out of the sexual marketplace.

The decimation of sex's market value has predictably led to a significant decrease in the number of relationships because the price of sex is so low that many people are deciding that transacting for it *isn't worth the effort*. Much like a homeowner in an unfavorable economy, many women would rather forgo a transaction than move forward at a perceived loss: receiving fewer resources than they would like in exchange for their sexual opportunity. While emotionally understandable, this strategy is often counterproductive, given the general effect of time on women's sexual marketplace values. Most women will never enjoy a higher valuation than they do today — and so incur a greater loss out of their unwillingness to suffer a smaller one.

By the same token, an increasing number of men would *also* rather forgo a transaction than move forward at a perceived loss: paying more resources than they would like in exchange for a given sexual opportunity. Since sex has been rendered so cheap, women would have to provide men with another desirable good of comparable value to offset the cost of men's commitment — which, due to certain reproductive realities, will always be more expensive than women's.[53]

53 Assuming she carries the child to term, a pregnant woman cannot exploit any other reproductive opportunities for the better part of a year — even if she wanted to. As a consequence, she assumes *no*

Unfortunately, many of the desirable goods that men of previous generations could reasonably expect from women in committed relationships — childcare, cooking, cleaning, femininity, pleasant agreeableness — have been recast by contemporary feminism as beneath the dignity of modern women to perform.

The upshot is that the cheapening of sex has led to a widening divide between men and women in the valuation of sexual relationships. Each side believes the other wants more for less — *and both are right*. This is because women are anchoring their valuation to historical precedents. From their perspective, modern men seem like unscrupulous cads who have no idea how to treat a lady. They believe modern men won't give them anything of value in exchange for their monopolized sexual commodity (i.e., sex). On the other hand, men are anchoring their valuation to current market conditions. From their perspective, modern women seem like greedy lunatics who refuse to read the writing on the wall. Men believe modern women won't give them anything of value in exchange for *their* monopolized sexual commodity (i.e., commitment). As the valuation gap widens, fewer relationships are transacted.

---

opportunity cost by committing to the man who impregnated her. From a reproductive standpoint, she loses little — and potentially gains a lot — by doing so. On the other hand, a man who impregnates a woman could potentially exploit hundreds of other reproductive opportunities during that same year. As a result, he assumes *an opportunity cost commensurate with his optionality* by committing to the women he impregnated. From a reproductive standpoint, he gains little — and potentially loses a lot — by doing so, especially in a social environment in which his resources are not necessary for the child's survival. Since these biological realities cannot be changed, a man's commitment will always be more expensive than a woman's (though this inequality can be mitigated under certain social conditions).

It probably wouldn't be overstating the fact to argue that nearly all of women's social progress over the past 60 years has been made possible by the proliferation of birth control. Among other things, this has allowed women to postpone marriage and motherhood until later in their reproductive windows and to establish themselves in the major spheres of social life. And women certainly have done well for themselves. Girls and young women are now significantly more likely than boys and young men to graduate from high school and college.[54] Single women are 40% more likely to own a home than are single men.[55] And perhaps for the first time in history, childless women under 30 are outearning men in the same demographic in many urban centers.[56] In many respects, the average young woman is now more successful than the average young man.

Unfortunately, these achievements are inseparable from certain consequences for the sexual marketplace. This is because men's and women's preferences for mates do not change as quickly or easily as the cultural zeitgeist. Three generations is no time at all relative to our evolutionary past, and our attraction remains heavily informed by selection pressures that have exerted their influence over millennia.

---

54 In fact, the undergraduate education gap is larger today than it was in 1970: it just now favors women. Source: https://www.brookings.edu/articles/boys-left-behind-education-gender-gaps-across-the-us/

55 Though this could be due, in part, to the fact that women tend to live longer than men. At least some of these single female homeowners may be widows who were bequeathed the property by their late husbands. Source: https://www.pewresearch.org/short-reads/2023/06/12/single-women-own-more-homes-than-single-men-in-the-us-but-that-edge-is-narrowing/

56 The new pay gap favoring women isn't significant, but neither was the controlled pay gap favoring men that we've heard about for decades. Source: https://www.pewresearch.org/short-reads/2022/03/28/young-women-are-out-earning-young-men-in-several-u-s-cities/

Women's collective success has made mating and dating more difficult and expensive — for both men and women.

In the first place, women's social success *has significantly reduced the pool of men that women would even consider as candidates for mating*. Despite their social advantages, women have not surrendered their hypergamous instincts: they *still* desire men who can elevate their lifestyles. A little girl dreams that one day she will meet a handsome prince; no woman fantasizes that one day she will financially support a man. In fact, many women don't see the point of entering into a relationship that isn't likely to significantly improve the quality of their lives — let alone one that would be a drain on their resources. Of course, the more success women achieve, the harder it becomes for them to find more successful men. That's bad for women because fewer eligible men significantly increases the intrasexual competition for a dwindling pool of potential mates. And it's also bad for men because many of them are simply being disqualified from the sexual marketplace. In a time when many women have ships, it's not enough for a man to have a boat.

One unintended consequence of this situation is that *an increasingly greater share of the sexual opportunity is being concentrated among an increasingly smaller number of men*. The most successful men who reside at the top of their status hierarchies are currently enjoying an unprecedented amount of sexual opportunity from an extraordinary number of women. And given their access and optionality, these highly desirable men are extremely unlikely to exchange their privileged positions for a monogamous relationship with any one woman. After all — whether or not they are aware of it — cultivating sexual optionality was the primary motivation behind these men's bids for power and status. After years of effort, why would they surrender the prize they worked so hard to achieve? The result is that women are increasingly disqualifying more men from consideration, which, in turn, increases the likelihood that the men who *do* qualify will disqualify *them* since the optionality these men enjoy drives up the price of their exclusive commitment. This results in fewer relationships all around.

As women are increasingly empowered to pursue their sexual strategies, societies will become increasingly polygamous: a greater share of all the sexual opportunity will be concentrated among a smaller subset of men. Polygamy is the natural end state of hypergamy. The reason why most societies are not (overtly) polygamous is because this end state has been "unnaturally" prevented by male-dominated, patriarchal social structures. This is because — from a utilitarian perspective — *monogamy benefits men.*

When women are prevented from concentrating their sexual opportunity among the highest-status men — which is what they tend to do when left to their own devices — a greater proportion of the male population is afforded opportunities for mating and dating. And in societies in which women both outnumber and outlive men, enforcing a "one woman per man" rule functionally ensures that women must mate *down,* affording more men with better sexual opportunities than they would otherwise be able to secure for themselves. Under strict monogamy, even the most unattractive men have wives, while many decent women go unmarried. Of course, monogamy is good for men *in general* — it typically does not benefit the men at the top of their hierarchies, who incur opportunity costs under monogamy that do not affect their lower-status peers. That said, successful men tend to find ways to work around the dictates of monogamy anyway (and usually with the enthusiastic participation of the women involved).

In any case, we can consider the institution of monogamy to be a kind of sexual socialism in which reproductive resources are redistributed across the masses. Though this comes at a cost to certain segments of the population, it improves the stability of society in general by (among other things) increasing the likelihood that enough children are born to replace the previous generation. However, just like political socialism, the "enforced equality" of sexual socialism can only be maintained through formal and informal systems of coercion and control. And with the collapse of traditional power structures, the evident rise in polygamy can hardly be surprising.

On the other hand, women's social success has also significantly reduced the pool of women that men would consider as candidates for mating. This is because men have not surrendered their reproductive instincts, either: they *still* desire women who are young and fertile. However, young and fertile women — empowered by an ideology made realizable by birth control — are increasingly uninterested in marriage and children. As previously discussed, a growing proportion of women now devote their 20s — the decade in which they are most likely to secure a long-term commitment from a high-value man — to hedonic pursuits (e.g., travel and short-term sexual relationships) or career development (e.g., higher education and full-time employment). Many of these decisions have significant downstream consequences.

Women continue to desire resources and emotionally compelling lifestyles. However, in the modern age, it is easier for a greater share of women to directly secure these goods *themselves* than to indirectly secure them *through men* — especially considering that unmarried men no longer significantly outearn unmarried women. When reproductive realities motivate many of these successful women to reevaluate their stance on children in their 30s, they often discover that finding a willing, satisfactory partner is more difficult than expected. These women occupy a disadvantaged position in the sexual marketplace relative to men, who — to the extent they are desired by women — reasonably expect to be sufficiently compensated for surrendering their optionality with something of comparable value to them: *an attractive reproductive opportunity*.

Contrary to popular belief, men can (and do) forgo their sexual optionality but only under the condition that the woman to whom each commits *represents a more attractive reproductive opportunity than any of his other non-exclusive options*. This is entirely rational: no man will freely choose to surrender more and more attractive options in favor of a single less attractive option. And when this *does* occur, it is generally the result of social coercion or emotional manipulation.

Though it should go without saying, here it is: *A 38-year-old woman is not an attractive reproductive opportunity to most men*. In fact, she is an extremely costly opportunity for several reasons. Not only are "geriatric" pregnancies associated with an elevated risk of a host of complications for both mother and child,[57] but they are more likely to require expensive fertility

57 This is often due to the increased likelihood of chromosomal abnormalities in "older" eggs. Source: https://my.clevelandclinic.org/

treatments to succeed. What's more, a 38-year-old woman has a significantly smaller reproductive window than, say, a 22-year-old woman. However, although the older woman can conceive fewer children, she still generally demands as much (if not more) in exchange for her reproductive opportunity *as the younger woman does,* namely: exclusive commitment over a lifetime (at a more fully extrapolated lifestyle). As a consequence, men who marry older women typically pay more for less. This covert calculus renders women increasingly more unattractive to men as they age, over and above the decline in their physical attractiveness as a function of time.

Contrary to popular belief, men are not intimidated by successful women. This is a rationalization employed by such women to emotionally cope with their encountered difficulties in the sexual marketplace. On the other hand, it might be true that men are not attracted to successful women. This is not because men find successful women unattractive *per se* but because successful women are older women, given success takes time to achieve. Men find — and will continue to find — the prospect of marrying a woman near the end of her reproductive window about as attractive as women find — and will continue to find — the prospect of marrying a man she will have to financially support. And this wouldn't be true *unless men exchanged resources for sexual opportunity and women exchanged sexual opportunity for resources.* Moral outrage or exhortations to the contrary will do nothing to change this.

As disturbing as the recent relationship trends might be, we will likely need to contend with them for the foreseeable future. This is because disrupting the decline in relationships

---

health/diseases/22438-advanced-maternal-age

would practically require the prohibition of birth control — which, in turn, would undermine all of women's social advances of the previous 60 years. Not only would supporting such a solution be tantamount to social suicide in today's political environment, but the idea would also be functionally impossible to implement in reality. The genie cannot go back into the bottle. At this point, a return to a male-dominated, patriarchal society capable of implementing such a solution would likely require such a horrendous catastrophe — something on the scale of global nuclear conflict or protracted civil war, in which most of the population is forced back into the game of survival, necessitating a return to traditional gender roles — that no sane person could prefer the cure to the disease. For better or worse, going back is not an option: we can only move forward and adapt to circumstances as they evolve.

ALMOST REAL LIFE

The promulgation of birth control has irrevocably altered the conditions of the sexual marketplace. By complex economic pathways, this technology has significantly altered the valuation of many components of the courtship process and has directly contributed to substantial reductions in the rates of committed relationships at the population level. On the other hand, as might be expected, birth control facilitated the practice (and destigmatization) of casual sex by dramatically altering the risk profile of nonmarital sex for both men and women. Fewer people were getting married, but — given the large increases in both the rates of nonmarital sex and the numbers of lifetime sexual partners in the wake of the pill[58] — it was obvious that men and women remained very interested in each other.

However, over the past 10 years, we have witnessed a precipitous drop in even *this* sector of the sexual marketplace. Millennials and Gen Zers are not only getting married less often than their parents, but they're having less casual sex as well. For instance, nearly one in three American men under 30 report that they have not had any sex in the previous 12 months, a proportion that has tripled in just the past 10 years.[59] Apparently, young men and women are growing increasingly disinterested in all forms of sexual relationships, as many succumb to frustration, confusion, and despair. What is behind these recent changes?

The technology that is responsible for this tidal shift in the sexual marketplace is *Web 2.0*: the stage of internet development characterized by person-to-person (p2p) connectivity, user-generated content, and social media. Remember: relationships are the media in which value is transacted. However, sexual relationships represent just one potential solution for securing that value. If people already possessed the value in question, or if they could obtain the value more cheaply, more easily, and more safely using other solutions, then we should reasonably expect a growing proportion of the population to abandon sexual relationships

58 These rates and numbers increased for both men and women. Source: Twenge, J. M., Sherman, R. A., & Wells, B. E. (2015). Changes in American adults' sexual behavior and attitudes, 1972-2012. *Archives of Sexual Behavior, 44*, 2273-2285.

59 The proportion of women who have been celibate over the past year has also increased significantly over the same period: from 10% to 18%. However, this still leaves five sexually active women for every four sexually active men in this age cohort. Source: https://gssdataexplorer.norc.org

in favor of these solutions. Recent developments in web-based technologies collectively constitute these solutions.

Think of it like this: No one really wants a job. People want a job because of what a job can give them: money. A job represents one potential solution to the problem of securing money. However, if people already had enough money, or if they suddenly could get money more cheaply, more easily, and more safely by other means, then they probably wouldn't go looking for a job. Of course, for most people, a job is the only way they know to get money. So they go looking for a job and look askance at anyone who suggests that a job might not be either strictly necessary or the best way of getting money. They create a virtue out of a perceived necessity, which, while not technically true, might be psychologically adaptive. In any case, it would be unreasonable to maintain that all people who no longer needed money would continue to work, which would result in fewer people seeking employment among this demographic.

This is comparable to the current state of the sexual marketplace. For potentially the first time in human history, men and women *don't really need each other*. I don't mean this at the population level: civilization would fall apart without a lot of men, and humanity would go extinct without a lot of women. Men need women *around*, and women need men *around*. However, modern man doesn't need *a* woman, and modern woman doesn't need *a* man. At least, not in the way that men and women needed each other even a few generations ago.

Throughout most of recorded history, men and women came together out of *necessity*, and that necessity was rooted in survival. Life was extremely difficult, and most people who have ever lived have done so at a subsistence level. Few can survive alone under such conditions. This is why poor folks form communities of assistance and strong interpersonal bonds. If you have little, you need other people; if you have a lot, you need other people less. This (at least partly) explains the clear inverse relationship between fertility rates and *per capita* GDP observed globally over the previous 70 years.[60]

Since men and women no longer have to come together because they need to, we're increasingly seeing that men and women only come together because they want to. And where there is neither the need nor the want, there is *nothing*. Of course, men and women continue to experience necessity and desire. However, modern technologies have disrupted how people go about satisfying both within the sexual marketplace, which has led to observed declines in all forms of intersexual relationships.

A disclosure from one of my recent consults exemplifies this issue. According to my client, when his wife filed for divorce, she told him that she could get everything she needed from a man "from Taskrabbit and Tinder." Though some might consider such a statement callous or cruel, it is difficult to completely disregard the possibility that it reflects an uncomfortable economic reality. Apparently, this woman believed it would be easier and less expensive to secure her needs on the open market than in a committed relationship. What's more, she could pay for these services (and more) using money earned by her ex-husband and awarded to her as alimony in the divorce proceedings. To the extent this

60 South Korea currently holds the title of the nation with the lowest fertility rate (0.91). Source: https://ourworldindata.org/grapher/children-per-woman-fertility-rate-vs-level-of-prosperity

woman saw marriage as a solution to certain problems of living (which marriage is and has always been), it would have been irrational for her to remain in the relationship, given the incentives under which she was operating and the alternatives available to her. This is not a particularly uncommon story. Existing relationships are threatened when more convenient and affordable solutions to personally relevant needs become available, and new relationships are less likely to form under such conditions.

However, these solutions have disrupted desire as much as necessity. Until very recently, people were limited in their search for sexual partners to those to whom they had direct access in their immediate vicinity. This created a natural restriction on individuals' optionality and set organic limits on intrasexual competition — both of which have been completely dismantled by dating apps and social media. Actors in the sexual marketplace now enjoy direct access to almost *every other single (and not-so-single) person in the entire world*. Whereas it may previously have been enough to secure a desirable reproductive opportunity by being a comparatively big fish in a relatively small pond, men and women now find themselves swimming in one gigantic ocean. Every man must now compete with every other man on the planet for the girl next door; every woman must now compete with every other woman in the world for their community's most eligible bachelor. Optionality that previously was only available to emperors or movie starlets as recently as 10 years ago is now taken for granted by ordinary men and women.

As might be expected, people were psychologically unprepared for the consequences of these changes. While limited optionality can certainly be problematic, too much optionality comes with challenges of its own, most notably: the greater the optionality, the greater the opportunity cost associated with *foreclosure* (the technical term for *premature commitment*). This significantly increases the stakes of any given decision, which drives down the frequency of committing to any one option. Since we all gamble with limited resources, raising the minimum bet would predictably lower the number of hands we are willing to play.

These technologies ensnare people with *the illusion of infinite optionality*. And this illusion has made desire even more important in the modern game of mating and dating than the elimination of necessity (by itself) ever could. If people don't need someone, and very desirable partners exist somewhere in that virtual marketplace of infinite optionality, then people have little incentive to settle for anything less than a *very desirable partner*. In fact, the costs associated with settling become increasingly prohibitive as optionality increases. Unfortunately, this predictably leads to a greater and greater share of overall interest being concentrated in a smaller and smaller number of highly desirable individuals, which results in far more people not getting what they want at the population level.

Since more and more people believe they don't need to settle for less, fewer people are entering into relationships — even for a night. Like it or not, forming a relationship with a real human being requires some degree of settling. No one can get everything he or she wants from a given relationship, but where to draw the line is always an individual choice. That said, those who prefer the potential inherent in infinite optionality to the limitations of an actual relationship often end up with nothing. Because that's what potential essentially is: *nothing*. It might become something in the future, but then again, it might not. And until it becomes something, it remains nothing.

The virtual optionality of the sexual marketplace makes people believe that they are suffering an enormous loss by trading the infinite potential for any given actual: by trading everything for just one thing. In reality, however, people achieve an enormous gain by giving up the infinite potential for a given actual: by giving up nothing for something. However, it will likely take time for our collective understanding to catch up with our technological progress.

While the illusion of infinite optionality is subject to deluding both sexes equally, particular web-based domains ensnare men and women at highly differential rates. It's easy to appreciate why this might be the case. While people want all kinds of things from relationships, in the sexual marketplace, men essentially trade resources for sexual opportunity, and women essentially trade sexual opportunity for resources. This remains true despite all the social and political advances of recent history. If either sex could get what they wanted more cheaply, more easily, and more safely using methods other than sexual relationships, then we should expect the number of such relationships to decline — which is precisely what is happening.

Two major culprits are behind this decline: *pornography* and *social media*. While obviously not always the case, it's generally men who have problems with pornography, and it's generally women who have problems with social media. Why might this be true?

If it's true that men attempt to exchange resources for sexual opportunity in the sexual marketplace, and if men could secure that opportunity more cheaply, more easily, and more safely without transacting with actual women, then we should expect men to increasingly abandon the sexual marketplace. Pornography provides this alternative to men by offering them *free, immediate, and dependable sexual opportunity*. What's more, advances in artificial intelligence, virtual reality, and humanoid robotics will only make this alternative more compelling to men in the foreseeable future.

Rather than transact his bundle of resources for the sexual opportunity of one actual woman, with pornography and simulated sexual experiences, a man can now transact his resources for the opportunity of an unlimited number of virtual women. Such a prospect will prove differentially attractive to men, given that it aligns with their biological incentive to secure as many non-terrible reproductive opportunities as possible. Furthermore, not only can men typically secure any given sexual opportunity from pornography far more cheaply than they would be able to do so from an actual woman (who generally requires at least some degree of investment prior to consummation), but — given the abundance of rejection and frustration that generally comes from seeking out sexual opportunity from women — they can do this far more safely, as well. If securing sex from women is both costly and high-risk, then it's little wonder why so many men are moving toward the cheap and low-risk sexual opportunities that virtual experiences represent. Moral arguments against pornography — or shame-based exhortations for men to "man up" — will do little to change the situation in light of these economic realities.

One could argue that pornography isn't really a sexual opportunity — just the *simulation* of one. I, personally, don't believe the two are comparable. However, the two are apparently comparable *enough* to entrap millions of men — and millions more are likely to follow suit as the simulation becomes increasingly indistinguishable from reality. In many respects, this situation is analogous to the perceived similarity between processed foodstuffs and whole food that is fueling the obesity epidemic: the two are apparently similar *enough* that millions of people can't tell the difference.

While pornography has been produced in many different cultures for thousands of years, only recent technological developments have made it possible to ensnare men at this scale by making it cheap, convenient, and safe. Finally, people generally only assume the risks and costs of hunting if they are *hungry* (or they understand that they are very likely to become so in the future). By providing men with an easy means of satisfying their sexual appetites without leaving the comfort of their homes, pornography has disincentivized them from entering the proving grounds of the sexual marketplace.

On the other hand, if it's true that women attempt to exchange sexual opportunity for resources in the sexual marketplace, and if women could secure those resources (like money, attention, validation, instrumental support, and emotional stimulation) more cheaply, more easily, and more safely without transacting with actual men, then we should also expect women to increasingly abandon the sexual marketplace. Social media provides this alternative to women by offering them *free, immediate, and dependable opportunities to acquire such resources*. And this alternative reaches its (logical) climax on platforms like OnlyFans, which enable individual women to market sexually explicit content directly to men on a global scale. This allows them to leverage their singular sexual opportunity an unlimited number of times through mechanical reproduction.

Rather than transact her sexual opportunity for the resources of one actual man, on platforms like OnlyFans, a woman can now transact her sexual opportunity for the resources of an unlimited number of men on the internet. At face value, this might be surprising, given that it seems to conflict with a woman's biological incentive to secure her single best reproductive opportunity. However, it's important to keep in mind that "single best" is context-dependent. For instance, it might be a woman's single best option to transact her sexual opportunity for a million dollars. That said, how she goes about transacting this opportunity will fundamentally depend on her available options. For potentially the first time in history, it may actually be easier for an ordinary woman to transact *one dollar from a million men than to transact a million dollars from a single man*. In this case, her "single best" option is the ability to transact at that price point: whether it is with one man or with many men has increasingly become anyone's guess in the contemporary sexual marketplace.

Such technologies also make the sexual marketplace significantly safer — a consideration that is much more salient to women than it is to men — for several reasons. In the first place, transacting in this way completely eliminates the risks of pregnancy — which are disproportionately borne by women — by completely eliminating the sexual encounter. Remember: in most relationships, women transact with their sexual opportunity only. As every man learns, buying a woman dinner and expressing (or feigning) interest in her life in no way guarantees that she will allow him access to her body. However, he is often willing to invest nevertheless because the *possibility* that she will allow him to do so remains. By doing away with even the possibility of an actual sexual encounter, women can now transact with men in the sexual marketplace without any reproductive risk for the first time in human history.

In the second place, utilizing technology to mediate the transaction significantly reduces certain social risks acutely felt by women. For instance, women seem to have a lower threshold for their disgust reactions than men do,[61] contributing to "the ick" phenomenon, which (at least partly) explains women's relatively higher standards for mate selection. However, by making physical contact with men unnecessary, these technologies allow women to transact with a greater proportion of the male population without feeling uncomfortable. Furthermore, since all the interactions occur online, women don't assume the social risks of associating with undesirable men, which could negatively affect her pSMV and potentially compromise her ability to secure more (and more attractive) resources elsewhere. That said, women run *considerable* risk to their social reputations if their activities on such platforms were to become widely known off-line (which is why certain contemporary social movements seek to destigmatize such behaviors as "empowering" to women). Consequently, many women still prefer to use less explicit platforms (like Instagram) to provide their actions with plausible deniability.

---

61 Apparently, women are more sensitive to sexual and pathogenic disgust than men are — but not to moral disgust. Source: Al-Shawaf, L., Lewis, D., & Buss, D. (2017). Sex differences in disgust: Why are women more easily disgusted than men? *Emotion Review, 10*(2), 1-12. doi:10.1177/1754073917709940

Finally, virtual interactions completely eliminate the risks of rape and sexual assault — victims of which are disproportionately women in the sexual marketplace[62] — since the nature of the exchange makes accessing the woman's body (consensually or otherwise) an impossibility. If securing resources from men is both uncertain and high-risk, then it's little wonder why many women are moving toward the certain and low-risk acquisition opportunities that virtual experiences represent. However, since it's generally easier for women to extract resources from men than it is for men to extract sexual opportunities from women, then we would expect fewer women to post content on OnlyFans than men to use Pornhub (which is certainly true).[63]

One could argue that social media platforms don't allow women to acquire actual resources — just the *simulation* of them. The money is definitely real, but the attention comes in the form of anonymous likes, the validation is provided by men with whom a woman might never otherwise choose to interact, and the connection is a mediated imitation of emotion. I, personally, don't believe the two are comparable. However, the two are apparently comparable *enough* to entrap millions of women — and millions more are likely to follow

---

62 The gendered rates of sexual violence vary significantly depending on the definitions used. However, outside of prisons, women are always more likely to be victims than men are. Source: Smith, S., Zhang, X., Basile, K., Merrick, M., Wang, J., Kresnow, M. & Chen, J. (2018). *The national intimate partner and sexual violence survey: 2015 data brief — updated release*. Centers for Disease Control and Prevention.

63 Apparently, between 60% and 98% of all men use pornography (compared to 30% to 90% of all women). Source: Ballester-Arnal, R., García-Barba, M., Castro-Calvo, J., Giménez-García, C., & Gil-Llario, M. (2023). Pornography consumption in people of different age groups: An analysis based on gender, contents, and consequences. *Sexuality Research and Social Policy, 20,* 766-779. doi:10.1007/s13178-022-00720-z

suit as virtual relationships become increasingly normalized in society.

And while the opportunity to promote themselves directly to men has been offered in many different cultures for thousands of years, only recent technological developments have made it possible to ensnare women at this scale by making these opportunities cheap, convenient, and safe. By providing women with an easy means of acquiring resources without leaving the comfort of their homes, social media has disincentivized them from entering the hunting grounds of the sexual marketplace. Moral arguments against these platforms — or shame-based exhortations for women to act like "ladies" — will do little to change the situation in light of these economic realities.

The upshot of all this is that people are increasingly replacing actual relationships with simulated relationships. Rather than transact resources for sexual opportunity in the real world, people are apparently preferring to transact simulated resources for simulated sexual opportunities online. Men and women have organically occupied virtual roles that mirror their actual roles in the real-life sexual marketplace. It's fascinating.

THE PATH FORWARD

Many of the realities of the contemporary sexual marketplace make people uncomfortable. Those who witness the goings-on at some remove often lament the superficial, transient, and materialistic nature of many modern relationships, especially when these relationships are viewed through the lens of traditional ideals or religious moralities. However, the disapproval of older generations and non-participants will do little to affect these realities, most of which are merely the (relatively) exaggerated expressions of dynamics that have existed for thousands of years. For better or worse, the phenomena described in this chapter aren't going anywhere anytime soon. In fact, the pendulum hasn't even started to slow in its sweep: it will swing even further from the center line in the foreseeable future.

The rates of all kinds of relationships will continue to decline for the "simple" reason that they are increasingly costly solutions to certain problems of living within the panoply of modern optionality. While marriage probably won't disappear entirely, it will likely become progressively irrelevant. Birth rates will continue to fall, and countries will need to resort to increasingly creative (or desperate) measures to mitigate the economic destabilization created when societies fall below replacement rates. The real variable of interest will be the rate of population decline: the more rapid the collapse, the more drastic the measures will be.

We will also need to collectively examine our relationship models. At this point, it should be abundantly clear that marriage — as conventionally understood — *does not work for a sizable portion of the population*. More than half of marriages end in divorce,[64] and half of those that remain intact aren't particularly happy.[65] A relationship structure with a one-

64 Probably around 40% of first marriages end in divorce. Attrition is higher in subsequent marriages, which bumps up the overall divorce rate. Source: https://ourworldindata.org/marriages-and-divorces

65 A well-conducted meta-analysis found no evidence across 18 studies that marriage sustainably increases subjective happiness, life satisfaction, or relationship satisfaction. Source: Luhmann, M., Hofmann, W., Eid, M., & Lucas, R. (2012). Subjective well-being and adaptation to life events: A meta-analysis. *Journal of Personality and Social Psychology, 102*(3), 592-615. doi:10.1037/a0025948

in-four success rate (at best) — and (often) disastrous consequences associated with failure — *absolutely should not be upheld as the ideal end state for all relationships.* Continuing to do so in light of these realities is reckless and irresponsible. However, in the absence of sane and compelling alternatives, many people will still choose to tie the knot — though we will likely continue to see a decline in all forms of relationships that tend toward marriage. Marriage is obviously problematic for many, but it may yet be preferable to the complete absence of intersexual relationships.

Fortunately, these are *not the only two options.* The capacity to see beyond this dichotomy — the choice between the way things have always been or nothing at all — is the opportunity inherent in the current relationship crisis. The idea would be to supplement marriage (and the conventional relationship pathway that leads to marriage) with additional relationship structures (and pathways) that optimize goodness of fit by solving certain problems of living. Ideally, people could then choose the arrangement that works best for them rather than attempt to force themselves into a single monolithic structure (or forgo structure entirely). Most of Western civilization has already created a precedent for this solution in the legalization of same-sex marriage, which fundamentally expanded what a large portion of these societies was willing to recognize as a "legitimate" union. We will see the potential of this moment fulfilled when this same tolerance and acceptance is extended to heterosexual relationships that deviate from the conventional ideal. Just as there is more than one way to be *queer,* there is more than one way to be *straight.*

To approach what these alternative relationship structures might look like, we must first understand why marriage tends to fail. After all, appropriate treatment follows from accurate diagnosis. In so many words, marriages fail because people want it to be *too many things*. The modern conceptualization of marriage is a hyperconflation of many disparate elements — almost all of which can (and do) routinely exist in nonmarital relationships. This complicates an inherently humble institution. When these elements can't be teased apart, the entire relationship — rather than the problematic component — is often discarded. And those who cannot (or will not) assume marriage in its entirety are denied the opportunity to enter into a fully recognized social relationship.

Among other factors, the marital ideal consists of a wedding, a legal contract, a solemn oath before God, emotional commitment, resource provision, sexual exclusivity, cohabitation, and child-rearing. This means that every spouse must be a celebrant, a business partner, a soulmate, a best friend, a sponsor, a monopolized lover, a roommate, and a parent. What's more, this ideal somehow expects each partner to unite the security and stability of companionate love with the passion and excitement of romantic love. And with the decline of civic communities and extended kin networks, each person is required to perform countless ancillary roles previously discharged by an entire village: nurse, therapist, playmate, cheerleader, activity buddy, chef, mistress, personal assistant. Finally, both parties typically expect a host of non-transactable goods — things like love and loyalty and friendship — from a relationship that might be predicated on attraction and lifestyle opportunities.

Unfortunately, no person can be all people, and no actor can perform all roles. A caring mother might be a disinterested wife. A family man might not be monogamous.

A loving relationship might be sexless. The institution of marriage has been overburdened with a weight that it was never designed to support. Much like a chain is only as strong as its weakest link, modern marriages are only as resilient as their most fragile component. The durability of the others too often becomes irrelevant if and when this component fails. Under such conditions, the outcome is generally a foregone conclusion: either divorce with all its attendant emotional and financial hardships, or a quiet resignation that has surrendered hope and responsibility.

We see a similar trend in contemporary attitudes toward work. For instance, the function of a job is *to provide people with the opportunity to earn money in exchange for a service*. That's it. Everything on top of that is additional weight that the institution of work was not designed to support. A job was never meant to be emotionally fulfilling, a source of meaning, or a container for passion. And it certainly wasn't designed to be fun and exciting. Rather, jobs were created to provide people with the opportunity to earn money in exchange for a service. From this perspective, we can understand that it isn't necessarily a problem when a job that pays well isn't fulfilling: the problem resides in expecting fulfillment from a job that pays well.

This is comparable to marriage. The function of marriage is *to provide a stable context for people to raise children*. That's it. Everything on top of that is additional weight that the institution of marriage was not designed to support. A marriage was never meant to be a partnership with your best friend, an exciting adventure with a lover, or a union with your soulmate — or any of the other ideals you're prone to hear at modern weddings. Rather, marriage was created to provide a stable context for people to raise children. It is fundamentally an instrument of social organization that became necessary once people started living in communities that exceeded Dunbar's number. From this perspective, we can understand that it isn't necessarily a problem when, say, a co-parent doesn't reciprocate sexual interest: the problem resides in expecting reciprocated sexual interest from a co-parent. This is why marriage fails: we want it to be more than it is, and so we expect our partners to be more than they are.

This is not a popular opinion. Despite its unenviable success rate, marriage remains a sacred idol in many cultures. Invested with romantic and spiritual ideals that may be precious and ennobling, the concept of marriage cannot be allowed to suffer any harm — no matter how inconvenient, wasteful, or unrealistic that concept becomes. When marriages fail — or they languish in unvoiced desperation — we typically believe this is caused by some flaw in the *individuals* in question. This judgment is reinforced by the many platitudes that masquerade as effective relationship advice: improve your communication, never stop dating, learn to compromise, don't go to bed angry. However, to my mind, it's equally plausible to consider that marriages fail because of some flaw in the *structure itself*. Rather than judging each other for our apparent inability to meet the standards of modern marriage, maybe it's finally time to judge modern marriage for its impossible high (and often paradoxical) requirements. Perhaps this will enable more people to remain married without outlawing divorce.

In the past, this wouldn't have been possible. Ironically, it's the contemporary relationship crisis that has created the conditions conducive to exploring what heterosexual relationships — including marriage — can look like. This would have been absurd to attempt during a time when intersexual relations were relatively stable. However, things are obviously falling apart. Just like we don't have to allow them to collapse entirely, we also don't have to build them up again just as they were — especially considering the possibility that their previous construction might be (at least partly) responsible for the current state of affairs. At the very least, I believe we may be forced to concede that marriage isn't for everyone, or to put it another way: *marriage only makes sense under certain conditions*. And when people avoid (or escape) the institution *en masse*, they are functionally communicating with their actions that they believe those conditions have not been met.

When I was a young man, I heard a great deal of public lamentation in the mainstream media about the state of the professional world. Apparently, business had become completely mercenary. Employers no longer offered their employees pensions for their years of service; they cashed in their integrity for a higher bottom line. Employees no longer served a single company for the duration of their careers; they were only loyal to the highest bidder. No one bought American. Greedy corporations were contending with an entitled workforce, and no one believed in an honest day's work for an honest day's pay anymore.

Of course, the pundits' moral indignation did nothing to alter the course of events. Thirty years later, the American marketplace is almost unrecognizable in its transformation. Americans now work an average of 12 jobs in their lifetimes,[66]

---

66 This is a slightly older statistic, but it's the most recent one I could find. I suspect that — with the advent of the gig economy — the number is

and no one expects a pension anymore. Globalism and digital technologies disrupted entire industries. Established businesses that refused to adapt were left behind, and innovative new companies sprung up to take their place. Greed and entitlement — neither of which were invented in the 1980s — persist today. People continue to work about as hard as they need to.

In retrospect, it's clear to see that the grumblers were wrong — or, at least, extremely myopic. Business has *always* been mercenary. Employees have always tried to secure as much money for as little productive labor as possible, and employers have always tried to secure as much productive labor for as little money as possible. The social conditions of the 1980s didn't create these dynamics: they *revealed* them. And this revelation was made possible by a confluence of certain economic realities.

For instance, when they did so, companies didn't offer pensions out of an abundance of gratitude or concern for their workers. They offered them because (given the influence of unions at the time) it would have been a liability for companies *not* to. However, as the power of workers' unions waned and a critical mass of companies stopped providing this perk, pensions functionally disappeared. Why? Because no one will pay more for a given option when it can be bought for less.

By the same token, employees did not devote their entire careers to a single company out of a sense of duty or allegiance to its mission. They did so because (given the incentives in play) remaining loyal was more personally advantageous

---

even higher for millennials and Gen Zers. Source: https://www.bls.gov/nls/questions-and-answers.htm#anch41

than jumping ship. However, as workers' optionality and portability increased, and it became easier to secure better terms for themselves by negotiating with a new company than by remaining faithful to an old one, lifers functionally disappeared. Why? Because no one will accept less for a given option when it can be sold for more. It wasn't national self-loathing that prompted people to stop buying American. It was the sudden availability of higher-quality goods sold at lower price points made possible by globalism (and the trade agreements that support it).

The pundits of my youth could only view current events through the lens of what they had known, which is why all they saw was ruin. The old ways were falling apart. However, every crisis is simultaneously an opportunity. Globalism may have signaled the end of America's consumer production industries, but it also marked the beginning of its digital economy. Every benefit is also a liability. Workers today might not enjoy the job security they once had, but they are also not practically constrained to devote the better part of their lives to a mismanaged organization. Success is possible under most any circumstances, provided the players are willing and able to adapt as conditions evolve. While those who could not (or would not) accommodate to change encountered difficulties, many others found ways to thrive in the new marketplace.

The point of this extended digression is that something comparable to the transformation just described is occurring in the sexual marketplace today. The old ways are falling apart. However, the pundits of the present day are as misguided as those of my youth. Contemporary social conditions have not created the intersexual dynamics discussed throughout this book: they have *revealed* them. Like it or not, men and women today are as opportunistic and self-interested with respect to whom they mate and date as they have ever been (or been allowed to be). Loyalty and integrity haven't changed as much as the network of incentives that differentially reward (or punish) their expression. People continue to commit about as much as they need to.

What's more, the disruption of the sexual marketplace is not an unequivocal disaster. Relationship structures that may no longer make sense in the modern day will give rise to new (and unknown) possibilities in the days ahead. The current decline in relationships is symptomatic of a transitionary period in which many previously successful strategies of mating and dating have been rendered obsolete but in which strategies effective under the new conditions have yet to be consistently identified. It is a difficult — and potentially painful — moment that we need to pass through, but it is not the way the story will end.

My prediction is that *something akin to the gig economy will emerge in the sexual marketplace*. Just as it now seems antiquated (or incomprehensible) that people used to work a single job for their entire lives (a job that may even have been chosen for them by their *parents*), before too long, it will likely seem outdated (or baffling) that people used to commit to a single person for their entire lives (a person that may even have been chosen for them by their *parents*). The grumblers will shake their heads and wonder what the world is coming to because they can only view current events through the lens of what they have known. They see the crisis but not the opportunity.

And just what is that opportunity? Nothing less than the chance *to get more of what you want*. Given human nature and individual limitations, it has never been — nor will it ever be — possible to get everything you want from a single person. Traditional marriage understood this, and its most enlightened response to this difficulty was to treat these frustrations and disappointments as an opportunity to self-transcend.

Your wife no longer has sex with you? Excellent! Use your involuntary celibacy as a chance to examine your own carnal attachment. Your kids leave you no time for yourself? Wonderful! Use your maternal responsibility as the means to overcome your residual selfishness. You're no longer satisfied with your relationship? Phenomenal! Use your dissatisfaction as an opportunity to realize that you are entitled to absolutely nothing in this life. And this perspective isn't necessarily wrong. Marriage *did* demand that people self-transcend — at least as long as they couldn't get out of it. And while it may not have been exactly what people wanted, the argument could be made that it just might have been what people needed in order to mature into fully functional adults.

The issue is that willingly entering into difficulty because it can be used as an opportunity for growth is about as appealing to most people as running a marathon on their day off. The possibility that they might be able to, say, improve their cardiovascular health and overcome certain mental weaknesses is not sufficient incentive for most people to run 26.2 miles that they don't need to. However, most people *will* run a marathon (or at least until the point of utter exhaustion) if they are forced to start and prevented from stopping. And among such people will be those able to create a virtue out of a necessity and who will helpfully explain to anyone within earshot that running this far is an excellent opportunity to *grow up*. However, in today's day and age, people are no longer expected to run marathons — and if they do start, they can stop whenever the ordeal becomes too painful or inconvenient. As should come as a surprise to no one, this has resulted in fewer people running marathons when they can do literally anything else in their free time.

So, fewer people are getting (and staying) married than ever before. Even casual sexual relationships are at historically unprecedented lows. The main reason for this is that people are continuing to rely on a previously successful mating and dating strategy that is becoming increasingly obsolete with each passing day, namely: *the optimization of value in a single individual*. If every relationship requires some degree of settling, then it's rational for people to refrain from entering into one until they meet someone who simultaneously maximizes value across as many different parameters as possible and minimizes the opportunity cost of their commitment, especially if relationships have become increasingly voluntary and unnecessary. This attitude is further reinforced by digital technologies that functionally guarantee that highly desirable individuals exist somewhere in the sea of infinite optionality. Unfortunately, reliance on this strategy only serves to significantly reduce the rates of all relationships and does little to justify staying in relationships that inevitably become (at least to some degree) unsatisfactory. This is because it's not possible to get everything you want from a single person.

However, it *might* be possible to get more of what you want from many people. The mating and dating strategy that will become increasingly effective in the foreseeable future is *the optimization of value across individuals*. Rather than attempting to find one person capable of effectively discharging all the hyperconflated roles of a modern marriage (which is a tall order, at best), people will progressively find many partners, each capable of discharging one (or some) of the hyperconflated roles of the same (which is a significantly more realizable goal). This prediction is value-neutral. For better or worse, those who are willing and able to flexibly adopt this strategy will thrive, and those who cannot (or will not) will encounter difficulties.

This strategy can be implemented consecutively, simultaneously, or both. For instance, rather than making a commitment for life — a commitment that, apparently, is too weighty for many to carry (especially now that they are living much longer)[67] — people might intentionally make a commitment for, say, 20 years to complete the task of raising children in a stable and sustainable context. The co-parents might choose to cohabitate during this time, or they might not. They might choose to be monogamous sexual partners, or they might not. They might choose to enter into a contract pertaining to their wealth and property, or they might not. They might cultivate a deep, abiding love for each other, or they might not. They might participate in shared interests and activities, or they might not. They might commemorate their commitment with a religious ritual, or they might not. They might assist each other in ways not directly pertaining to their duties as co-parents, or they might not. And when their mission is complete, they might go their separate ways, or they might not. In any case, separation wouldn't require

67 Improvements in life expectancy aren't entirely attributable to reductions in infant mortality. Life expectancy has significantly increased at all ages over the past century. Source: https://ourworldindata.org/life-expectancy

a painful or expensive divorce: the term of the agreement will have simply expired. Who knows? We may even end up celebrating the end of such an arrangement at least as much as we currently celebrate the beginning, given that doing so would recognize a relationship that actually completed what it set out to do.

This is the opportunity inherent in the crisis: people might be able to get more of what they want. The catch is that they won't be able to get more of what they want from a single person. With the dissolution of marriage as a monolithic social institution, individuals might finally have sane and compelling alternatives to the "everything or nothing" Hobson's choice that still dominates the sexual marketplace. While some people will continue to seek all the hyperconflated components of a modern marriage in a spouse, more and more will attempt to secure these components piecemeal in multiple, nonmarital relationships. Both approaches will have their benefits and liabilities, risks and rewards. However, in another generation or two, it's highly probable that such arrangements will have become completely normalized.

In this chapter, I argued that people don't really want relationships: they want the value that relationships provide. If that value can be secured more cheaply, more easily, and more safely in other ways, then people will increasingly abandon the sexual marketplace in favor of these solutions. Certain technological developments — like birth control and p2p internet platforms — have brought about a precipitous decline in sexual relationships by significantly altering their valuations through unforeseen economic pathways. However, this crisis also contains an unexpected opportunity:

the possibility of reimagining our relationship models for the modern day.

If you'd like to further explore the topics presented in this chapter, please scan the QR code to access a curated playlist on the PsycHacks channel on YouTube.

EPILOGUE

THE COIN OF CAESAR

There is a story in the life of Jesus,[68] and it goes like this:

One day, a group of people approached Jesus and asked, "Is it right that we should have to pay taxes to the emperor?" They were trying to trap him with his words.

In response, Jesus requested that they show him some of their money. He asked the group, "Whose image is on this coin?"

The people answered, "Caesar's."

So Jesus continued: "Render unto Caesar what is Caesar's, and unto God what is God's."

When they heard this, the people were amazed, and they let him be.

68 Matthew 22:16 — 22

ACKNOWLEDGMENTS

A book is always a collective work of many efforts, and this volume is no different. I am indebted to many people for their contributions in the service of its realization.

Jennifer Jas did an excellent job editing the manuscript. She demonstrated an extraordinary attention to detail, and her suggestions helped make the text even more clear and incisive than it otherwise would have been.

Tracy Kimball Smith designed the lovely cover art for the book. She also formatted the finished draft for ebook and paperback publication, thereby protecting my sanity.

Nauman Jamil created the graphs used in chapter 11, and he designed my professional website, as well. I'm happy with the clean elegance of both.

Bruce Abbot edited and mastered the audiobook for distribution. His skill and expertise are evident in the finished product.

Rich Cooper, Shawn Smith, and Andrew Mills all graciously shared their self-publishing experience with me. Their advice was instrumental in positioning this book for a successful release.